Candi,

Find your joy!

Barbara

Praise for
Tristan's Letters from Heaven

This is a wonderful journey of one angel who came to earth and changed the lives of everyone he came in contact with and continues to do "angel work" through his mom on earth. A MUST READ for any parent who has ever gone through the devastating lesson of losing a child.

— **JAMES VAN PRAAGH**, Spiritual Medium, Best Selling Author

As pure souls, our natural propensity is to love others and serve. Our relationships are opportunities to cultivate our spirituality and overcome our personal defects. This book demonstrates that the higher spirits are actively involved in our lives. The communications from Tristan contained in this book will significantly transform your life and help you to progress spiritually. His channeled messages offer insight and wisdom easily applicable on a personal level.

— **REVEREND STEPHEN A. HERMANN,** international medium, teacher and author of *Mediumship Mastery: The Mechanics of Receiving Spirit Communications: The Ultimate Guide* and *Mediumship Mastery II: Advanced Techniques That Work.*

After the tragic loss of her son, Barbara reached into her deepest heart to find the treasure of his love. It is through this love and his guidance that her gifts of mediumship unfolded. This book also contains profound insights about the education, religious and criminal justice systems in our country. By reading this book you will gain the courage to heal from deep loss and the inspiration to be a better parent.

— **TERESA BROWN-KONELL**, intuitive medium and author of *Discovering the Power Of Ceremony.*

Beautifully researched and written from the heart. This book answers the WHY we are living in a broken society. The awe-inspiring research gave me an education on how none of our societal systems are working for us. They work against us while we lose our freedoms. The family's journey through this process and Tristan's letters of wisdom will touch your heart. This book is a gift that will keep on giving in your life.

— **ELAINE WITTWER**, Clarification Facilitation Counselor

Tristan's Letters from Heaven

A Mother's Story of Her Son's Life and Afterlife

by Barbara Bruni

To my family and friends who shared in the adventures of Tristan—and still do!

To our sons Alex and Chris, I am so grateful for all the joy you have brought to our lives and for joining us on this sacred and wild journey called family.

And to Jack, it is only with your love, support and technical assistance that this book became a reality.

CONTENTS

Tristan Robert Bruni
1999-2018.
Fifteen years old.

INTRODUCTIONS

TRISTAN'S INTRODUCTION

Hello, my name is Tristan Bruni. Well, it was *Tristan Bruni* when I was on this Earth plane, as you all are now. I will help my mother write this book about life: yes, my life, her life, how she is handling things now after my departure, as well as how she managed my trials and tribulations. I do have a story to tell, and it's not just for me. Really, that is secondary. It is for humanity. As many of you are aware, we are going through a planetary shift of consciousness. This book continues my work, as I came in at this time for this purpose: my mission that I embarked on when I accepted this lifetime from our Creator.

I was honored to do it, but it was hard—harder than I expected— yet the outcome will certainly help to ignite the fire in the hearts of many to keep fighting the good fight. To shine the light through the darkness. To unify your thoughts, words and actions to bring peace, not to get caught up in the nonsense that is fed to you through your media—both local and national—the fear-based gossip, thoughts and beliefs that have been spoon-fed to you from birth. I say to you, do not fear—fear fuels the agendas and continues the atrocities. You may not agree with your neighbors, coworkers and family. But if you love and want a better world ruled by peace and benevolence, then ride the current of truth that underlies it all. Leave the distractions and noise outside of your relating to others. Love them—see your reflection in all people. Treat each other with respect and compassion, even if you don't agree with them.

Many on this side are working tirelessly (we don't really get physically tired) to feed the light and organize meetings and events. Don't pick sides—that makes someone a loser. Walk with truth and use your intuition and discernment.

Through this book, I will help to shed light on sensitive topics. This is where my story is interwoven through the realities of what our systems and leaders have created for humanity's so-called reality. It is not real—it is an illusion. Only love is real. Follow my life and see the threads of how it is all interwoven. You will see your life in there as well.

Take loving action to stop the hate (even hate in the name of love.) On this side we love all people. We love ALL people. May peace blanket our beloved Earth. It is up to you—it is all inside of you.

Love, Tristan

BARBARA'S INTRODUCTION

I really wish I wasn't writing this book. I am writing it because my son has passed away. However, I am honored to write it because God gave me such a precious gift in my son Tristan that I must share it. The happiness, joy and wisdom stay with me as I pass this on to help do my part to create a better world: one where we can see the truth and empower ourselves and each other. This is a book about reality. It is really my experience of my son's life. It is not a New Age book, a metaphysical book or a religious book. When I speak of Indigo children or channeling letters from my son, I know that many of you will put this book down and classify it, and me, as one of those people who believe in weirdness, UFOs, conspiracy theories or even heresy. Hopefully, you will read on, as the information in this book about my son's life, our experiences of the systems, and historical and scientific research is very valuable. It can change your life, help your children and change your perceptions of what is real. For those who have the courage to read on, you will experience many emotions—laughter, joy, sadness, disbelief and anger. This book is meant to serve as a catalyst for us, as a culture, to take notice of the truth of the world we have been living in. It is an impetus for action in small and large ways to move us a bit more quickly through the shift of consciousness. We have been led to the dark and left there. But this is changing. There is so much information now available regarding the shifting consciousness on Planet Earth.

Tristan's story brings to light what is really happening to our children and our world. Tristan was a very loved, amazing person who came into this world to show us our mistakes and to mirror back to us our thinking. He was so strong and courageous. He was kind of on the front lines of the shift, and the system devoured him. Keep an open mind as you read. Realize that we thought—just like you, perhaps—that the systems and authorities, even with all of their dysfunctions, were basically working on behalf of the people. We believed that even though they were not perfect, they were effective and ultimately were there to help the citizens they served. I have since awakened from that utopic dream. I have experienced a completely different reality. We have accepted outdated and harmful ways that have created systems that are destroying our children, societies and cultures. We were taught to accept these systems and adapt ourselves around them, but young people are not accepting the status quo. Not because they are rebellious, but because they are wired differently energetically. At this time we are charged to invent and create new and improved systems that will uplift humanity so that no one and no one's child will ever suffer what Tristan so bravely endured until the end of his life. May his love, joy and courage be a healing balm as we live through these times.

Hopefully this story will reach parents who have also lost children. It is the worst pain imaginable, and there is no one who will understand the depth of it and the all-encompassing way it changes your life unless they go through it themselves. Tristan has helped me lighten the load of grief. The death of a child is not an event that you eventually move on from. It is a pain that never goes away. I envision a large backpack, heavy with grief, sorrow, guilt and all the myriad emotions, that you carry with you every moment of every day. As time goes by it lightens, but it will be with you the rest of your days on Earth until you cross over and greet your child once again in a joyful reunion. But until then, we must find a way to move on with the backpack and still find joy, enthusiasm and ways to make our life meaningful. They truly want that for us. Hopefully the messages from Tristan in this book will help to take some of those heavy bricks out of your backpack and make your load lighter. He wants us to know that souls heal and experience joy and bliss when they cross back to home. Death is not a punishment. They are once again in the hands on an ever-loving God who passes no judgment. We go to school "over there" as well and get to be with our loved ones who crossed before us. Most importantly, Tristan wants us to know that they are still a part of our lives, whether we are aware of it or not.

After Tristan's death, I was searching online for a certain book on our school systems and came across James Van Praagh's book *Growing Up in Heaven*. James is an internationally known gifted medium and has written many books about loved ones who have crossed over. I did not purchase it, though; I only purchased the book I initially was searching for—or so I thought. A few days later a package came with the book I had ordered, but *Growing Up in Heaven* was also in the package. Apparently, someone some-where was insisting I read it! I devoured that book in just a few hours, as it is about children who have died. In the book he advises to write a letter to your child in Heaven from your heart, address it however you want, then put it up for a week. In a week you are to pray and meditate, and then just start writing your response back from your loved one.

I have always been intuitive, but it can be overwhelming, so I became pretty good over the years at suppressing it. Also, I have always had a deep interest in spirituality and looked deeper beyond what religions were offering. I used my gifts for my own personal spiritual growth and healing, and used my mediumship capabilities for myself, but never thought how I would be moved to use them beyond that. But when your heart is broken, the idea of experiencing your child one more time is extremely appealing. With tear-filled eyes, I wrote Tristan a letter on a Sunday afternoon. The following Sunday, I just didn't feel like I could do the response back. It seemed overwhelming, and I didn't want to get let down if nothing came through. That night I had a dream that Tristan was handing someone a letter. I woke up immediately, knowing that he wanted to give me his letter! I grabbed a notebook, and in the dark I scribed his letter. I wrote so fast—the thoughts just seemed to come through me to the pen. I was not in control of the words I was writing.

Here is his letter:

Dear Mom,

I want to tell you that I am here—always here for you. I know you got some answers from Teresa [a friend of mine who is also an intuitive medium]. *I want to let you know that I am sorry for what happened and what I put you and Dad through. I ask for your forgiveness. Not that I think you are mad at me or that you think you need to forgive me—it is just the way it is done. Forgive—each other and ourselves. Nothing is ever any one person's fault. We all come in and play the parts for each other's soul progression. It doesn't always turn out like we expected or really, in reality, what we truly ever would want or choose for ourselves. There is free will on such a chaotic planet.*

Let me tell you first that I like it here—no fear or darkness, you see the big picture. I love all people. Yes, my heart was broken in this last lifetime. I chose to be this way, but it was indeed difficult. We love each other and know I love you for that, and Dad, and my brothers. We are a soul group and will continue to be such.

Grateful. Please know that. Please don't be sad for me. Yes, it was horrible what I went through. I learned many valuable lessons. Van is here with me and we understand that many were hurt by our actions. [Van is Tristan's friend who died in the tragic accident you will read about in Chapter 1. Tristan also then said a few things about Van's parents not taking responsibility for what happened. I have chosen to omit what he said, as it is of a personal nature.]

I was so sad and had anger and resentfulness, yet I knew people still had goodness in their hearts, but they were too fearful to show it [after the accident]. *I want to come back for sort of a re-do and complete the errors made. To let love come through foremost and not violence. People need to love and support each other—not persecute. There is no other way. I would have liked to live longer but not under these circumstances. It was too hard, and I know you would be hurt and miss me terribly. Your sunshine, yes, you are my sunshine, my only sunshine, you make me happy when skies are grey—you never know dear how much I love you, please don't take my sunshine away. I am not away—I have loved you through eons of time and will continue to do so. Don't let one lifetime of bad choices harden your heart. Yes, I made bad choices, but I truly needed to do that to learn and evolve my soul. Allow me to do that. I am so grateful for the space you held for me to do that. Some things are not what they seem. Love underlies all. My love to you—all the love of the Universe is right here for us to hold and bring forth.*

I love you, I see all that is going on. I support you and appreciate you wanting to continue my story and efforts. Please continue on with your life. It is just a short blink of the eye, but yes, we have a mission. And sometimes that mission brings us to uncharted territory for our soul as we continue the ongoing fight for freedom on the planet. It all comes from love and yet perseverance for us and each other. "Our Brother's Keeper"—you know. Thanks for the cool tattoo—it is an honor. Keep fighting the good fight. All will end well. Yes, there is work to be done—don't get lost in it, yet continue in a manner to hold the light—your light. I will continue—the work continues with all who are aware and awakening. We must clear the darkness.

I know you miss me terribly—and I you. But love endures. Find a way to be in peace with me being on this side. I love that you are trying to stay in touch with me. I will stay in touch with you as much as I can as I have a lot of work to do on this side too, you know. Many lifetimes of work to thread together before I come back in to pick up a new thread and help to sew the tapestry of my soul into that of all humanity. I know I am getting heavy but that is the truth of the matter. I want to come back in a more passionate way—not so rebellious too. In a way of togetherness. To ease the pain of the world rather than to stir it up. These are not the words exactly, but I think you know. I will never just be passive—too much work to do at this time.

Yes, you keep wanting to show people the horrors I went through and the bad systems of this world and this is true. Also, to clear my name. I appreciate that. Please continue this work as it needs to be done, and I appreciate it. I will be doing the support work on this end, but my request to you is not to get lost in it. Take care of your soul and the big picture. The way things are now can't last forever—they will destroy themselves as they are not sustainable.

I love you. Let's keep writing letters. This is a great way to communicate. Keep feeling for me—I will be there—loving and still taking care of you. Your forever loving son-shine, Tristan

Kiss baby Mittens and all the dogs—even Pedro—for me—haha.
My love to Dad.

The next morning when I read these words I thought that I probably wrote the entire thing. But I soon realized that these were not my words! This was indeed Tristan. I didn't remember writing any of it. It is so beautiful. As you read his writings, you will see that he still has his witty sense of humor, yet he is all loving. After he died, before we started writing letters, I would sit out by the garden that our family planted in his honor. In deep thought, I would hear him say things to me that were profound, so I knew that he wanted to communicate. Knowing that he still wanted to be in our lives brought me peace, although nothing could ever replace his physical presence, which is still the most difficult part. When you lose your child, you lose all of them: their past, present and future. All you have left, besides your memories and a few belongings, are their photographs—and the last one is just that. There will never be another photograph. All your plans and dreams for their future are gone. You miss how they felt when you hugged them, their voice and laugh, how their hair felt and their scent. I keep a shirt of Tristan's that has "his scent" in a plastic bag and open it sometimes when I just want to experience some sort of physical presence.

I believe Tristan was an "Indigo" child. In this book I will explain about Indigo children, and why life can be difficult for them. I will talk about my experiences raising Tristan, and about the final seventeen months of his life after surviving a horrendous gun accident and the subsequent gross inhumanity that he endured. Through my story you will get a glimpse of how corrupt our systems are—specifically, our school, religious, legal and criminal justice systems—and how they fail us. I also briefly touch on "science."

This is not new news. But it is now being exposed at such a head-spinning rate! The old systems are crumbling so that we can create new, benevolent, compassionate ones. Our job is to further expose the corruption so we can hasten the process. When we don't take responsibility, we become victims of the systems, and we allow them to continue. We are the ones responsible for creating a better life with improved ways of living. Many say we are fighting the dark. Perhaps so. However, I think that we are witnessing extremely bad human behavior, which has held the reins for centuries, going down fighting, kicking and screaming until the last breath. It reminds me of the massive bloom a tree has the season before it dies.

Much of what I am writing about are just stepping-stones for continued research and increased awareness. I am just one stone on the path that has been laid by many others who have helped me to understand my personal situation and what is happening on a global level. What I have learned is that resistance is futile. Better to embrace the changes, let go of fear, and learn new ways of living, parenting, teaching, working, etc. We can choose: awake or asleep. It is easy to stay sleeping unless something happens to us or a loved one. We either help to create a positive environment, or we stay sleeping and lose our freedoms—because human greed is always awake and looking for another opportunity to gain power and money at the expense of the greater good.

Sometimes there are brave people who show us, willingly or unwillingly, where the dark is. Their light exposes it. That seems to have been the case with Tristan. His light was extinguished here on Earth, but not in spirit. This book is being written so that what happened to us will not happen to others. Let no one diminish your Light! I will continue his legacy because it has a purpose. Every single person has a story, and this is Tristan's. Apparently, we are writing this book together!

SECTION I

Beginnings

"I hold that when a person dies
His soul returns again to earth;
Arrayed in some new flesh-disguise,
Another mother gives him birth.
With sturdier limbs and brighter brain
The old soul takes the road again.

JOHN MASEFIELD

CHAPTER 1

The Beginning of the End: The Accident

*"Love cannot be expressed through acts of violence,
not even in play."*

-TRISTAN

BARBARA'S STORY

It was the day before Thanksgiving, November 23, 2016. Tristan was seventeen years old at the time. Our son Christopher was visiting from Miami, and we were sitting around in the kitchen that morning discussing the day's plans. Tristan walked in and told us that he was going to drive his friend Van's girlfriend, Regina, to work at Chick-fil-A, as he did most mornings. She lived in our neighborhood, and Tristan did this as a favor for Van because he lived too far away to do it. Besides, Tristan just loved to have any excuse to drive his new Jeep, and he would do anything for his friend. He told us that after he dropped her off he was going to Van's house for a while, then would be back to do things with us later.

My gut instinct immediately told me "no." I was uneasy about Tristan going over to Van's that day. He told me that they were just going to hang out as usual, and he was going to teach Van how to change the oil in his car. Besides, Van was joining the marines, and they only had another month or so to spend time together. I reluctantly agreed but asked him to make it a short visit. I've looked back a thousand times and admonished myself for not listening to my intuition. But I tended to worry a lot raising three boys, so I was always a bit unsure—never quite knowing the distinction between true intuition and just being a worrying mom.

In this case, one of my reasons for worry was that I knew Van's family had a lot of guns. I had mentioned to my husband Jack many times that I couldn't wait until January when Van was leaving for bootcamp, because Tristan would no longer be around the guns. Tristan always reassured me that there was nothing to worry about, because Van's father kept the guns safe and was always around when they worked with them. Looking back, I see more clearly that this was from a seventeen-year-old who wanted to play with guns, and who admired Van's father; he told Tristan that he was like a son and he trusted him, which made Tristan feel mature and respected.

At around 2:00 that afternoon, Jack was outside working in the back-yard when he received a phone call from Van's father, Hain Lugner. Jack came to the kitchen door and told Chris and me that Tristan had been shot. Time stood still. We all looked at each other in pure helplessness and shock. The first words I remember saying were, "Is he alive?" Jack asked Hain, and he said yes, that Tristan was going to be OK. Hain was frantic as he told Jack that Van, however, was dead.

Then he told us that Tristan had been shot in the face and was being taken to the hospital. Jack left our house immediately to go there, and coincidentally ended up driving behind the ambulance that had Tristan in it. He followed it into the hospital emergency room driveway in time to see his son being taken out of the ambulance. He ran over to see him but was prevented by police. Jack went to the surgical waiting room and waited there during the entire nine-hour operation to save Tristan and rebuild his face. I stayed at home with Chris, waiting to hear any information from Jack. When Tristan came out of post-op, I drove to the hospital. I braced myself before I went into his room, not knowing what I was going to see, but knowing that Tristan's life and our family's lives were never going to be the same.

We watched our son for agonizing, grief-filled hours. Eventually, he woke up from the anesthetic. My beautiful, happy, funny, full-of-life son was gone. His eyes said it all: they were full of terror, pain, confusion and grief. Unable to speak, Tristan used his phone to communicate with me. The first words he wrote were: "Van's dead?" He couldn't even cry because he was stuck in traumatic shock. Additionally, he had a titanium plate in his jaw, which was all sewn together, and a trachea tube breathing for him.

Over time, Tristan wrote on a paper exactly what had happened. His story was unchanging from that moment through the seventeen months leading up to his death. Here it is:

After he dropped Regina at Chick-fil-A, he drove to Van's house. As usual, unknown to us, they "messed" with the guns. This, come to find out, was standard procedure at the Lugner's house: unsupervised gun play. Guns were not locked up, and anyone at the house could access them. (Hain had taken the day off work because he wasn't feeling well, but he was in his bedroom.) Tristan and Van then went to the auto store to get oil for Van's car. (We have the receipt from the auto shop to verify this. Besides getting a copy of it from the store, we found the original receipt in the pocket of the pants Tristan was wearing that day when we got his clothes back after Tristan's death from the sheriff's office, who had kept them for evidence. I was surprised to find the receipt still there, indicating that Tristan's clothes had never been searched by investigators. This would be just like Tristan: buying oil for his friend's car so he could teach him how to change it. The browser history on Tristan's phone also showed the YouTube link to how to change oil in an Audi, which is what Van had.)

After changing the oil, they went inside to make Eggs Benedict for themselves and Van's father and fourteen-year-old brother. (This was also substantiated by Tristan's phone, which showed an Eggs Benedict recipe in his search history.) Hain came out of his bedroom long enough to eat with the boys.

After breakfast, Tristan and Van cleaned the kitchen and decided they would go to Sports Academy before Tristan had to go home. They walked into Van's bedroom to get his wallet and whatever else he needed to bring with him. Tristan said that there was one gun remaining on the dresser, so he picked it up with the intention of putting it away. It was a snub-nosed .357 Magnum with a hair trigger. Unfortunately, along with the lack of adult supervision, the next moment in the series of errors that happened was that when Tristan picked the gun up, he put his finger on the inside edge of the trigger guard.

Tristan had the pistol in his right hand. Van came up next to him and grabbed Tristan's hand. Tristan told us that Van said, "Is this gun loaded?" Tristan said that he was pushing the back of his finger forward against the back of the guard—away from the direction of the trigger—but that the way Van grabbed his hand (maybe Van didn't know Tristan's finger was in the trigger guard) caused the gun to go off and shoot Van in the face. Van fell and died instantly. Stunned and grief-stricken, Tristan's first thought was that he would not let his friend die alone. Reacting as a seventeen-year-old with no ability to handle such a traumatic shock, Tristan put the gun under his jaw and pulled the trigger.

Tristan said that at first, he was so confused because of all the smoke and noise that he thought he had died and was looking around for Van's spirit. But he soon noticed Mr. Lugner, who had come in after hearing the shots, and realized he had not died. However, he was severely injured. The bullet had decimated his jaw.

Mr. Lugner later reported that Tristan was going after the gun to shoot himself again, saying, "I don't deserve to live." However, Tristan told us he was unable to even think that at this point, and with his jaw hanging open from the shot, there was no way he could have spoken.

Mr. Lugner walked Tristan outside to the front yard, then left him there alone! According to the evidence and depositions, Lugner apparently went back into the house at that point. He made some phone calls, including calling 911, but we don't know the order in which they were made. We do know that Lugner's attorney, Patrick Batemans, was already in the waiting room at the sheriff's department when Lugner was taken there, approximately an hour after the accident. And we found out that Lugner had put all the guns into his bedroom closet, even the one that had caused the accident. (On the recording of the 911 call, Lugner told the dispatcher he had already moved all the guns, so it seems he did that before calling for an ambulance for Tristan.)

When we first heard what happened, we naively thought that everyone realized it was a horrible accident resulting in one teenager's death and another's trauma and critical injury. However, unbeknownst to us, within an hour a conspiracy was brewing to charge Tristan with manslaughter and attempted suicide. The sheriff's investigator, Lillith Dusta, was apparently creating a character defamation portfolio on Tristan with various potential motives. One was that Tristan loved Van's girlfriend, so was trying to get Van out of the way. Another was that Tristan was depressed and felt like a jilted gay lover and was planning to take them both out. These were incredible allegations, completely unfounded in fact. At this point, she had no evidence and had only done a brief walk-through of the scene. (Later we discovered that she had found Van's cell phone in the garage, where the boys had been changing the oil. The phone wasn't password protected, and she went through it without a warrant, illegally. The boys tended to use quite a bit of creative swearing as humor, and she concocted stories around their absurd adolescent texts.)

My sister, a surgeon in southern Florida, told me that she had told Tristan's story to one of her patients who is a police officer. He said that this was an obvious accidental discharge, but we should still hire a defense attorney. We were shocked. If Van's death and Tristan's trauma and injury were not enough, now we were dealing with the possibility that Tristan might be charged with manslaughter? Meanwhile, Mr. Lugner was not being charged with anything? We proceeded to find a lawyer.

Tristan was at Sacred Heart Hospital for nine days and then was transferred to a rehabilitative hospital for two more weeks because he still had a tracheotomy. He also had a feeding tube in his stomach, which had been put in place with a second surgery after a few grueling, unsuccessful attempts by nurses to insert it nasally. Jack and I took turns staying with him around the clock. There were two reasons for this. First, obviously, we wanted to be there for Tristan emotionally and medically. Second, we were there for protection. Our attorney had told us that the police might try to question him; then they could twist his words to be used against him.

Tristan was discharged in the middle of December. He came home with his feeding tube and on a heavy dose of opioids. He stayed in bed around the clock except for feeding and wound care. He was in tremendous physical pain as well as mental and emotional pain from post-traumatic stress and the grief of losing his best friend. The physical pain came from the original injury to his bone and soft tissue, as well as the titanium plate they had put in his jaw. Also, most of his teeth on the left side and front were cracked and broken, causing an incredible amount of nerve pain. Jack and I were heartbroken for our son's physical, mental, emotional, and spiritual suffering, and terrified about the possibility of him being charged with a crime.

A few days before Christmas, the sheriff's investigator, Lillith Dusta, showed up at our home unannounced, asking to take a DNA swab. We had to wake Tristan up to come into the living room where she and her partner were waiting. She was completely clueless about the severity of Tristan's injuries. We wondered, did she really think that she would find Tristan up and around? Why was an unannounced call necessary? Also, she wanted to push a cotton swab into his mouth—one that he could still barely open! He asked if he could take the swab and do it himself. Thankfully, she agreed. (Unbelievably, we later found out she had told Van's family that Tristan only needed cosmetic surgery.)

The first week of January, Tristan had to have another major surgery. The titanium plate was holding his jaw together, but his jaw would soon deteriorate because there was no blood supply to the bone and soft tissue on either side of the hole. Both the plastic surgeon and the oral maxillary facial surgeon who had performed the initial trauma surgery worked on Tristan for eight hours. The plastic surgeon took bone out of Tristan's hip and connected it to the loose end of his jawbone, while the OMF surgeon removed more of the broken teeth.

After the surgery, a nurse called us into the recovery room because Tristan was in terrible pain and they didn't know what to do. We walked in to find him wailing in agony. Apparently, the staff hadn't received any orders for pain medication on the computer, so he hadn't had any! It turns out that since he was only seventeen years old, the prescription had to be written manually, and the nurse didn't see it. They finally gave him the appropriate pain meds. It was a grueling experience, to say the least, and now Tristan needed a cane to walk and had difficulty even lying in bed due to pain from the bone in his hip being removed.

A week after the surgery, our attorney called to tell us that Lillith Dusta was filing a charge of manslaughter against Tristan. He advised us to have Tristan down at the sheriff's office by 3:00 p.m. Otherwise, they would come to the house and arrest him. They were going to charge him as a juvenile. One of the many problems with the juvenile system (and there are too many to list here) is that when a youth is charged, they must spend the night prior to their court appearance in jail. We were frantic, as Tristan was still on heavy opioids, needed a cane to walk, and still had a feeding tube.

We called the juvenile detention center and spoke with a nurse to tell her about Tristan coming in that afternoon. We asked what the conditions would be for someone with his medical issues. She told us that he would be in the medical section of the ward, but he was not allowed to bring in any of his medications. However, he could bring his feeding tube supplies. Tristan still had open wounds from the tracheotomy, plus new open wounds in his mouth and hip, as well as the hole in his abdomen from the feeding tube. Also, his food supplies had to be kept sterile, and we worried that wouldn't happen in the center. We needed to know what they would do in case Tristan went into severe withdrawal from the opioids that he had been on for approximately seven weeks, as well as how they would treat his pain. She said that there was nothing they could do except give him Tylenol and call 911 if he showed signs of distress or seizures. We hung up but called back later because we had more questions. The supervisor of the center told us not to call again, and said she was informing all staff to not take calls from us! We couldn't believe that this is how our youth is treated. Is this really our system? We were finding out that the reality is, those accused of a crime are treated as if they are guilty until proven innocent, rather than the other way around. We feared for our son's physical and mental health, and we were angry that this was happening while he was still in such terrible shape. We didn't understand why the sheriff's office had filed charges so soon—it's not as if Tristan was a flight risk.

We asked our attorney if anything could be done. He said that he would call the assistant state attorney, which he only does in very special circumstances. The state attorney was not in when our attorney called, so he left a message. We could hardly breathe while we waited for a return call. We were hoping that it would come in before 3:00 p.m. The only thing we could do was pray. We knew there was no way that Tristan could survive a night in jail. I had heard many stories about addicts dying in jail because no one paid attention as they went through withdrawal; we were terrified that this could happen to Tristan if he suddenly had to stop his pain medication. Shortly before 3:00, the state attorney called back and said that he would hold off on charging Tristan for another day—but that he would have to be tried as an adult instead. When someone is charged as an adult, they don't have to spend the night in jail. When they're arrested, they go to their court appearance, get processed, and wait in a cell just until bail is posted—unless they don't have the money for bail; then they wait in jail for their court date, no matter how long it takes. It is hard to believe that we were grateful for this option, but we were.

The next day at 1:00 p.m., we brought Tristan in to get arrested. He appeared before the judge, bail was set for $75,000, and he was escorted—handcuffed and limping on his cane, with a feeding tube—to a cell. Jack and I immediately posted bail. We waited for Tristan's release, checking in with the receptionist every hour. The clock ticked very slowly. At 5:00 p.m., the daytime staff left and only the small night shift remained. Each time we asked at the window, no one had any answers for us as to when Tristan would be released. In fact, they told us when we asked about his health that they were unable to locate him. Finally, at 11:00 p.m., we were told that he was being released, but they weren't sure which door he would be coming through. There were two exits, one through the lobby and one through a single door near the back of the building, with a long walkway to the parking lot. Jack waited by the inside door and I waited out by the parking lot so I could have a view of both doors. In a while, the outside door opened and out walked Tristan with his cane—and no one to assist him.

Tristan told us that he sat alone in a cell on a cement bench for around ten hours, and only once did someone come by and offer him a sandwich. When Tristan told him that he was unable to eat because of a feeding tube, the person offered him some water, which he couldn't drink. (When one has a feeding tube, even fluids must be administered through the tube.) There had been no special notation for the jail staff letting them know of Tristan's medical condition.

Once again, we were shocked. This is legal barbarism. Why wasn't the jail staff notified of Tristan's condition? Why was he left alone and unsupervised for hours, in a cold, unsanitary environment, when he had open wounds? Why did we have to wait so long for our sick child to be released after we had posted bail? Ten hours was too long for someone in his state to go without fluids, food, or pain medication. He could easily have passed out or gone into withdrawal, possibly causing further injury. I shudder to think what happens to the poor children who must go through an entire night in jail cells before their hearings, or to sick people whose families don't have the means to post bail.

Shortly thereafter, Tristan developed a fistula at the injury site. A fistula is a hole that develops through the skin at a wound site; it drains infection. It's likely that he picked up the infection in that jail cell. We were told that he would need another operation to flush the wound out, and that there was a staph infection and Tristan would need a special port in his arm for antibiotics. Tristan's plastic surgeon was performing this operation, and he only had operating room privileges on certain days at two different hospitals. We were told that it would be easier for him to get Tristan on his schedule if we came in through the emergency room at Baptist Hospital early in the morning.

We were there at 7:00 a.m. We waited in the ER until almost 7:00 that evening. It was yet another case of gross miscommunication, a problem we encountered all too often in hospitals. Our doctor had told us that he would have another surgeon there to place the port, but when we spoke to the admitting nurse, she told us she was unaware of the port and had no doctor there to insert it. She also told us that Baptist was not a pediatric hospital, and since Tristan was seventeen, he couldn't be admitted to spend the night. Our doctor had forgotten how old Tristan was. Finally, they found a surgeon to place the port. Thankfully, it was a fairly short surgery and Tristan was out by 10:00 p.m. The surgeon set up an appointment with an infectious disease doctor for the following morning at 9:00 a.m., as that was the only time available. Here we were with Tristan coming home at 11:00 p.m. after surgery instead of being admitted, then having to go to a doctor's appointment the following morning.

At the infectious disease doctor's office the next day, she told us she didn't have the labs, but she would treat it as a staph infection. Tristan would need to go every day for intravenous antibiotics. Up to this point there hadn't been a coordinated effort or comprehensive plan for Tristan's care; we were bouncing around from doctor to doctor for different issues and no one was following up on him. We were concerned because he wasn't healing well, so we searched for someone who could give us a better level of care. We were able to get in for an appointment with an oral maxillary facial surgeon in Wellington, Florida. He was shocked, not only at the negligent medical care, but also at how mismanaged Tristan's case had been. This doctor was able to help lessen Tristan's pain. Then my sister (the surgeon) was able to get Tristan in to see Dr. Robert Marx, an internationally known OFMS in Miami. Even though he was seven hundred miles away from our home, we were grateful for the opportunity. Finally, we would have a team and a plan of care. We were able to get permission from the prosecutor to leave Pensacola, as Tristan was in no way a flight risk.

When we got to Miami, we met with Dr. Marx and multiple other professionals, who worked together to devise a plan of treatment. This would include extraction of many more teeth, getting the right labs done (which showed Tristan had had MRSA, an antibiotic-resistant form of staph infection, in his jaw all along), surgery to rebuild his jaw, and eventual fitting of upper dentures.

On July 17, 2017, Dr. Marx and his team, including a vascular surgeon, removed the bone graft from the January surgery—it was infected and failing—and the existing titanium hardware, and installed new hardware to properly re-set Tristan's mandible. They took veins from his right wrist via free flap microsurgery to place in his jaw, so he would have blood supply there, and put a skin graft from his leg on the wrist. He also had more bone taken from his hip.

Here is a lesson we learned: new residents start at hospitals in July. If you can avoid having surgery in July at a teaching hospital, by all means do so. On this surgery, there were new resident anesthesiologists. They took Tristan out of the anesthesia too quickly—especially for a trauma patient—causing him to buck, which made the free flap rip. The vascular surgeon was driving home when he got the call, and he sped back to the hospital. He told us later that he was livid with the staff. By the grace of God and his remarkable skill, he was able to repair the damage, but Tristan needed to have an emergency tracheotomy and a blood transfusion. The vascular surgeon told me at the post-op appointment that there was no way Tristan should have lived through that; that it was only God who had saved him.

The entire surgery lasted fifteen hours and Tristan was extremely upset when he woke up to find himself in the ICU with a tracheotomy and feeding tube again. It would be a long recovery. Fortunately, my sister lived nearby, and we were able to stay with her so she could keep an eye on him after he was released from the hospital.

Along with all of Tristan's life-threatening injuries and physical and emotional pain, we were also dealing with the charge of manslaughter. In criminal and civil cases, there is a process called discovery. It is a formal process of exchanging information between parties about the witnesses and evidence that will be presented at trials. This is when interrogations, depositions, requests for production and requests for admission occur. Among the many specialists we hired to help with the evidence of the accident (since the state wasn't doing their due diligence because they were pressing their unsubstantiated agenda) was a tech specialist to enhance the audio recording of the discussion between Hain Lugner, Investigator Lillith Dusta, and Lugner's attorney Patrick Batemans at the sheriff's department about an hour after the accident. Parts of that conversation follow. You will see that even through unspeakable shock, grief and horror, Mr. Lugner was focused on how to protect himself and blame Tristan for everything. Along with his attorney and the investigator, they began to create a narrative of murder and attempted suicide.

Allow me to preface this transcript with the fact that Mr. Lugner was on probation for a DUI at the time; he should not have had alcohol in the house. It is a gray area as to whether he was allowed to have firearms in the house.

The written transcript of the conversation at the sheriff's department approximately one hour after the 911 call between Hain Lugner, his attorney, Patrick Batemans, and sheriff's investigator Lillith Dusta:

First, Lillith Dusta is in the interrogation room alone with Hain Lugner.

He tells her: "The attorney said to ask to speak to him before I spoke with y'all."

She verifies Lugner's name, birthday, and the fact that Van was his son and Tristan was Van's friend. Dusta continues: "OK. So I'd really like to start talking to you, just because you're not a suspect in anything, I don't need a lawyer for a witness, and I'd like to figure out what's going on so we can get this information to the other officers as soon as possible."

Lugner reiterates that he wants his lawyer first.

The conversation turns to who would tell Van's mother, Heather, since Lugner did not want to be the one to do it. When Dusta calls the attorney, Patrick Batemans, to inquire about his estimated time of arrival, he says that he is already there in the waiting room.

When Batemans enters the room he says to Dusta: "Could I chat with him just for a quick second?"

Dusta replies: "Oh, sure, no problem, uh-huh. And as far as we're concerned, he's not a suspect in something like this, so I told him he didn't …"

Batemans interrupts: "Yeah, I know, but I just need to calm him down." (At this point, Dusta apparently leaves the room.)

The conversation continues, with Batemans questioning Lugner as to where his younger son and Lugner's mother are.

Then Lugner says: "Here's the problems that I see, Patrick."

Batemans: "OK."

Lugner: "I caught my son smoking weed, my younger son."

Batemans: "Yeah."

Lugner: "I took it from him, got rid of the pot, but the stuff is still in this little box that he kept it in."

Batemans: "OK."

Lugner: "There's guns all over the house."

Batemans: "OK."

Lugner: "We have a lot of guns."

Batemans: "Uh-huh, OK. Are they stored properly? I mean, your son was obviously eighteen. I don't know about the other boy. Do you know how old the other boy is?"

Lugner: "Seventeen, maybe sixteen…his jaw is shot off."

They continue to discuss the situation of the younger son.

Batemans: "You don't have any clue about what happened, do you? Going back to the pot, your youngest son's pot, where is it at?"

Lugner: "It was in my closet."

Batemans: "Well, they can't just go around searching the house, OK? . . . You don't need to bring up the pot, just answer the questions about just what you heard and what happened. And is there anything else? I mean, were the guns stored in gun shelves or cabinets?"

Lugner: "They're—they're stored—no, they're—they're in corners of walls and in drawers and stuff. But they were playing with their guns. They were—you know, had them out. I was sick, and I was in my bedroom."

Batemans: "How do you know they were playing with them?"

Lugner: "They had them out, they were cleaning them."

Batemans: "Cleaning them?"

Lugner: "Yeah."

Batemans: "How long have you known the boy that shot your son?" (Note the presumption that Tristan shot Van, prior to any investigation.)

Lugner: "A couple of years."

Batemans: "What's the boy's name?"

Lugner tells him Tristan's name and Jack's name.

Lugner: "Do I need to call my probation officer? I don't know if I'm supposed to do that, I don't know what."

Batemans: "You're not in trouble, Hain. Just let them come in. What's this deputy's name?"

They call the deputy in and discuss where to send Van's body and other heavy details.

Dusta comes back in and asks Lugner if Van had been depressed. Lugner said he was depressed, that he and his girlfriend were having a little trouble, but not too bad, and that Van and his brother were arguing. He also said he believed that Van was scared about going into the Marine Corps.

Dusta then asks Lugner to go through the accident from the beginning.

Lugner says: "I was sick, so I was staying in bed and I—I was sitting in my chair, my easy chair, watching TV when I heard, you know, a gunshot. And I froze for a second and then I said—I jumped up, I had a dog in my lap and then the dog fell down then, you know, barked and then I started running out of the bedroom. And I said, hey, hey. And then I heard another gunshot and I stopped. I don't know why. And then I took off running and screaming hey, hey. I don't know what. And I come around the corner and Tristan was in the threshold of my son's bedroom door sitting like this and his face is open, you know. He's shot in the face and his jaw is apart and hanging down. And I see Van laying there, and I didn't know, I saw some blood on him but I didn't know if—it didn't look like a lot, you know. But I went over there and he—he had a bullet hole right here, I think. And—and I was seeing—you know, I know he was dead, you know. And he was bleeding out and he was bleeding and turning white. He wasn't breathing. And I just grabbed him and started saying, my baby, my baby. And then I jump up and I turn around and I look at Tristan, and he's looking at me kind of blinking, going like this. And I was like—I grabbed him and was freaking out, you know, are you OK, are you OK? It's stupid now, but oh he's OK, you know. And he—he started talking and moving and stuff. And it took me probably, probably—probably like fifteen seconds, it felt like twenty minutes to figure out to call 911, you know. And I called 911. And I tried to keep him with me because he was trying to say I've got to kill myself, I've got to kill myself, I've got to kill myself. And I was worried because, I mean, I've got guns, you know, and he'll just go back in there. I let him go a few times. It was hard to watch him, because I don't want to roughhouse with him, you know....But he's combative and he wants to go back in there and kill himself. And I'm trying to—I'm trying to talk to her, you know, [the 911 operator] and I was like, I got to go, I got to go, but I didn't want to hang up because I was worried that if I did somehow something would get miscommunicated where they wouldn't know where to go to or whatever. I know now that that was one of the first things I gave them. So I kind of walked and then I took him out in the yard and sat him down in the grass so that it would give separation. And then I just started calling people, called his parents. The paramedics said they're taking him to Sacred Heart."

Dusta: "Uh-huh. When you first saw Tristan, was he sitting in the threshold or was he standing?"

Lugner: "Sitting."

Dusta: "Sitting. And did he have a gun at that point? Did you see him with a gun in his hand?"

Lugner: "I didn't...But he may have, but I just immediately went...I went right over the top. Well, no, I remember. I went right over the top of him and went to Van to check on him. It seems like he might have been moving when I went by him…the first time. But I saw him, saw his face. I went straight over to Van and saw him."

Dusta: "Do you know what gun was used?"

Lugner: "Uh-uh."

Dusta: "OK. Is there a .38 in the house?"

Lugner: "Uh-huh."

Dusta: "There was a mention that that might be the one that was used. OK. Did Van—or not Van. Did Tristan say anything else about why he wanted to kill himself or why he had to go kill himself?"

Lugner: "He just said, I don't deserve to live. He was hard to understand.…I'm assuming he is OK. I mean…"

Dusta: "He's in surgery is all I know. I know he was talking to a nurse prior to going into surgery, but still unknown of, you know, what's going on with him. Did you know of either one of them being suicidal or wanting…"

Lugner: "No, just suffer with depression and stuff, yeah.…But I never thought, never in a million years."

Dusta: "You would have not thought anything about maybe like a suicide pact that maybe he was…"

Lugner: "No."

Dusta: "—to kill and then kill himself or…"

Lugner: "I don't know anything. No, I would have never assumed that."

Dusta: "I don't know if you know about Tristan, but do you know if Van was—was he looking into seeing somebody for his depression or did he talk to anybody about his depression?"

Lugner: "No. We didn't think it was that bad. I mean, he's joining the marines and that stuff can mess you up, I think. And he didn't want—me and his mother are getting divorced, so we're going to a psychiatrist, me and his younger brother, and so we see someone. And I mentioned that, you know, to Van and he was—because he didn't want to mess up."

Dusta: "Mess up his chances?"

Lugner: "Yeah. And that would have."

Dusta: "Yes, definitely."

Lugner: "And—and—but I never, never thought he would do that."

Dusta: "He never actually came out and said he wanted to kill himself, he just seemed a little—"

Lugner: "No."

Dusta: "—down?" The conversation continues for a bit about depression in the family and their issues. Then Dusta continues asking about the day.

Dusta: "When did Tristan come over?"

Lugner: "9:00ish."

Dusta: "So they were just hanging out in the room?"

Lugner: "They were going to go work out. We were going to try and watch a movie maybe that afternoon and go have pizza at my mom's apartment."

Dusta: "What is their relationship? I know you said they're friends, but…"

Lugner: "Best friends."

Dusta: "Just best friends?"

Lugner: "Uh-huh, really close."

Dusta: "Nothing more than friends?"

Lugner: "No."

Dusta: "OK. Did you ever know Tristan to be—you said he was depressed sometimes, too?" They then discuss the concept of Tristan being depressed, and Lugner tells Dusta that he thought that Tristan saw somebody.

(The truth is, Tristan had had early adolescent depression, but he had out-grown it and was having the best time of his life. He was almost done with high school, was looking into going into the police academy, and had good friends. He was growing up and felt like life was good.)

Dusta continues: "And did—I know you said you were sick in the other room. Do you know what they were doing in the room? Do you know if they were cleaning guns, you know, looking at the guns, doing something of that nature?"

Lugner: "I think they were—they were cleaning guns is what I thought . . . This is only because I could hear them in there."

Dusta: "Did you hear any of the conversation that was said while they were in there?"

Lugner: "No."

Dusta: "Do you know if they were laughing or if they were arguing, anything?"

Lugner: "No, it was kind of quiet."

Dusta: "So if they were to argue about something and one of them was mad at the other, you would have probably heard some type of argument?"

Lugner: "If they raised their voices, yeah."

Dusta: "You'd have heard it from where you were at?"

Lugner: "Uh-huh."

Dusta: "And that room that Van was in, that's his bedroom, or is that a spare bedroom or your bedroom in the back where he was located?"

Lugner: "Yeah, he was in his bedroom."

Dusta: "OK. And your bedroom—is your bedroom on the opposite side of the house?"

Lugner: "They were in his brother's bedroom, and they were in his bedroom and the living room and kitchen, you know, they were kind of going around."

Dusta: "I'm going to give you a little break. I'm going to go check on the search warrant. We have to conduct a search warrant before we can go, you know, gather anything from the home. But does Van know how to use guns?"

Lugner: "Uh-huh."

Dusta: "Does he practice and go shooting all the time?"

Lugner: "Uh-huh."

Dusta: "The .38, does that belong to you, or is that one that they use at times, or is that something that he would have gravitated toward, for some reason that they would have had that one?"

Lugner: "I don't know why they would gravitate to it. I don't know. There's a bunch of guns."

Dusta: "OK. And—and like I don't know if you're worried about that. We're not worried about that, OK?"

Lugner: "OK."

Dusta: "So just have peace knowing that that's not what we're looking at, OK? All right. All right, I'll be right back. I'm going to give you a little bit of a break. Do you need anything?"

Lugner: "No. Thank you, though." (Dusta apparently leaves the room.)

Batemans: "They're still, of course, investigating. It looks like it's possible that—is that a call coming in?" The call is Lugner's wife, but he refuses to answer because he doesn't want to talk to her. He says he is not sure if she has found out or not, and is not confident in what her reaction would be.

Batemans: "OK. So she'll probably leave a voicemail and you can call her back. But it looks like it may be shaping up that Tristan shot Van and then shot himself as opposed to Van killing himself. That's the way it's looking right now. They're getting a search warrant affidavit because of the homicide that occurred in there."

(Listening to this audio, we wondered, was there a set up here? The lawyer says it's shaping up to be a homicide and then a suicide attempt—without any crime scene investigation at this time! There is absolutely no discussion about the possibility that it could have been a terrible accidental discharge, then a shock-stricken teenager reacting in pure terror. We were astonished to hear the investigator tell the man who is on probation but has alcohol, pot and loaded guns in his house—and let them be used by teens without supervision—that law enforcement is not concerned about that, and that he shouldn't worry! This is the real crime here and these, in my opinion, are the real criminals. Mr. Lugner allowed it all to happen, and his attorney and the sheriff's investigator put the wrong person—Tristan—on trial. It was a spectacular failure of the justice system.)

Batemans continues: "Now, it happened, there's really no basis for them to have to search your room. You say you took that pot away from—"

Lugner: "[my younger son]."

Batemans: "—from [his younger son]."

Lugner: "Uh-huh."

Batemans: "And how much from [his younger son]?"

Lugner: "I flushed it, it's gone."

Batemans: "OK. So what's still there in your closet?"

Lugner: "There's just this little pipe in a box that he had it in."

Batemans: "OK. Paraphernalia?"

Lugner: "Uh-huh."

Batemans: "All right. But they shouldn't even want to search anywhere other than the vicinity. It there anything else in the house that would have [inaudible] that you know of?"

Lugner: "I have alcohol in the house."

Batemans: "You're not allowed to drink alcohol on probation."

Lugner: "Yeah, I have a little bit of Scotch—a little bit of Scotch and then I have a little bit of beer…I drank the night before or the day before."

Batemans: "You were good at not drinking. Understand that it's going to be tough for you not to take a drink, but…"

The conversation continues about family issues. Then Lugner asks, "What do I say if they ask me about alcohol or drugs?"

Batemans: "They should only ask you as it relates to Tristan, whether or not—she's calling again. Do you want me to answer it?"

Lugner chooses not to answer the call. He is still concerned about protecting himself: "I'm still a little nervous about the alcohol and the pot. I really just need to tell them."

Batemans asks: "I mean, the kids weren't drinking?"

Lugner: "No."

Batemans reiterates: "You didn't let the kids drink, did you?"

Lugner: "No."

Batemans: "OK."

Lugner repeats: "No."

Batemans: "[inaudible] alcohol, do you understand me?"

Lugner: "Yes."

Batemans: "They'll find the alcohol, but that's not what they're looking for."

Lugner: "OK."

Batemans: "That's not the cause of this. Quite frankly, I don't know what they're going to do. They'll search for the gun [inaudible] this is a homicide."

Lugner: "OK."

Batemans: "Apparently, it's not a suicide, it's a homicide. Tristan, they suspect, killed Van and then tried to kill himself."

Lugner: "But why?" (Even he knew how much the boys cared for each other and how Tristan had watched over Van as his parents were going through a messy divorce. He couldn't believe that Tristan would ever do such a thing, but I think he sees an out for himself by going along with his attorney's narrative. He could have said that Tristan was like a son to him, and until all evidence was in, he was going to wait. But he didn't. He chose to allow a seventeen-year-old boy to go to prison for a crime he didn't commit, rather than put himself in jeopardy.)

Batemans: "Tristan didn't try to kill himself, OK, because he shot his jaw off. This is—if this is what turns out to be the case, then you're looking at a homicide charge."

(We were stunned to hear this line of reasoning. Can you imagine a teenager shooting his own jaw off under any circumstance? This felt like pure evil conjecture on his part.)

Lugner: "OK."

Batemans: "And so anything having to collect on it or anything associated with. How many bottles of [inaudible] had you had?"

Lugner: "One that has about that much in it. There's hardly any, just one."

Batemans: "Where is it at?"

Lugner: "In my closet."

Batemans: "Master bedroom?"

Lugner: "Uh-huh."

Batemans: "[inaudible]"

Lugner: "Yes, and it's just one bottle."

Batemans: "People have alcohol that's sitting around their houses for years, not necessarily the same case with beer."

Lugner: "OK."

Batemans: "[inaudible]"

Lugner: "OK."

Batemans: "[inaudible]"

Lugner: "OK."

Batemans: "Yeah."

Lugner: "All right. I'll take care of it."

Batemans: "I don't want any [inaudible] in the house is going to be [inaudible]."

Lugner: "OK."

Batemans: "You can answer those. When is the last time you had a drink?"

Lugner: "Yesterday afternoon."

Batemans: "OK."

Lugner: "OK."

Batemans: "[inaudible]"

Lugner: "OK."

Batemans: "Your probation [inaudible]."

Lugner: "OK."

Batemans: "[inaudible] not the focus of suspicion and they're not trying to make it any harder for you, unless they're going to say you were giving alcohol to these kids."

Lugner: "Yeah."

Batemans: "[inaudible] give them a drink?"

Lugner: "No. Not to my knowledge, no. But Van, no."

Batemans: "OK, all right. We'll see. When was he scheduled to go to boot camp?"

Lugner: "January 30. OK. So I want to get this over with."

Batemans: "It could be that it was—what was it, Tristan? Tristan is the one who just killed—maybe he thought Van wanted to die. But that's—this is a whole…"

Lugner: "Yeah."

Batemans: "It's a homicide, it's not a suicide, it's a homicide." (I have always wondered how Batemans seemed so sure of his theory, as he had only had knowledge of the accident for about an hour. The crime scene investigators had barely been to the scene, and it's questionable if the medical examiner ever did go there. Whom had Batemans spoken with to be so sure, and to tell Lugner how this was going to play out? I question, did Lillith Dusta tell Batemans or did Batemans tell Dusta how it was going to go? It was extremely premature to call this a homicide before all the evidence was in, especially that from the medical examiner.)

(Investigator Dusta enters back into the room.)

Dusta: "You guys OK?"

Batemans: "Just for Hain's benefit, how much longer do you think before we'll be done here?"

Dusta says she only has a couple more questions. She asks what kind of phone Van had. (We wonder why she asked that question, as we now know she had gotten Van's phone from the garage and had already gone through it without a warrant.)

There is more discussion about getting the news to Van's mother. Dusta receives a phone call regarding Van's mother and says, "No, just—just go ahead and make the notification and then if Tristan's family happens to show up, then yes, I would need to talk to them. But they're probably going to be at the hospital."

Dusta continues to question Lugner about Van's cell phone, and Tristan's cell phone as well. Then she asks, "How—how much time passed between the shots? You said the one shot you jumped up, started walking that direction and then the second shot…"

Lugner: "I heard the shots and I jumped like that and then I jumped up and ran out and grabbed my door. And as I was going through my door, which I didn't grab my door, it was open. I get to my bedroom door and I'm just—I'm running, and I heard the next shot."

Dusta: "OK, all right. Let's see if there's anything else I need to ask you and then we'll cut you loose so you can get out of here and get where you need to get going, OK?"

Lugner: "When are you going to tell me when—what you know, and what happened?"

Dusta: "As soon as I figure out what's going on with Tristan once he's out of surgery, hopefully they'll be able to talk to us and let us know."

Talk resumes regarding Lugner's mother coming to pick him up. His mother calls him, and what she says to him is inaudible.

Lugner: "As soon as I get downstairs. All right, as soon as I get downstairs, we'll—we'll leave. And I'm assuming I need to go to the hospital."

Lugner's mother: "Why?"

Lugner: "Because I need something."

Lugner's mother: "[inaudible]"

Lugner: "Yeah."

Lugner's mother: "Then yes, you do." (This has always been a mystery to me. What, exactly were they talking about? What did he need?)

In this interview, they floated the theory that possibly Tristan had been suicidal. However, two days after the accident Tristan had a psychological assessment with Dr. Robert S. Benson, who determined that he was not suicidal and "does not have psychiatric symptoms that would require treatment with any medications at the present time…The circumstances of the shooting do not indicate suicidal ideation and he does not indicate a plan for harm to himself or others. He does not require suicide precautions and does not meet criteria for involuntary placement under the Baker Act."

No one from the sheriff's office had spoken with Tristan to get his side of the story, so any theories as to his state of mind were just conjecture. We hired a defense attorney, and he had told us not to let any law enforcement officials question Tristan, as they often twisted a defendant's words to use against them in court. Additionally, Tristan was unable to speak and highly sedated; plus, we didn't want to upset him any further since he'd had a tracheotomy and wasn't breathing on his own. Of course, investigators did show up, and we had to turn them away.

Jack was planning on going to Van's memorial. At this time, we were under the impression that everyone knew it had been a horrible accident and was grieving Van's passing and also concerned about and praying for Tristan, who was closer to death than most people realized. Jack wanted to pay his respects to Van's family and tell them what we had learned about that day so that at least they would know exactly what had happened to their son. We even thought (naively, it turns out) that there would be an apology for allowing the boys to use the guns and an admission that if there had been adult supervision, this probably could have been prevented. Since the Lugners were "devout Christians," or so we thought, we assumed that there would be forgiveness on both sides. But just before Van's service, Lillith Dusta told Jack that our family would not be welcome there.

Dusta had been telling us that she was praying for Tristan and doing her best to work the case, but we now know she had already decided to charge him with a crime. To this day we don't know why she did this. Was she was coerced or bribed, or just an eager cop wanting to close a case fast to further her career? Ironically, she had been chosen Law Enforcement Officer of the Year a few years prior. But a few years after Tristan's case, she was demoted to court security officer due to her mishandling of another case.

Also, we found out that Hain Lugner had chosen to go with the get-out-of-jail-free card and tell everyone that Tristan had murdered Van, then faked a suicide attempt, and all he needed was some cosmetic surgery. We felt that we were victims of a witch hunt mentality and were beginning to realize that Tristan was not being considered "innocent until proven guilty." Evil gossip was everywhere, and Tristan felt every bit of it. A little support would have gone a long way in his healing process, both physically and mentally, but outside of our family and several close friends, there was none to be had.

While our attorney worked diligently on the discovery process, we tried to keep Tristan as far removed from it as possible except for answering the attorney's questions. He needed all his strength to heal, and he was already deeply distraught, missing his best friend immensely, and suffering from PTSD.

There were many discrepancies that came to light during the discovery process, but the investigators ignored them. Among the disclosures that surfaced were two almost identical photographs taken by the CSI team the night of the accident of Hain Lugner's nightstand by the easy chair in his bedroom. One of the photographs showed a half-full glass of brown liquid, a gun and a Bible. Another photograph, taken by a different photographer, showed the same glass, the gun, the Bible and a bottle of Chivas Regal Scotch. This made us question, what happened to the bottle of Scotch, who moved it, and why wasn't it collected as evidence? The bottle didn't appear in the evidence inventory. This is unbelievable to us, since as I said earlier, Lugner was on probation for a DUI. Now a death had happened in his house when he was apparently drinking, and no one followed up on that?

Another one of the many discrepancies was that the guns were all found in Lugner's bedroom closet, which contradicts Lugner's original statement to Batemans, that "the guns were in corners in walls and drawers and stuff." This means that after he put Tristan outside (alone, with his face blown apart) he apparently moved all the guns. This was an active crime scene. Wouldn't that be considered tampering with evidence? There were also bullets on the living room floor, which Lugner said must have fallen out of the gun as he was moving it. The gun expert we hired said that bullets never fall out of a gun. So now we wonder if the gun had been tampered with before the police got to the scene.

Also, Tristan's blood was in Lugner's shower. How did that happen? Tristan didn't go in there after he was shot. And, the boys were always on their phones, but there was a fifty-minute gap between the last activity on either boy's phone and the time Lugner called 911. He couldn't have called 911 immediately, as he claimed. Why not, and what was he doing? No one ever asked.

The autopsy showed gunshot residue on Van's arm, which substantiated Tristan's account of how Van had grabbed Tristan's hand, as the powder angle on Van's arm was consistent with how Tristan explained the direction his arm was pulled. There was also no stippling (a small dot pattern of red marks from gun residue) on Van's eyelids or below his lower lip (as if his head had been down upon the shot), meaning that the shot was unexpected.

I kept thinking that, with all of this evidence mounting, the district attorney, the prosecutor, and the judge would throw the case out. But another day would go by, and still nothing would happen.

In April we had a change of prosecutors. A special prosecutor, Tyron Devlin, was assigned to the case. Devlin called us. We thought it was to say that he had reviewed the evidence and was dismissing the case. Instead, he tried to pull what I now know is the plea bargain scheme. He had upped Tristan's charge from manslaughter to second-degree murder, and wanted to place a four hundred-thousand-dollar bail on Tristan or keep him in jail until trial. He asked us if Tristan wanted to take a plea bargain down to manslaughter in return for a reduced prison term. We couldn't believe it! This is the criminal justice game. As you will read in the chapter on the criminal "injustice" system, this is how prosecutors plow through casework. Remember, there's not much money to be made or career advancement for prosecutors unless they get convictions. These prosecutors appear to have no compassion; they are playing with people's lives as if they are playing a of poker.

Tristan was still sick, traumatized, in excruciating pain and having to eat a special diet because of his missing teeth and jawbone. He still had many very serious surgeries ahead of him as well. Our attorney asked Devlin what made him up the charge, and all Devlin could say was that he had reviewed the case. Our attorney told him that Tristan still had hundreds of thousands of dollars' worth of medical procedures left, and the county would have to foot the bill if Tristan were in jail. Besides, he was obviously not a flight risk. Fortunately, Devlin pulled back on increasing the bail, but he kept the charge of second-degree murder. We tried to keep the news from Tristan, but eventually we had to tell him. It was heartbreaking.

Meanwhile, we did our best to create an environment of structure and some sort of normalcy in Tristan's life. He was unable to go to school, so he took (and aced) the General Equivalency Diploma test. He also worked part-time managing the front desk at our Pilates/Myofascial Release studio. His first love was the Jeep that he and Jack had purchased several months before the accident. He taught himself how to embellish it with lights, a winch, a lift kit and more. He loved to drive around in it and look for people who needed help, like being pulled out of a ditch. He also hung out at a vape shop, where he made true friends who listened to and supported him. (Later, though, they told me that it was really Tristan who had counseled them. He is such an old soul.)

The heaviness of those days was truly unbearable. Even though we were trying to live our day-to-day lives, the upcoming major surgery and murder trial loomed over us like an approaching hurricane. Still, I prayed that this charge would be dismissed, that somewhere in the system someone existed who would realize that this was an accident and there was no evidence of a murder and suicide attempt. But it just kept heating up. The pressure continued from Van's family to get "justice," based on their made-up narrative and Lugner's unwillingness to admit any wrongdoing. Devlin told our attorney that he was glad he didn't have to come up with a motive, because he saw none. All they had was character defamation. Tristan made multiple appearances in front of the judge and prosecutor, but each time our lawyer asked for a continuance so he could have more time to gather evidence. Sometimes the prosecutor asked for a continuance as well.

Dr. Gary Cumberland, a retired medical examiner, heard about the case and volunteered his time to help us. He truly believed that this could be nothing but an accidental discharge and an impulsive overreaction by Tristan. He was astounded to hear that the case wasn't being thrown out and he wanted to help. He ran an independent analysis of the scene photographs, the autopsy report, and witness depositions, and visited the scene to do technical investigations noting the trajectory of the bullet, the placement of the boys in the room, gunshot residue, and more. He also re-enacted the incident with Tristan. After this, he concluded that all the evidence was consistent with Tristan's story and firmly stated that this had to have been a horrible accident. We were extremely grateful for his efforts and support.

The next major surgery happened in Miami on December 14, 2017. This was to be the last attempt to save Tristan's jaw. (The rest of the journey would be to implant teeth once the jawbone had formed, and then do advanced facial plastic surgery.) The surgeons made an incision from ear to ear, then pulled Tristan's facial skin up to work on the jaw. They removed his titanium plate and did a bone graft using tissue engineering (combining cadaver bone and stem cells harvested from Tristan's hip). They also screwed upper dentures into the roof of his mouth. Then they wired his jaw shut.

While the surgery was successful and we were very thankful for the surgical staff, again there was miscommunication. They had forgotten to insert the feeding tube into Tristan's stomach. After a horrifying attempt to put it through his nose despite his repeated pleas not to, they inserted it through his stomach—with no sedation. In order to make sure the tube was inserted properly, they had to inject dye and X-ray the area. The dye, combined with pain medication on an empty stomach, caused severe nausea. This necessitated an immediate emergency procedure to cut the jaw wires so Tristan wouldn't aspirate on vomit. I was staying in the lounge chair in his room that night, and he was just crying and pleading with me to make it stop, that he couldn't take it anymore.

After two days my sister (the surgeon) drove down to Miami from her home in West Palm Beach and explained to the doctors where they had gone wrong. The interventional radiologist was insisting that Tristan go in for another X-ray with more contrast dye to see what the problem was. My sister was able to pull up the previous X-ray, which showed the tube was in the right place. She was met with strong resistance from the radiologist but fortunately was able to explain to her that another X-ray with dye would torture Tristan and make him sicker. My sister also told Tristan's doctors what medications to give him. They followed her advice, and in a few hours he started to feel better and was able to relax. I could write an entire additional book about the medical world and its problems, but I will leave that for another person. My son was alive and that was good. We returned home to Pensacola.

On January 2, 2018, Jack and Tristan flew down to Miami for the follow-up with his surgical team. He still faced a long recovery from this surgery, and his next surgery was scheduled for six to twelve months out. Also, the criminal case against him continued to intensify. Needless to say, his fear and anxiety about this, coupled with PTSD, pain from all the surgeries, and pain from the initial injury plus exposed nerves in his mouth, were all taking a toll. Tristan started using medical marijuana, which I supported because I felt that it was better than continuing to take opioids. He had weaned himself off opioids between surgeries; the cannabis seemed to help his residual pain and PTSD. But after this last surgery, Tristan was in such pain, he had to go back on opioids. He had built up quite a tolerance because he'd been on them for so long, plus he was a large-framed young man. He began to go to Dr. Bill Wilson because Dr. Wilson prescribed narcotics more freely than other physicians. I was unaware of exactly how much Dr. Wilson was prescribing.

The trial was scheduled for March 15, 2018. Jury selection was held on March 5th. Tristan had to sit through the entire grueling process. But after selection was finished, the jury seemed to hold people who would be sympathetic toward Tristan. For the first time since the accident, I saw a glimmer of happiness and hope in Tristan—but it was short-lived. When Devlin realized there was a strong possibility that this jury would deliver a verdict of not guilty, he asked Judge Malvin Bundy to postpone the trial. He used the excuse that his gun expert witness from Tallahassee had come down with the flu. Much to our surprise, Judge Bundy agreed, and moved the trial date to the first week of May with jury selection on Monday, April 30th.

Additionally, the judge heard multiple motions regarding the trial. Judges have the authority to deny or allow motions, which are basically requests from the prosecutor (the state) or the defense on what will be allowed for the jury to hear at trial. In effect, the motions creatively determine the story that the jury will be told. Judge Bundy allowed the following motions requested by the prosector:

- The judge shall not tell the jury what type of sentencing would be imposed.

- There shall be no mention of the marijuana found in the younger son's room.

- There shall be no mention of a "dummy grenade" found in the Lugners' garage.

- There shall be no mention of a bat with nails in it that was located in the younger son's room.

- There shall be no testimony as to the defendant's ongoing medical treatment, and limited testimony as to any previous medical procedures. (Lillith Dusta was telling the family that Tristan only needed slight cosmetic surgery, and Hain Lugner was telling the boys' friends that Tristan went to kill himself but chickened out and only shot his chin off. Tristan's extensive injuries would reveal those stories to be untrue.)

- There shall be no opinion testimony solicited as to whether the firearms were stored properly.

- There shall be no mention of "silencers" or "noise suppressors" or "flash suppressors" located within the Lugner's home.

- There shall be no testimony solicited as to what crime the defendant was arrested for. (Which would have revealed that the charge had been upped.)

- There shall be no mention as to Mr. Hain Lugner wanting his lawyer at his interview.

- There shall be no mention of or testimony solicited as to any of the firearms located within the home possibly being stolen.

- There shall be no mention of or testimony solicited as to Mr. Hain Lugner being on DUI probation or the terms of that probation. DUI is not a felony conviction or a misdemeanor involving dishonesty and therefore is not a prior conviction for impeachment purposes. (However, I say it shows completely irresponsible behavior!)

- There shall be no mention of or testimony solicited as to text messages that were downloaded from any of the phones without proffering testimony. (We have a heartfelt text from Van to Tristan regarding how much their friendship meant to him, and they did not want us to use it at trial.)

- There shall be no mention of or testimony solicited as to any alcohol consumed or marijuana smoked on any previous occasion by Van Lugner, [the younger son], [another friend], or Hain Lugner.

- Dr. Gary Cumberland, retired Medical Examiner, …shall not be permitted to testify as to what the defense counsel told him or what the defendant may tell him prior to trial as this would constitute the reliance on hearsay…Dr. Cumberland shall not be permitted to testify as to his opinion on the cause and manner of death of Mr. Van Lugner if it is based on such hearsay.

Our defense attorney formally requested dozens of motions. Most of them were denied by Judge Bundy.

Our defense attorney had another month to prepare for the case and prepare Tristan as well. He hired a psychodramatist to help Tristan to deal with his emotions, so that he could handle being on the stand. This work also provided a safe environment to draw out memories regarding the incident. Tristan made many visits to see the attorney as the questioning became more frequent and intense. On April 26th, Tristan had a practice cross-examination to prepare him for the realities of the trial. It was brutal, but they needed him to know what to expect.

Tristan took a break from the prep that day and went to see Dr. Wilson, unknowingly picking up the fatal cocktail that would end his life several hours later. (Wilson had not only given him opioids, he had also given him Xanax and Ambien because Tristan was experiencing major anxiety and stress and couldn't sleep.)

The cross examination continued for hours. When someone has PTSD and is still in shock, the worst thing that can happen is for the wound to be reopened viciously and callously, yet it had to be done to prepare him for the trial. By around 10:00 p.m., Tristan still wasn't home. I knew that he was being tortured and had had enough. I texted and asked him when he was going to be done. He texted back "IDK" (I don't know). That was the last text I would ever receive from him. Jack texted the attorney and asked him to end the prep and let Tristan come home.

Tristan arrived shortly after that. I met him at the side door and I hardly recognized him. He seemed listless and his eyes were empty. He was all discombobulated and said that he still had to read Hain Lugner's deposition and more; he had a whole file full to read before the next day of prep. I put my hand on his back and said, "No, that can wait until tomorrow. You need to eat and get some sleep." He went upstairs. That was the last time I would ever see my beautiful son alive. Tristan ate dinner and watched television with his brother Chris, telling him that that had been the worst day he'd had in his entire life.

Throughout the day, Tristan had taken seventeen opioids for pain. Then he took a Xanax and two Ambien before bed. Around 6:30 the following morning, I heard him snoring very loudly. I wanted to go in and move him but I knew that he needed sleep. I went out for an errand and came back home around 1:00 p.m. I was in the kitchen and Jack was in his office when Chris went upstairs to wake Tristan up so they could go to an afternoon movie, as they had planned the night before. Chris yelled for me and Jack. When we got upstairs, we saw Tristan's lifeless body. I climbed in bed next to him, hugged him, and told him how much I loved him. Chris had called 911 and the paramedics said to start CPR. I did, despite the fact that his lungs were filled with fluid. I just had to. The paramedics came and took over. They were followed shortly by the police.

We were treated harshly by the Pensacola police, despite our beloved son's body lying warm in his bed upstairs. They even taped off his room with crime scene tape so we couldn't go in. It took many weeks to get someone out to the house to remove the tape so we could go into our son's bedroom, despite multiple requests.

Hain Lugner had created the perfect environment for an accident to happen, and yet the legal system was undeniably in his corner from the start. As I relay this story now, I continue to be as shocked as we were then by the absolute mistreatment of Tristan on every level, by almost everyone, including deputies, the medical examiner, the CSI, the hospital staff, the Escambia County Sheriff's Office—especially the detective in charge of the investigation, Lillith Dusta—the state attorney's office, and the juvenile offender retention facility.

Even social media was harsh, and Tristan read everything. When the local media ran their stories online reiterating the falsehoods put out by the sheriff's office, people responded with remarks like, "Where is he, I'll go over and finish the job for him," calling him a coward, and worse. Harsh words can be sharper than a sword. Statements like these were extremely damaging to Tristan's heart and soul, at a time when he was trying his best to hang on.

The fact that the prosecutor continued this case despite no evidence—despite all evidence pointing to accidental discharge—seems to indicate that they had an agenda that was more important to them than the truth. This entire experience should never have happened. And the financial and emotional outlay required to defend our son in a case that most jurisdictions would have recorded as a tragic accident was outrageous. It's also shocking that nothing happened to Hain Lugner, whose lack of supervision of his sons and visitors, as well as his stockpile of openly accessible guns and other weapons, had made this horrible accident possible. After Tristan's death, he went his merry way without ever looking back at the total destruction left in his wake.

Before we move on to Tristan's story, I want to share information that sheds further light on what happened and validates Tristan's case, as well as a recent update on Dr. Bill Williams.

First, I have been given permission to share the following letter written by Dr. Cumberland, MD, to the state attorney, First Judicial Circuit of Florida. It is dated May 3, 2018, one week after Tristan's passing.

Dear Sir,

I wanted to address issues that continue to bother me in reference to the above scribed case. As you are aware, the state had charged Tristan Bruni with second degree murder and was scheduled to be tried this past week. As an acquaintance of the Bruni's, I had agreed to look over the forensic evidence, pro bono, and give their attorney any help that I deemed appropriate. I cautioned that I would look at the scene, investigation and autopsy reports objectively and would not sugar coat my impressions.

After reviewing the records, and visiting the scene with Tristan's defense attorney and your assistant state attorney, several things began to bother me.

1). Both your office and ESCO [Escambia County Sheriff's Department] seemed to have jumped to conclusions about the lethal shot much too quickly before examining all of the evidence. They failed to compare the incident to all of the possible scenarios, the most important being accidental discharge of the weapons vs intentional discharge (which your office seemed to blindly accept as the ONLY story that fit the circumstances.) This, I think caused them to push for second degree murder rather than a lower charge. In point of fact, based on my thirty years of experience, I felt that the incident was really more consistent with an accidental discharge rather than an intentional firing. I saw nothing in the records to indicate that any thought had been given to this or other possibilities. Thus, I saw no evidence that your office or the ECSO did anything to rule out scenarios which would cause you to consider a lower level of homicide or even realize that it was, as I believe, just a tragic accident. Instead they seemed to spend large amounts of time trying to come up various motives for intent—not one of which could withstand the light of day.

2). I am not a lawyer nor do I claim to be one, but as I observed the case, I saw the prosecution assuming an "I am going to win this case based on my early impressions regardless of the truth" mindset. Once he set his mind on an intentional discharge of the gun he showed no interest in other possibilities. One of the reasons that I so admired Judge Rimmer when he was a prosecutor was that he always took the time to sit down to discuss our cases before going to trial. This gave us an understanding of what we could say while dismissing items that didn't fit with our mutual perception of what had happened. This was obviously a foreign concept to your assistant prosecutor.

3). Finally, I need to tell you that your Assistant State Attorney on this case was arrogant beyond any level of appropriateness. During hearing he would assume a condescending attitude to Tristan (the defendant), Tristan's defense attorney, and most importantly, Tristan's parents. The Bruni family is a strong, contributing middle-class family in this community and has been for years. The dismissive, rude way they were treated should be an embarrassment to your office. They were and are a traumatized family who deserved much better.

The poor handling of this case from the ECSO to the State Attorney's Office to the presiding judge resulted in plenty of blame to spread around. I believe the system let Tristan and the Bruni family down in multiple ways. The circumstances surrounding Tristan's recent death this last week only deepens my conviction.

I have never written a letter like this ever before and I hope that I never have to again. Please accept this criticism in the spirit in which it is intended. If you feel that this doesn't apply or that my ignorance of the legal system has given me a distorted look at the process, feel free to trash this letter knowing that this is the only copy and will not be shared with anyone other than the Bruni family. You guys work hard and do a remarkable job handling all of the burdens of the judicial system in our four counties. Sometimes, though, it's important to have a perspective from someone on the outside looking in. Unfortunately, it is my considered opinion that in this particular case, you and your office failed miserably. It is this failure to be both objective and respectful that demeans the office you are duty bound to lead. Ultimately, a dismal failure occurred that should never, ever be repeated, lest our community be victimized again by such injustice.

Sincerely,

Gary D. Cumberland, MD MS CPE
Forensic Pathologist

The following is an excerpt from a *Pensacola News Journal* article published on July 9, 2018, about firearms being confiscated from two residents under the state's "red flag" law. The high school student mentioned in the first case is Mr. Lugner's younger son, and the adult man mentioned in the second case is Mr. Lugner. Note that the article refers to what happened with Van as an "accidental shooting."

"Escambia County authorities have sought risk protection orders to confiscate firearms from two residents since Florida's 'red flag law' came into effect earlier this year in response to the Parkland shooting.

"The two petitions were both sought the same day—May 22—in two separate cases. One was against a Tate High School student who had an AR-15 and was reportedly stalking his ex, and the other was against a father accused of having a history of unsafe gun storage and mental health issues following the accidental shooting death of his teenage son.

"Risk protection orders allow law enforcement officers to petition a judge who can then decide whether the subject is a risk to themselves or others at a level that warrants temporarily confiscating their weapons. …

"The first case involved a juvenile who, at the time, was a Tate High student. Two school resource officers submitted sworn affidavits to Circuit Judge Thomas Dannheisser urging for an order to be put in place to remove an AR-15 hanging in the boy's bedroom.

"Court documents do not give the boy's name or age, but one SRO wrote that another Tate student told him that her boyfriend of three weeks was stalking her after she broke up with him. She said he was stopping her in the halls, repeatedly contacting her via social media and, at one time, he allegedly attempted to punch a boy who was seen with her.

"Three days before the order was signed, the boy allegedly threatened to post naked photos of the girl on social media if she didn't get back together with him and said he would kill himself if she didn't return to him.

"The girl also said her ex-boyfriend posted photos of the AR-15 and a bullet on social media.

"The girl's mother said she didn't want to press charges but wanted the behavior documented.

"The deputies took the boy to the Lakeview Center on May 22 under the Baker Act, which allows law enforcement to involuntarily hold a subject for up to 72 hours if they are an immediate danger to themselves or others. When the boy's mother arrived at Lakeview to take her son home, she reportedly said she was 'glad she won't have to come home and wonder if her son was dead.'

"In a court hearing three days later, the boy's mom said all firearms had been removed from the home and wouldn't be returned until the court allows.

"In the second case, the ECSO removed more than 50 guns from a man whose teenage son had been killed accidentally in their home.

"The 42 year-old father had been experiencing substance abuse and mental health issues since the death of his 18-year-old son in November 2016, according to court documents.

"The father told police his son and a 17-year-old friend were in his son's bedroom when he heard a gunshot. He said he jumped up from his chair and ran into the room, but as he opened the door, he heard a second gunshot. He found both boys had been shot in the face.

"He told police he ran to his son and held him, but he already knew he was dead. The man then called 911 and grabbed the son's friend. He later told police the surviving boy was trying to kill himself and repeatedly made statements including 'I don't deserve to live.'

"The 17-year-old friend faced a manslaughter charge in the death, but he himself died before the case was resolved.

"The father's risk protection order documents cite his son's death and a divorce as a catalyst for post-traumatic stress and anxiety. Both he and his still-living son, a 14-year-old, allegedly have violence and mental health issues that have caused concern to police.

"The father also faced manslaughter charges in his son's death due to accusations he had improperly stored and secured firearms in the home, but those charges were not prosecuted.

"ECSO confiscated 54 weapons at the time the order was filed in May, and Dannheisser later denied a request for a longer period of confiscation after two hearings when he determined the man wasn't a significant risk to himself or others. The man's weapons have since been returned to him."

The following is a filing by sheriff's investigator Lillith Dusta associated with the risk protection order to remove Lugner's guns from his home, described in the news article above. I find it incredible to see how differently she describes Lugner's behavior, the circumstances surrounding Van's accident and the subsequent investigation. Remember that at the time of the accident, Dusta said she never saw Mr. Lugner under the influence, and she seemed completely unfazed by all the guns lying around the Lugner home—she even told him "we're not worried about that, OK?" when he mentioned having a lot of guns. Also, remember the discrepancy in the evidence photographs, where a liquor bottle was visible on the nightstand by his chair in one photo, yet mysteriously missing in another? Interestingly, it shows up in her statement here.

Filing # 72528008 E-Filed 05/22/2018 05:37:46 PM

IN THE CIRCUIT COURT OF THE FIRST JUDICIAL CIRCUIT, IN AND FOR ESCAMBIA COUNTY, FLORIDA

IN RE: PETITION FOR RISK PROTECTION ORDER
AGAINST ▓▓▓▓ ▓▓▓

AFFIDAVIT

STATE OF FLORIDA

COUNTY OF ESCAMBIA

    I, ▓▓▓▓▓ ▓▓▓ in my position as an investigator with the Escambia County Sheriff's

Office, swear and affirm that the following facts are true and correct.

    1.   ▓▓▓▓▓▓ poses a significant danger of causing personal injury to himself/herself or others by having a firearm or any ammunition in his/her custody or control or by purchasing, possessing or receiving a firearm or any ammunition. The following specific statements, actions, or facts give rise to a reasonable fear of significant dangerous acts by the respondent:

    On November 23, 2016, I responded to ▓▓▓▓▓▓ Pensacola, Florida in reference to a death investigation where 18-year-old ▓▓▓▓▓ was shot to death by 17-year-old T▓▓ B▓▓ T▓▓ B▓▓ also shot himself but survived his injuries.

    Throughout my investigation, I learned ▓▓▓▓▓▓▓▓▓▓▓▓▓ was home inside his residence of ▓▓▓▓▓▓ at the time of the shooting. A search warrant was conducted on ▓▓▓▓▓ residence where approximately 54 firearms were located unsecure inside the residence. I observed firearms and ammunition in both of ▓▓▓▓ son's ▓▓▓▓ and ▓▓▓▓ bedrooms. ▓▓▓▓ was 14 years of age at the time of the shooting and along with firearms on the floor of his bedroom, marijuana was also located in his bedroom. Located inside ▓▓▓▓ bedroom were multiple firearms inside the dresser drawers and on the floor. Inside ▓▓▓▓ bedroom were multiple firearms laying on the floor of his closet. All the firearms inside the residence were not secured properly and T▓▓ B▓▓ had possession of a firearm belonging to ▓▓▓▓▓▓▓

    I learned that at the time of the shooting, ▓▓▓▓▓ was on probation for DUI,

2016 MM 002197 A, and located inside his bedroom was a glass and bottle of alcohol on the nightstand next to the recliner that ████████ claimed he was sitting in at the time of the shooting.

Since the shooting, I have spoken with ████████ multiple times and each time he appeared to be under the influence of either drugs or alcohol ████████ also appeared to be mentally unstable and requested counseling services for him and his son, T███ H████. I referred him to Escambia County Sheriff's Office Victim's Advocate Leanne Sprague. After review of the documentation provided to me in reference to the interactions with ████████ and Leanne Sprague, I learned that ████████ and ████████ had already been seeing Doctor ████████ for mental health care prior to the shooting. I observed that ████████ requested a referral for psychiatric care for medications due to ████████ not being able to prescribe the medications ████████ disclosed to Leanne Sprague that he believes he has PTSD and anxiety following his divorce along with ████████'s death. I observed that Leanne Sprague also documented her observations in which she stated ████ sounded very manic on the telephone."

During my investigation, I spoke with ████████'s ex-wife, ████████ who also raised concerns about the mental health of her estranged husband and the fact that he has multiple firearms in the residence with her young son. Initially, ████████ wanted ████████ to also be charged for his part in the death of their son stating that he was responsible as well as T███ B███

████████ 14-year-old son, ████████ has been arrested for marijuana possession, carrying a concealed weapon, brass knuckles, ████████ and disorderly conduct involving a fight at school ████████

At this time, the return of ████████ firearms would be a concern in many ways as his and ████ ████ mental health are cause for concern. ████████ has also been arrested for a second DUI (2017 MM ████████) and appears to have a substance abuse issue.

Lastly, ████████ also faced charges of Manslaughter for the death of his son, ████████ for improperly storing and securing the multitude of firearms at their disposal ████████ had a duty as a gun owner and an adult parent in the home with juveniles to prevent this tragedy. Ultimately, ████████ was not charged for his part in the death of ████████

2. Affiant is not aware of any existing protection order governing the respondent under any applicable statute.

3. The quantities, types, and locations of all firearms and ammunition the petitioner believes to be in the respondent's current ownership, possession, custody or control are as follows:

Quantity	Type	Location
1	Sig Sauer Mosquito with Magazine	Escambia County Sheriff's Office
1	CZ-CZ52 with Magazine	Escambia County Sheriff's Office
1	HK 45 CT with Magazine	Escambia County Sheriff's Office
1	12 Gauge Remington	Escambia County Sheriff's Office
1	Round 5.7x28 Ammo	Escambia County Sheriff's Office
1	Round DPMS .380 Win Ammo	Escambia County Sheriff's Office
1	Round Winchester .45 Ammo	Escambia County Sheriff's Office
11	Rounds assorted live Ammo	Escambia County Sheriff's Office
17	Rounds 9MM Luger Ammo	Escambia County Sheriff's Office
19	Miscellaneous Magazines	Escambia County Sheriff's Office
20	5.7x28 FNB Ammo	Escambia County Sheriff's Office
24	.410 Rounds Ammo	Escambia County Sheriff's Office
25	Federal Target Live Load 12 Gauge	Escambia County Sheriff's Office
29	LC 5.56x45 rounds ammo	Escambia County Sheriff's Office
38	Rounds Remington 38 special Ammo	Escambia County Sheriff's Office
48	Rounds Remington 32 Auto Ammo	Escambia County Sheriff's Office
6	Rounds 38 Special and P Federal Ammo	Escambia County Sheriff's Office
6	Rounds Hornady .45 Colt Ammo	Escambia County Sheriff's Office
6	Rounds Reminton 870 Ammo	Escambia County Sheriff's Office
7	Rounds Winchester .45 Ammo	Escambia County Sheriff's Office
8	Rounds .45 Auto Ammo	Escambia County Sheriff's Office
9	7.62x39, 8 Wolf, 1 Tulammo Rounds Ammo	Escambia County Sheriff's Office
1	Enfield 2A1 firearm with magazine and Bayonet	Escambia County Sheriff's Office
1	Ruger 357 Magnum Revolver	Escambia County Sheriff's Office
1	556 Drum Magazine	Escambia County Sheriff's Office
1	7.62, 25 Win box live Ammo	Escambia County Sheriff's Office

1	American Eagle Box containing miscellaneous Ammo (11.8 lbs)	Escambia County Sheriff's Office
1	Ammo Can containing miscellaneous Ammo	Escambia County Sheriff's Office
1	Anderson Firearm with magazine AM 15	Escambia County Sheriff's Office
1	Arsenal Firearm with magazine	Escambia County Sheriff's Office
1	Beretta 9MM Firearm with magazine	Escambia County Sheriff's Office
1	Beretta 12 Gauge Shotgun	Escambia County Sheriff's Office
1	Beretta Stampede .357 Firearm	Escambia County Sheriff's Office
1	Beretta Tikka T3 7MM Rifle with scope	Escambia County Sheriff's Office
1	Black ammo box with miscellaneous ammo (12.0 lbs)	Escambia County Sheriff's Office
1	Black ammo box with miscellaneous Ammo (13.0 lbs)	Escambia County Sheriff's Office
1	Black ammo box with miscellaneous ammo (18.2 lbs)	Escambia County Sheriff's Office
1	Black ammo box with miscellaneous ammo (19.2 lbs)	Escambia County Sheriff's Office
1	Boot box with miscellaneous ammo (12.6 lbs)	Escambia County Sheriff's Office
1	Box of various ammo	Escambia County Sheriff's Office
25	Rounds .38 Special rounds ammo	Escambia County Sheriff's Office
1	Brown Federal box with miscellaneous ammo (7.2 lbs)	Escambia County Sheriff's Office
1	Miroku Browning Arm J A Bolt Rifle with scope	Escambia County Sheriff's Office
1	Bulk magazines	Escambia County Sheriff's Office
1	Bushmaster Camo XM15-E2S with magazine	Escambia County Sheriff's Office
1	Bushmaster XM-15 with magazine and Bayonet	Escambia County Sheriff's Office
1	China SKS	Escambia County Sheriff's Office
1	Colt 32 Pistol	Escambia County Sheriff's Office
1	Colt Police Positive 38 Special revolver	Escambia County Sheriff's Office
1	Crickett Rifles Davey Crickett .22 Rifle	Escambia County Sheriff's Office
1	Flash suppressor/silencer firearm accessory	Escambia County Sheriff's Office
1	FN Hershal Test Fire Sample	Escambia County Sheriff's Office
1	FN Herstal 5.7x28 Pistol	Escambia County Sheriff's Office
1	Gesichert Luger 9MM firearm	Escambia County Sheriff's Office
1	Glock 23 .40 caliber Firearm	Escambia County Sheriff's Office

1	Green ammo box with miscellaneous ammo (22.4 lbs)	Escambia County Sheriff's Office
1	Green ammo box with miscellaneous ammo (32.0 lbs)	Escambia County Sheriff's Office
1	Green canister with miscellaneous ammo (2.6 lbs)	Escambia County Sheriff's Office
1	Green canister with miscellaneous ammo (23.6 lbs)	Escambia County Sheriff's Office
1	Harrington and Richardson Topper 410 Gauge Rifle	Escambia County Sheriff's Office
1	Hecklentkoch .45 Test Fire	Escambia County Sheriff's Office
1	Henry Repeating Arms 30/30 Win Rifle	Escambia County Sheriff's Office
1	Hornady box miscellaneous ammo	Escambia County Sheriff's Office
1	Keltec KSG Firearm	Escambia County Sheriff's Office
1	Kimber Raptor II .45 ACPP Pistol with Magazine	Escambia County Sheriff's Office
1	Lowe's box with miscellaneous ammo (39.4 lbs)	Escambia County Sheriff's Office
1	Marlin 3361Y Firearm	Escambia County Sheriff's Office
2	Marlin .22 Rifle	Escambia County Sheriff's Office
1	Mauser 98, 7.92x57 Rifle	Escambia County Sheriff's Office
1	Mossberg 500 12 Gauge Shotgun	Escambia County Sheriff's Office
1	Mossberg 500A	Escambia County Sheriff's Office
1	Orange ammo box with miscellaneous ammo (20.4 lbs)	Escambia County Sheriff's Office
1	Orange ammo box with miscellaneous ammo (29.4 lbs)	Escambia County Sheriff's Office
1	PW Arms M91-30 firearm with Bayonet	Escambia County Sheriff's Office
1	Remington 710	Escambia County Sheriff's Office
2	Remington 870	Escambia County Sheriff's Office
1	Remington box of ammo	Escambia County Sheriff's Office
1	Remington 700	Escambia County Sheriff's Office
1	Rock Island Armory .38 Special revolver	Escambia County Sheriff's Office
1	Rossi Survival Firearm	Escambia County Sheriff's Office
2	Ruger .22 Rifle	Escambia County Sheriff's Office
1	Ruger .38 Special revolver	Escambia County Sheriff's Office
1	Savage Arms 308 Win Rifle with scope	Escambia County Sheriff's Office
1	Savage Arms Sprg Rifle with scope	Escambia County Sheriff's Office
1	Sig Sauer 5.56x45 Rifle	Escambia County Sheriff's Office
1	Smith and Wesson 357 Mag Revolver	Escambia County Sheriff's Office

1	Smith and Wesson M&P Rifle	Escambia County Sheriff's Office
1	Smith and Wesson .45 Pistol	Escambia County Sheriff's Office
1	Speed Loader (6) .38 Special	Escambia County Sheriff's Office
1	Speed Loader (6) Hornady .45 Colt Ammo	Escambia County Sheriff's Office
1	Speed Loader (6) Winchester .45 Colt Ammo	Escambia County Sheriff's Office
1	Springfield Armory .45 Pistol	Escambia County Sheriff's Office
1	Springfield with Magazine	Escambia County Sheriff's Office
1	SPSM with Magazine	Escambia County Sheriff's Office
1	Stagarms – Stag 15 Firearm	Escambia County Sheriff's Office
1	Stoeger .45 Revolver	Escambia County Sheriff's Office
1	Silencer (homemade)	Escambia County Sheriff's Office
1	Taurus Milleniu .45 ACP with Magazine	Escambia County Sheriff's Office
1	Upper Receiver Firearm Accessory	Escambia County Sheriff's Office
1	Various Rounds of Ammunition	Escambia County Sheriff's Office
1	Winchester 37A	Escambia County Sheriff's Office
1	Winchester Ammo (12G)	Escambia County Sheriff's Office

AFFIANT HEREBY CERTIFIES UNDER PENALTY OF PERJURY THAT THE STATEMENTS AND FACTS IN THIS AFFIDAVIT AND IN ANY ATTACHMENTS ARE TRUE AND CORRECT TO THE BEST OF MY KNOWLEDGE.

Dated: 5-22-18   Signature of Affiant:

Sworn to or affirmed and signed before me on _may 22 nd 2018_ by _Inv._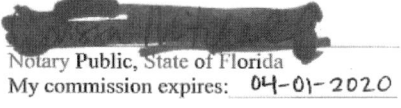

who ✓ is personally known to me or ___ presented _____, as

identification.

Notary Public, State of Florida
My commission expires: 04-01-2020

Finally, here is an excerpt from an article published in the *Pensacola News Journal* on October 12, 2021, regarding the arrest of Dr. Bill Wilson, the physician who prescribed the drugs responsible for Tristan's overdose. The death referred to in the article is Tristan's.

"A doctor, his wife and their son have been arrested after a two-year investigation into an alleged pill mill being run out of a medical center on University Parkway in Pensacola.

"William Wilson, 68, and Beverly Wilson, 66, were arrested Tuesday in Norfolk, Virginia, and their son, James Wilson, 48, was arrested in Pensacola.

"At least one overdose death has been traced directly back to opioids illegally prescribed at the

Wilson Family Medical Center, said Florida Department of Law Enforcement Pensacola

Special Agent in Charge Chris Williams at a press conference Tuesday afternoon announcing the arrests. The investigation remains ongoing.

"Williams said the clinic operated as a pill mill where patients, in many cases without a documented history of pain, were pre-scribed pills and were double-billed, paying both in cash and with a charge to their insurance. …

"Williams said there were complaints on and off about the medical center for years, but when they became more frequent and some pharmacies stopped taking prescriptions from Wilson due to concerns about his practice, the agency launched an official investigation in 2019.

"FDLE agents executed their first search warrant Sept. 11, 2019, at the University Parkway clinic, where they allegedly found significant evidence the Wilsons had been operating an unlicensed pain management clinic prescribing hundreds of thousands of Oxycodone, Adderal and Xanax pills to patients without a documented history of pain.

"The clinic was closed down after the search warrant in 2019. Since then, Williams said agents have been pouring over the extensive evidence and have had expert physicians evaluate patient files to build the case and document enough evidence to charge the three suspects.

"Williams said he personally was present at the first search warrant.

"'I can assure you it didn't look like any legitimate doctor's office I've ever been to,' he said.

"The Wilsons are each charged with conspiracy to traffic in Oxycodone, unlawful use of a two-way communication device, culpable negligence-inflicting actual injury and scheme to defraud.

"Williams said the three have not been charged in the death of the 18-year-old who was prescribed opioids at the clinic in 2018 and died of an overdose the following day, though he said further charges could come as the investigation continues.

"Williams did not say how many patients had appointments at the clinic, but in 2018 alone, the clinic prescribed 106,000 Oxycodone pills, 100,000 Xanax pills, and 29,000 Adderall pills, he said.

"He gave examples of one man who attended the clinic between 2015 and 2019 without any documented chronic pain who was prescribed 20,000 pills, and another who attended between 2016 and 2019 who received 9,000 pills.

"State Attorney Ginger Bowden Madden said the state is involved in prosecuting the charges and is taking the crimes very seriously."

TRISTAN'S MESSAGE

It all happened so fast . . . the gun shot . . . me turning it on myself. I didn't even really think about it. I just did it . . . so fast . . . I couldn't think. I felt all was lost . . . my best friend . . . like a brother at that time. We were only teenagers who were trying to formulate a deep and lasting friendship like we had both never experienced before. When he went down, nothing else mattered. I felt I would never be able to live with this event. I would see Van getting shot in the face the rest of my life. I couldn't stand the thought of letting Van's dad down. I just couldn't face any of it . . . yet it was just a reflex action to shoot myself . . . not thinking, really, about living or dying . . . just to get out of the nightmare as fast as I could. It was horror, complete horror, Mom. I had no thoughts about anyone or anything else . . . just end this horror immediately. I went unconscious. When I was coming back to consciousness, I thought I was dead too, so I was looking for Van's spirit, but I couldn't find him. Mr. Lugner was in the room moving things around when he saw me. I realized I wasn't dead and the pain was here now . . . the reality along with the horror of Van's death. I really did want to die then.

[*"If this too hard, Mom, we can stop."* Me: "keep going, I'll try."]

When Mr. Lugner walked me outside and left me there I was hoping to just die but it wasn't happening. Mr. Lugner had gone back inside and then I saw myself in the Jeep's mirror. . . dear God . . . please, I thought, just let me die, please. I wasn't dying and I was in so much pain and I was so scared . . . beyond fear, really . . . no words. It seemed like an eternity outside, but people started coming. I could hear the sirens. Pain, fear, horror, humiliation . . . "please kill me . . . let me out of this". . . I was hoping.

My worst fears were when I realized that I was being treated like a criminal by the cops and the EMT staff. My world came down hard . . . nothing left in me. Like an animal caught in the traps and being tortured, knowing his life was over and surrendering to be slaughtered. I wanted to just fade out and go numb but also my deep human trait of survival was running. I stayed alert so I could keep aware of what was happening and going to happen to me.

Thoughts of "Van is dead, Van is dead . . ." was so overwhelming . . . such grief and shock that my own needs were really secondary. So fast. . . the ride in the ambulance . . . the going into the hospital . . . seeing the line of doctors in masks . . . so fast . . . so surreal. "I hope I die."

But I didn't. I woke up and Dad was there, and you came in. The sadness was beyond belief. I knew my life was never going to be the same. But thanks for being there for me. I mean it—in case I never let you know that. Let's stop here today.

A fisherman from the start. Six months old.

Enjoying fishing on the pier at two years old.

Everyday he was out on the water was a good day — even when
he caught something unexpected! Twelve years old.

The last photo of his time on earth was of his biggest catch. Image that?

This photo was taken two days before he died. Eighteen years old.

CHAPTER 2

The Creation of Our Family

"The Opportunity of a Lifetime . . . think on that expression."

-TRISTAN

BARBARA'S STORY

My husband, Jack, and I adopted Tristan from birth. We already had adopted two boys and felt extremely fortunate to have been blessed with two beautiful and amazing sons. As far as having a family, it couldn't get any better. In April of 1999, when they were eight and six years old, I started having powerful dreams that we were going to have a third son. The dreams were completely random, unexpected and unrelenting. I used to lie in bed wondering what his name would be. I even went so far as to go to my OB/GYN and discuss the possibility of in vitro fertilization. I felt silly bringing the subject up, as I was in my late thirties, had fertility issues, and already had two wonderful children. Life was good.

A few days after my visit to my doctor, I came home from work to find Jack sitting at his desk in his home office. He had news to give me about a phone call he had received earlier in the day. He had a controlled calm about him, knowing what kind of reaction he was going to get from me. Someone we knew had called him wondering if we would be interested in adopting a baby boy! I suppose you can imagine my reaction.

It might seem like a bizarre coincidence to get this sort of call out of the blue as I was thinking about having a third child. But it wasn't exactly out of the blue. Shortly prior to my dreams, I had happened upon an acquaintance, Tom. We had met six years earlier when Jack and I bought an older house and renovated it. Tom was one of our contractors, and he and his wife Tammy had spent many weeks working in our new home. One day I was driving home and saw his truck at a neighbor's house. I stopped in to say hello. We had a short conversation about renovations, and that was it—or so I thought. But that was what kicked the pebble—we don't know how Spirit is always working. I realize now that Tristan was channeling to me even then—before he was born—as he is now, after his death.

It was Tammy who had called Jack that day. Their daughter was pregnant—expecting in mid-June—and had made the difficult decision to put the baby up for adoption. We were the fourth potential parents, as due to various reasons, each adoption referral had fallen through. They were getting worried since the baby would be born soon. They knew that we had adopted our two sons, and felt that we would make good parents. Apparently, they hadn't thought of us earlier, but when I spontaneously stopped to say hi to Tom, they remembered us. They didn't know how to proceed, so we told them that we would contact the attorney who had handled our younger son's case in Fort Walton, a city an hour away.

The next day we phoned the attorney. She remembered us and was thinking that perhaps we wanted to go back on the waiting list for another referral. I told her that we had found our own referral, or rather they had found us. She was surprised when I gave her the name of the birth mother. It seems the birth mother, Jane, had originally gone to see our attorney many months ago. Our attorney had found a referral and started the process, but Jane was reluctant because the couple was of a different religion, and after much thought realized that she didn't want her baby raised in this particular religion. She pulled the referral, and our attorney hadn't heard from her since. In fact, she had just pulled out the file, and it was lying open on top of her desk. She was about to call Jane to find out what the status was with her baby since the birth was only a few weeks away. You don't always know when miracles are happening. They are a gift from God.

Adoptions are not for the weak-hearted. They are difficult for both the birth and adoptive families. The media has tended to portray the birth family as sad victims and the adoptive families as lucky and entitled. The birth family indeed grieves the loss of a child, and the adoptive family is indeed extremely fortunate. But the emotions are very deep on both sides, and the adoptive families go through difficulties as well. Even when you receive a referral, there is always a sense of trepidation. The excitement is similar to finding out you are pregnant—but in adoptions everything is totally out of your hands.

Before we adopted our oldest son, Jack and I had had the painful experience of having the birth mother of a prior adoption, change her mind three days after the birth. We had been on the waiting list of a private adoption attorney. One day we got the call that a baby boy was to be born in about three months; she wanted to know if we were interested in pursuing it. We accepted and began the process. We were only in our late twenties and were totally new to adoptions, but we so wanted to have a family. We discovered that in private adoptions, the adoptive parents pay for everything—with no guarantee that they will ultimately bring home a baby. In this case, the birth mother was uninsured, so we paid her medical bills. (Personal health insurance doesn't cover someone else's medical expenses.) We also covered maternity clothes, groceries, and psychological counseling, as well as all the attorney and legal fees. It is quite a large sum.

Jack and I enthusiastically set up a nursery and bought everything we could think of, from a crib to a stroller to diapers. After the birth of the baby, we spent three days in the hospital caring for our new son until it was time to bring him home. That morning came, and as we were packing up the car we received a phone call from our attorney saying that the birth mother had changed her mind and decided to keep the baby. Her stepmother had put pressure on her to keep the baby and had said that she would care for him. To say we were devastated is putting it mildly. Then the birth mother told me that I would never know what it was like to love a baby, because I couldn't have one of my own, which poured salt in my wound.

We sadly returned all of our purchases. We were so distraught that all we could do was go out for a long walk that evening. Above us was a double rainbow. We both claimed that it was a message from God that he would bless us with two children. A short while after, a fainter third rainbow appeared a bit farther down from the other two . . . we didn't realize its meaning at the time! Now we do.

After losing that adoption (in addition to going through seven years of infertility treatments prior to that), Jack and I felt we should take time off from pursuing another one. We had spent close to thirty thousand dollars and never had any of it returned to us. Also, we were heartbroken. We rejected a couple of offers from our attorney because they sounded uncertain.

Eventually, we did get a referral. My sister worked for an OB/GYN and a young woman came in who was due in three months and had decided to give her baby up for adoption. The doctor knew of our situation and offered the referral to us. Initially we were reluctant, but we felt deeply that this was the soul that was meant to be our son, and the adoption went through.

Our first son has been a blessing and a joy. We initially felt that his name was Alexander, and his strong, loyal personality has certainly fit the name. He was three days old when we were able to come to the hospital and bring him home. When we pulled up to the door, there were three nurses standing there with a precious little swaddled baby in a nursery cart. The nurses told us how much they all had held and fed him and that they had fallen in love with him during his few days in their care. They handed him to us along with some formula and told us how happy they were for us and to feed him at 5:00! That was it—no care manual! We cautiously put this fragile little five-pound baby boy in his car seat and drove him home. The moment had finally arrived! Everything seemed so surreal and miraculous. At last, we had our family.

When Alex was almost two years old, we thought we should put our name on the waiting list because it can take years to get another referral. We let our attorney know that we were interested in pursuing another adoption. To our surprise, we received a phone call a couple of weeks later. A woman who was due in about eight weeks had just come in. We accepted that referral and began the process of adopting our amazing, talented second son.

At the time, we had just purchased an older home in need of repairs and were in the middle of moving in. We were living with a demolished kitchen and unpacked boxes everywhere. Every wall, door and trim still needed repainting, and every room needed new floors.

Jack's parents had come to visit and spend time with Alex. On the day they were to leave, Jack was driving his parents to the airport when I received the call that the birth mother was in labor. She was at a hospital in a city that was about eight hours from us by car. The birth parents had requested that we be present; they wanted to hand the baby over to us rather than hospital staff. This was before cell phones, so I had to wait for Jack to get back from the airport to give him the news. Thankfully, this was also before 9/11 and TSA security measures. Jack quickly drove back to the airport. The plane that his parents had boarded had just closed the doors. He explained to the attendant at the gate what was happening, and they contacted the pilot, who agreed to let Jack's parents off the plane. They were so excited to stay home with their little grandson while we went to pick up the new baby and to be able to meet the newest one upon our return.

We boarded a flight from Pensacola the next morning and had to change planes in Tampa. As we were walking through the Tampa airport, we realized that everything was happening so fast that we hadn't yet thought of a name. As we passed a gift shop we saw a large bottle of Christian Dior cologne. That was it! His name would be Christian because it just felt right.

When we arrived at the hospital, our attorney had to hide us because the birth grandmother had shown up and wanted to take the baby. She hadn't supported the young couple through the pregnancy, but after the baby was born she had a change of heart. I believe that happens frequently in adoption cases; the grandparents don't want to lose their grandchildren. I cannot harbor hard feelings toward that. It's just that they are babies for such a short time. Then they grow up and take a lot of work and resources, and often the child ends up in the situation that the birth parents were trying to avoid.

When Jack and I were initially told about the grandmother, we were crushed. We figured that we were going to lose yet another baby to a grandparent who steps in at the last minute. However, the birth parents were firm in wanting to give their baby to us. We had met them prior to the birth as part of their wishes and knew we could give him a good home. The birth grandmother was being held back by security. We were taken to the hospital room, where both birth parents were holding their new baby. In adoptions the adoptive parents get to choose the name of the child, but the birth parents get a record of birth where they can put the name that they wanted the baby to have. They told us they had named him Christian. We told them that Christian was the name we had chosen as well. We all felt that this adoption was divinely planned.

A nurse came in with a wheelchair to take the birth mother downstairs, as she was being discharged. She sat in the chair and handed the little swaddled baby over to me. He was just twenty-four hours old. At the moment he was in both of our hands, he wriggled his little arm out of the swaddled blanket, stuck it up in the air, and cried. A good-bye and a hello. There wasn't a dry eye in the room. The birth parents were escorted out, and I sat there and held baby Christian. Jack was instructed to go get the car and wait by the back door as I was escorted out, in case the birth grandmother showed up. As Jack was walking to the parking lot, the birth father, who was just nineteen years old at the time, was driving by on his way to pick up the birth mother. He stopped and thanked Jack for caring for his son and said that he just wanted to make sure that he would take him fishing. Jack promised him that he would take good care of his son.

This is the part of adoption that is most difficult. It is such a bittersweet time; as you are receiving a miracle, someone else is losing one. To watch a birth mother give up her baby and grieve is heartbreaking. You feel both your joy and her pain at the same time. It is extremely emotional. I realize now after losing Tristan that I have witnessed and experienced mothers and fathers losing their children. It is terribly hard. I don't know why I have experienced this in my lifetime, but I am sure that my soul has its reason.

We boarded the flight back to Tampa with our new little bundle of joy. It was a small airplane, and the pilot made an announcement welcoming our new baby. Everyone was calling it the Stork Flight. We were still reeling in the extremes of almost losing this baby to the grandmother and witnessing the grief of the birth parents plus the miracle of our newest blessing. Our next flight, from Tampa to Pensacola, would take us over the Gulf of Mexico. It departed around 9:00 p.m. There were severe thunderstorms as we boarded this small thirteen-passenger plane. We were sitting in the very back of the plane, and it was tossed about by the winds with these quick drops that took our breath away. At some point I handed the baby to Jack because I felt that I didn't have the strength to hold on to him with the harsh movements of the plane. Finally, we landed in Pensacola. Everyone sat there stunned for a moment, then applauded that we had made it. As we exited, we overheard the flight crew saying that the automatic righting of the plane had gone out, and they had been manually adjusting the plane over the Gulf.

When we arrived home we could barely speak, we were so shaken up by the day. I placed Christian in a cozy dresser drawer next to me by the bed. That was his big entrance to the world! As days went by we would call him Christian, but it just wasn't fitting anymore. I asked my mother-in-law who the patron saint of travel is, and she told me Christopher. That was it! He would be called Christopher, as both he and the safe arrival of that airplane were miracles!

We were attending Christopher's kindergarten graduation when we got the call from Tristan's birth grandmother that her daughter had gone into labor and was going to the hospital. They wanted us there for the birth. We waited until the graduation was over, then arranged for a babysitter to stay with Christopher and Alex. As soon as we could, we drove to the hospital. We arrived fifteen minutes after his birth. It was hard to believe that this little baby boy was going to be our new son! His birth mother wanted me to stay in the hospital so that I could bond with the baby. I didn't think that the hospital would allow it, but they did. The baby would go back and forth from my room to the birth mother's room. I was on pins and needles wondering if she would change her mind. In the end she signed the papers, and we were able to bring the baby home to join our family.

Tristan was one of those easy and fun babies. He would laugh himself to sleep as a newborn. He slept well and ate very well. Jack found a mother's milk bank out of Colorado, something that had not been available to us at the time our other two boys were infants. A hospital program collected donated milk from mothers, froze it, and shipped the bottles out on dry ice for next-day delivery. I am forever grateful to these moms for their selfless help of little adopted babies and other ill young children. Many of these mothers had lost their infants and wanted to give their milk so other children could live healthy lives. Most of them gave gallons to the program! We never knew who they were, but we appreciated them enormously. The service cost thousands of dollars, yet the mothers didn't get financially compensated. It was a gift of pure love.

A couple of weeks went by, and our baby still wasn't named. We knew that his middle name would be Robert in honor of Jack's father. There were four or five names we were thinking about, with Connor and Tristan our favorites. We would call him a different name every day, waiting to see which name fit this sweet, precious, funny little baby. One day as I was giving him his bottle, Christopher was standing by my side watching. The baby always giggled as he was falling asleep. I told Christopher that when the baby was done with his bottle we were going to say all the names that we were considering one by one, and whenever the baby laughed we would choose that name. He laughed when we said "Tristan." That is how he named himself! What a strong soul. He chooses us to adopt him and then chooses his own name!

About one month after Tristan's death, as I was sitting in meditation, I saw Tristan and I trading presents wrapped in white with colorful ribbons. I heard him say to me, "Mom, when I crossed over we gave each other a gift—that was a gift. Think of everything I did for you as a gift as you were my mom—that was my gift. We love each other tremendously. If I chose you as my mom, and I navigated my way to you from spirit, don't you think I capably navigated my way out—back home—just as well?" He knew I needed to hear that. As a parent, the minute you have your new baby in your arms, your life changes forever. There is never a moment that you aren't aware of them, even as they grow older. You are concerned about everything: their health, happiness, spiritual understanding, safety, education, clothing, sleep, friends, food, location, transportation—it's endless. When they die, you feel helpless and totally out of control. Even with my faith in God and spirit, I was worrying how Tristan was, where he was, who was with him, etc. So he let me know that I had nothing to worry about. (However, I still do, and until the day I cross over and he takes my hand, I still will.)

To those of you wondering about someone's ability to converse with the spirit of someone who has crossed over to Heaven, I encourage you to have an open mind. Everyone truly has the ability, and most are doing it without any awareness of it. A thought, a memory or a dream may happen, which could be your loved one saying hello or giving you some information that would help you. We have been discouraged from believing in this. I believe it is a gift from our Creator that we never really lose our loved ones. Tristan tells me that he is always here for me. Whether you believe it is a benevolent system of God or you tend to think in terms of quantum physics, frequencies and other dimensions doesn't matter. Maybe God is the master physicist.

Apostle Paul writes in 1 Corinthians 12:4–11, "Now there are varieties of gifts, but the same Spirit; and there are varieties of services, but the same Lord; and there are varieties of activities, but it is the same God who activates all of them in everyone. To each is given the manifestation of the Spirit for the common good. To one is given through the Spirit the utterance of wisdom, and to another the utterance of knowledge according to the same Spirit, to another faith by the same Spirit, to another gifts of healing by the one Spirit, to another the working of miracles, to another prophecy, to another the discernment of spirits, to another various kinds of tongues, to another the interpretation of tongues. All these are activated by one and the same Spirit, who allots to each one individually just as the Spirit chooses."

In 1 Corinthians 13:8, you find the message "Love never ends." Yes, Love never ends because Love is all there is. All the rest is illusion.

TRISTAN ON FAMILY

What can I say about family? There is a bond that is so strong that it can only be shattered by the ego. All other outside interference should be unable to break this sacred bond between family members. Remember family comes together for a reason. It is not and never is random or haphazard. Each life is carefully calibrated so fine it is difficult to fathom on the Earth plane. So much detail goes into planning each lifetime. It is a sacred privilege to meet up with old friends and loved ones on the Earth plane of existence. But let me tell you, once you are on the Earth in a body, the importance—the deep meaning of that lifetime is lost. We have been led to believe that a new soul is born with each new birth of a baby—no—souls are eternal. We have been a part of God from the beginning, which really there is no beginning. We are allowed to travel the Universe and experience worlds for our Creator. We create for God. We take on missions. So many—or most—on Earth have taken on the mission of raising this planet—like raising a family. We are raising the family of Earth. It is not a quick mission, except in the view of eternity it is. We come in together time and time again. Sometimes we play the villain, like the child who needs tough love, and sometimes we are the good kid. We are all that. We are a big family, yet that is forgotten when you enter the Earth. We forget because how else could we learn if we knew all the answers to the tests? As we learn we evolve our souls. Our souls keep these lessons in a sort of bank account of lessons—we call it wisdom. You can access the wisdom if you know how to do it.

Anyway, we make all the plans and details while in, shall we say, Heaven. We bring our guides with us too to help us navigate through the dark, so to speak. As a baby and young child you are still very sensitive to Spirit so you know so much more about what is going on around you spiritually. Like you say about dogs—if your dog doesn't like someone then maybe they are giving you a message. Well, attention should be paid to your little ones because they are more sensitive than your dog! They are fresh from spirit. They are just getting used to maneuvering around in a new human skin.

Soul groups are just that. Groups who have a sacred bond on this side who keep coming in together either to make changes or accomplish a certain Earth task or to learn a particular lesson (not a fan of that expression), maybe to learn a certain aspect of being… Sometimes a soul comes in just to help another, like a support system—a bodyguard, if you will. Maybe it's a return of a favor or maybe it is because of love—nothing more. Almost a sacrifice. We never know on Earth what our relationships have been in the past—other lifetimes with the family we are with now. Sometimes family is difficult—everyone knows about families and holidays—because we are here to teach the most valuable lessons to each other. We give the hardest exams to the ones we love—like me to you, Mom. That is hard. How to experience the death of a child. Yes, isn't that a tough one? We ask why we would pick such difficult life lessons. Well, there is always karma—or a balancing of energies, really. When a lesson wasn't complete when we left the body last time or sometime in the past, we come in to balance it. Enter your friends on the other side coming in as family to help you. You help each other as we weave a complexity of lifetimes and experiences to create the life we are to play out. We are our brothers' keepers again—so important to remember. That is one of our themes—you and me—lifetimes back.

So it matters not how you come together. Sometimes through your mother or through adoption of some sort, like an aunt, cousin or a complete stranger. Genetics is not everything. It is the love bond from the soul that makes one a family. Sometimes you are so close because of past life and spirit life connections. But sometimes a soul who you haven't had much connection with comes in as a family member to bring forth a lesson and you just don't have the same heart connection. It is there, but it is different. But you talk about ancestry and the blood line. Yes, there is that, but it is not everything. There is a karma that runs through bloodlines— some call it miasmas. It is passed through the DNA. So when you are adopted there is that aspect of ancestral DNA but that too is planned on this side as to how you will work with that DNA and be in a different blood family. But it is not a big deal; DNA on Earth is all relatable anyway. We come in to heal ourselves—our past and our future. We heal all that as we heal or balance the energies— karma—in us. It is not so cut and dry—or black and white—like this happens so that happens. It is a melding of energies. You find your family through bloodline births or adoptions. Love supersedes all. Remember, souls choose their parents, not the other way around. And yet that is all preplanned on this side as well.

Much goes into a lifetime. Never take a life for granted. It is a gift—a gift of love—an opportunity of a lifetime! Think of that expression. Yes, some are cut short maybe because they were planned that way or maybe due to free will things get off track and we choose to exit on a soul level. It is like we get called home early. But no matter—love the ones you're with!

Cherish the moments. They are sweet. Don't take the hardships personally. Hold the love and light for your loved ones. Don't get lost in the minutia or problems of life—the small stuff. Know your family is a family on Earth and on this side. Be grateful that you have earned another lifetime together to enjoy the experiences of this beautiful planet together. To work through the difficult times together and to bring out the best in each other even when you feel like it is being forged in the fire. We are all forged in the fire, so to speak. Love continues. We come back—pick up somewhere where we left off, and the spiral of time (not linear time) continues. I am your son, but we have also been other relationships to each other as well. Some lives we come together and others we don't. Sometimes we stay in spirit and guide our family member from this side. Actually, sometimes we marry, sometimes we're siblings, grandparents, cousins, best friends, even co-workers but as a group—a soul group. We are each other's homies—love that! You are my homey, and I love you for that. Always know love underlies all and supersedes all.

Love, your son T

Welcome to your new home Tristan! Alex — eight years old,
Tristan — eleven days old and Chris — six years old.

It's official — adoption day! January 2000.

Bedtime stories with his big brother Alex. August 2001

Exploring with dad on a boy's day out. August 2001

Christmas 2001

Rub-a-dub-dub two boys in the tub — with lots of bubbles! October 2002.

My three sons — such precious gifts from God.

I could always tell when they were up to something! October 2007.

Alaskan cruise summer vacation. July 2010.

Our last family photo with Tristan. Alex's college graduation. April 2016.

CHAPTER 3

All God's Children

"We need someone to just put their arm around our shoulder and say that we are OK and that we are loved and supported."

-TRISTAN

BARBARA'S STORY

Have you ever heard of Indigo children? When I discovered what an Indigo child is, there was no question in my mind that Tristan was most likely one. It was a relief, because knowing that helped me understand him better. I think that maybe our two older boys are Indigos, but there was no doubt about Tristan.

Many of you who are reading a book that involves God, Spirit and channeling have most likely encountered the term "Indigo child." And even if you haven't, you have certainly met them. Many people do not believe this. It truly does not matter. Whatever you call them, there are definitely people who have a distinct type of personality and behavioral traits that fall under this category. Many people call them entitled, spoiled, ADD, ODD, and a myriad of other labels, and are exasperated by this "new breed" of young people.

The description of "Indigo" was coined by a woman named Nancy Ann Tappe. She was born in 1932, and when she was twelve years old a doctor diagnosed her with a condition called synesthesia. This is a condition of joined sensations in which an external stimulus is experienced by two or more senses simultaneously, creating a sixth sense. Her Scottish grandmother had the same condition, so not too much was made of Nancy's diagnosis. Synesthesia is not an overactive imagination or psychic ability. It is an actual physical trait of the brain, not a disease or medical condition. The most common form is a visual link between colors and letters of the alphabet. Other forms manifest as a combining of color and sounds or color and tastes, as well as shapes and flavors. For example, someone with synesthesia may hear music and see colors in their mind.

In Nancy's case, she saw colors around people. She spent most of her adult life studying and clarifying her system with psychiatrists and universities and authored a book, *Understanding Your Life through Color.* Initially, she saw eleven colors. She explained that most people's colors change throughout their lifetime, but that everyone has one color that remains unchanged. She referred to that as their "cradle to grave" color. She was able to isolate generalized behavioral and personality traits pertaining to each color. In the late 1960s and early 1970s, she began to notice many individuals coming in with a new color she hadn't seen before: indigo. Of course, many Indigo children are now adults.

At first the New Age community created myth-type personality traits about these new Indigos, such as that they had indigo auras and were magical, psychic, loving, dreamy and sensitive. This may or may not be the case because the other generalization, which I believe is more accurate, is that they are "systems busters" sent here to show us new ways of doing things, to shake things up and help to tear down the old guard to enable future generations to create better ways of living. They are trying to blaze new trails without a road map and can find it very frustrating as the "good old boy" structures don't tear down without a fight.

Indigo people are here to help others, but they have a warrior-type personality that can be intimidating. They cannot tolerate injustice. They often choose careers in fields like the military, police, and emergency services. You can certainly be sure they are whistle blowers and defenders of truth. They usually are very energetic. They start out life naturally happy and exuberant, but the years of being misunderstood and labeled by the same old-school systems they are here to change take a toll on them.

I see this as similar to the Renaissance Period, which pulled us out of the Middle Ages through advanced thinkers and artists such as Leonardo da Vinci, Leonardo Bruni, Shakespeare, Galileo, and Copernicus. And let's not forget Giordano Bruno, who was burned at the stake for his scientific and philosophical views. I end with Bruno because my intention is to draw a comparison of the popular opinion of advanced thinkers throughout history and today's opinion of advanced thinkers. Today, instead of being burned at the stake, they are medicated, labeled, shamed, humiliated, censored, imprisoned for petty charges, and emotionally tortured. Is that over the top? Perhaps, but if you know young people whose ideals have been crushed and who have given up hope, you can easily make the connection. Why did we have the Renaissance Period? Why are there now a majority of people here with similar personality traits, pushing for change? Perhaps it is a random evolutionary force. Or maybe it is not so random.

Whether or not you believe in this color system, most people agree that the children of today are of a different breed than the children of years ago. Indigo children are characterized by the following attributes.:

- Have strong self-esteem

- Have an obvious sense of self

- Have difficulty with discipline and/or authority

- Don't like to follow orders or directions

- Are very impatient

- Get frustrated by structured systems, routines, or processes that require little creativity

- Often see better ways of doing things at home, school, or work

- Resist conforming to others' desires or trends
- Always want to know "why," especially when asked or told to do something
- Get bored easily with routine tasks
- Are very creative
- Are good at mental multitasking—can do many things at once
- Display strong intuition
- Have strong empathy for others, or have no empathy for others
- Exhibit developed abstract thinking very young
- Are gifted, talented, and/or highly intelligent
- May have been identified or suspected of having attention deficit disorder (ADD) or attention deficit/hyperactivity disorder (ADHD)
- Are talented daydreamers and/or visionaries
- Have spiritual intelligence and/or psychic skills
- Often express anger outwardly and may sometimes have trouble with rage
- May need support to facilitate self-discovery
- Are here to help change the world—to help us live in greater harmony and peace with one another and improve life on the planet

This list was adapted from attributes originally developed by Wendy H. Chapman, MS, and can be found in the book *Indigo Children Ten Years Later* by Carroll and Tober.

I believe that these children are demonstrating to us what no longer works. They are starving for us to find a way to care for them successfully. They are refusing to be molded by our old, outdated authoritarian control, which attempts to dominate them. They cannot be forced into submission as past generations of children once were. They use mischievous humor, ingenious rebellion or all-out resistance as a means of refusing to let go of their inner knowing. This strong sense of inner knowing can make it difficult to do what they are told to do or what they "should" do.

Parents often feel completely helpless as to how to raise and guide these children, and it is difficult to find meaningful support. However, lately something called Conscious Parenting has emerged. For those of us raised with the authoritarian model, this can be a tough pill to swallow, but it's necessary. Conscious Parenting is basically inner work for the parent so they don't pass on their issues, limitations and fears to their children. (Think of the father who wants his son to be successful in sports because he wasn't as a youngster.) A turnabout from authoritarian, know-it-all, control-based discipline, it encourages taking responsibility for mastering your emotions that your child could be mirroring to you. This is deep work for the adult. These wonderful souls are using their experiences to increase our awareness and to bring balance to a world on the precipice of extreme change. They make us think!

In our society we have been taught to show a good face, behave a certain way, and repress our truth. This causes us to put up filters in seeing the truth in others and in ourselves as well. Indigos are more vulnerable because they don't have these filters. They have a heightened sensitivity and an intuitive sense of truth. They can see through the masks people are wearing.

If Tristan had a motto, it would be "To Thine Own Self Be True" (to borrow a quote from Renaissance man Shakespeare). He did not live to please others; although he loved to do so, it was not his mission. He was born with a high consciousness of who he was, more so than most people I have met. He didn't need validation from others to make him feel whole or define who he was. He didn't seek the approval of others. He didn't need the gold star at school to feel good about himself (I don't think he ever earned one!). He had integrity, something most people search an entire lifetime to find.

Tristan loved people and animals, too. He was all about joy and living. Tristan was always there to make you smile or laugh but also question yourself. He showed people a brilliant mirror to their deepest selves, but most denied it and refused to look at their behaviors and realize their inadequacies. They blamed the messenger.

He didn't define himself through the expectations of others. However, he was human, and years of others trying to take his confidence away took its toll—like water dripping on a stone. But it wasn't until the accident and the subsequent betrayal by friends, humiliation, and fear he experienced that his spirit was crushed. Even after the accident, when he was in unfathomable pain, had PTSD, and faced the charge of murder, he still wanted to help people. He would take his Jeep out after storms to help move tree limbs, or find people to pull out of the sand on the side of the road. He was also a good listener and advisor to his true friends. He never bragged about these things. We found out about many of his actions and kindness from friends and acquaintances later, after his passing.

We are all God's children with many different colors, feelings, personalities and gifts. We are indeed a rainbow of beautiful colors and a symphony of sounds. We are here to learn to accept and love ourselves and each other. We are charged with the responsibility to create the ways and means to do so. Let us choose these with wisdom, compassion and love.

TRISTAN ON CHILDHOOD (11/18/18)

*W*ell, first of all, you don't know that you are called anything. You don't know or have even heard of Indigos.

That would be silly to an Indigo because we are who we are. We are a bit confused that not everyone sees things the way we see them. We are confused and in fact bewildered, like "what planet is this?" Why are all these people walking around like they have no idea of what is going on? I came in wanting to just love life—like a huge big world just waiting to be explored. I had a great time, really, but man it got increasingly hard because not everyone understood how I wanted to experience things. I saw humor and happiness in almost everything, and I wanted to experience everything. I know you sure do have your stories, and I realize now that you and Dad had your hands full. Thinking about some of the things I did I realize how smart I was or so I thought. I could do anything I wanted but I kept meeting roadblocks. Why couldn't people see how easy life would or could be if they could just let themselves see and speak the truth? I could tell that people were living all locked up inside like the zombies. These children that some call Indigos are becoming more aware of who they are because they are getting older and there is more information out there for them to find and explain a bit about who they are.

As you know, I never felt that I fit in. I knew it but could never figure out why. I would have a good friend or two but never wanted to be around a large group. Large groups were too much energy to absorb—it is like wearing 3D glasses all the time because everything is so much more intense. I liked to be the class clown because it could disperse some of the heavy energy and what I interpreted as nonsense in the classroom. Other kids felt it and appreciated me taking the edge off sometimes even though I'm sure the teachers weren't too happy about it! It's like I always wanted to show them a better way but it was met with disapproval. As I got older I tried to make the best of it but I never took school seriously because it is such doldrum. I'm like this— doesn't anybody understand me? Why are not more boys curious? I loved to take engines apart, rebuild them, paint them, ride them— go carts, tractors, build treehouses, etc. Life was to be explored. School was horrible—like the death of my soul. I used to get sick with belly aches and constipation with just the thought of school. Most teachers dreaded me but a few who knew my heart and had integrity in their words and actions just loved me.

Indigos are people who need extra love and care even though we seem extremely independent. Our souls are very sensitive, and we need so much love because we are taking on such a big task of seeing the wrongs of this world. We need someone to just put their arm around our shoulder and say that we are OK and that we are loved and supported. Because that is not the message we receive verbally and nonverbally by those we encounter. Our energy is strong and can disrupt the apple cart of the status quo. But that is our mission—you are calling me a trail blazer because of how much I loved my Jeep. I loved to go out on the trails so that is a good analogy—I like it. Like I said, we don't know we are trailblazers. We just want to speak and live the truth, do what feels right and help people live in a better way. That all sounds good but the world isn't always ready for the change that is before them, so no one likes the messenger—you know what happens to them usually. Uggggh. People get comfortable with being comfortable, and even if it's uncomfortable they want to stay in that comfort zone. That is about the mass population because the people in charge of this world know exactly what they are doing to keep people feeling comfortable and fearing change. Fear of the unknown. Even when they are shown a better way. The leaders of this world have kept the people of this Earth in bondage with small ideas, false histories, fears of God—really, I can tell you that God is not fearful. There is nothing to fear in Spirit or over here in what has been called Heaven. It is all love and God is all love—the Source of everything. Only love. Religions taught us to fear God. But that is wrong. Love God and love each other. Love nature, love Earth, love yourself. That is all Indigos had as a mission really—like "damn the torpedoes full speed ahead" kind of mentality. They just have met with a lot of opposition which makes them frustrated and angry to see things the way they are and seemingly no one listening to them. There are so many Indigos on Earth. I was one of them who just didn't make it. I know that is hard to write, Mom. But it is true. Our mission was a difficult task and sometimes we just can't move on. I sure did unearth a lot of evidence of lies, dishonesty, what isn't working and what needs to be cleaned up. Thanks for taking the torch for me, and I will continue my work as my soul needs to finish its mission. As you heal, Mom, I heal and vice versa. We are so close in spirit—we all are, it has just been shut down. We have been told that communicating with those of us on the high frequency side in spirit is crazy or of the devil. Nothing can be further from the truth. It is a beautiful gift that is of our Creator that we never really leave the ones we love and that our soul's purpose is still our soul's purpose whether we are in human body form or spirit. It is a fine veil and getting finer. You can tell who the Indigos are on Earth. Don't judge them—they are trying their best with their mission and in a place where most of the time they are not appreciated. Maybe you could put an arm around their shoulder and tell them that they are loved and appreciated for me? To keep going—that they are honored over here on this side. A lot of them are the same courageous souls who fought in the world wars who came back in and picked up a new mantle of bringing change to the world in a different way. That of change without war. To stop the wars really. To lift the rocks where the rats and insects are hiding and say, "these are the war-creators—don't *believe them." Look up and look within, we are still beating our drums—now it is all for love and evolution of this beautiful planet. Thank you Mom, I love you. -Tristan*

As I was editing this chapter, Tristan had more to say. This is an excerpt (3/6/19):

● ● ● S*weet Mom, you did the best you could. I was a tough kid. Coming in with that temperament and the world doesn't know how to work with that energy yet. Yes, it could have been better—but that's part of the purpose, is it not—of an Indigo (names don't matter) to bring awareness to the new energies. So that is part of the process, the mission so to speak—that of a trailblazer—exactly that—there is NO trail! It will get easier for future generations because of the time going by when parents who are now adult Indigos are learning new ways to parent. Yes, the new term is Conscious Parenting. I'm not a fan of that name—as if parenting in the past was unconscious. Just parenting that is, really, not just so old school. Like just on cruise control doing things like they've always been done even though it is not working. Let's call it Awareness Parenting, or Specific Parenting, or Mature Parenting, or Appropriate Parenting or Systems Busting Parenting—HAHA.*

So this was part of my mission—to know that things weren't going to be perfect or a rose garden because I chose this path—where no one knows how to work with this type of energy—rebellious, but only rebellious—not mean or violent. It seemed rebellious in as much as I am saying, "I can't work in this manner, in this environment." The tide (many new souls) is coming in and breaking down the old sand castles (new metaphor!) so that as the tide recedes we have an open canvas—more space to work with and to build new castles, new ways. I did love to jump the waves with Dad when I was little. Good memories, hold on to those— they are all in the now. Feel them—so much love. I'll leave you with that. I'm around—just feel and ask. Not going anywhere. - Tristan

Always loving life and bringing a smile. Could it get any cuter?

Everything he colored was intricately colored in rainbows.

Picking apples in Michigan. Note the rainbow orbs to the right!

His Jeep Rubicon was his everything. He certainly has crossed the Rubicon.

SECTION II

Awakening to the Harsh Realities of Our Systems

"Finding myself to exist in the world, I believe I shall in some shape or other always exist; and, with all the inconveniences human life is liable to, I shall not object to a new edition of mine, hoping, however, that the 'errata' of the last may be corrected."

BENJAMIN FRANKLIN

CHAPTER 4

Uphill Battle

"This is why we are writing this book - to help explain what is happening and how to live in peace with it all in these times."

-TRISTAN

BARBARA'S EXPERIENCE

I want to talk about our educational, religious, and criminal justice systems, as well as gun laws and science, and how they are dysfunctional and harmful. There are other institutions that need to change, but these are the ones that I feel compelled to share my experience with and research on. These are the systems that I personally watched destroy Tristan's life. (There is also the healthcare system and its many failings, but that is too vast a topic to cover here, and many others are doing their best to expose the problems and create new, more humane health systems.)

We have adapted to these dysfunctional systems. We are, in fact, adaptors. We adapt to our environment, our relationships and our physiology. We adapt to the rules that are imposed upon us. This is how we develop our unique personalities. We have, to a great extent, adapted to our institutions because of fear. Fear is indoctrinated into us from childhood. As children we are taught to fear—and especially to fear others: other cultures, nationalities, races, religions, political societies. There are numerous divisions. We have been taught to divide and separate. Divide and conquer. We absorb the beliefs and fears that our fathers and mothers have. Yes, there are indeed real dangers, such as vaccinations, abductions, the sex trade, guns, drugs, wars, etc. These result from separation, and this separation is bred and spread by governments, religions and corporations (such as the pharmacology industry). We pick sides and fear all others. When enough fear is created, we can be brainwashed into wars and into killing our fellow man. We must learn how to tune in and listen to the Divinity within us. We must honor our true selves and realize that there are as many differing opinions as there are people.

Fortunately, we are leaving behind the old energy of complying to others' dictates when they go against what we know is right for us and our loved ones. Pleasing others while denying that which is in our own heart is not living authentically. That old energy is based on fear of rejection. The need to be accepted and loved has been so instilled in us that we follow the crowd's ideas and opinions without much thought. We are reluctant to express ourselves from our hearts. We have been taught to keep our opinions to ourselves if they differ and are losing the ability to have meaningful conversations with others. Disagreements turn into name-calling and choosing sides. When we hold back our true feelings, we are choosing to live in fear and limitation. When we keep quiet, we give our power away. Yes, we don't want to be shunned for being weird. But, if we don't speak up, then who will? We must realize that in order to follow what we believe is right for us, we must be fully responsible for every one of our words and actions. We are our brothers' keepers and we have the sovereign right to live an authentic life while being respectful of others' rights and honoring their own experiences.

We all have free choice. We can choose to continue to go along with the status quo, continue to acquiesce to the dictates of others, and not experience the freedom of living authentically. We can also choose to look toward a higher consciousness and find new and better ways of living. We are indeed separating that way: to stay the same or to evolve. There is a fight happening. It isn't against evil, or between individuals. It is between those controlled by dark fear-based consciousness and those who follow a higher consciousness and see this new way of being. Currently, those who have "seen the light" still have to live surrounded by outdated and fear-driven behavior. This planet has been ruled a long time by controlling with fear, and those in power do not want to give up control.

I believe that change is happening. While the world appears to be in great chaos, I believe it is because the light is increasing on this planet and exposing the dysfunctions, deceit and outright horrors that have ruled the day. The dark is fighting mad and does not want to give up the reins, but it is inevitable. That is my great faith. I believe that compassion and healthier behaviors will win out. We are evolving into an improved way of life.

We must come from compassion, not the ego, revenge, or anger, in order to make a better planet—to make a difference, to be a part of something bigger and better. Let the negative dark things of this planet show themselves so that we can eliminate them. Let the ugliest horrible hidden things that are going on show themselves so we can look at them and demand that they go away. Let society agree so that they will disappear. Let the unconscionable things that are happening to our children stop. When the negativities emerge into the light, know that it means we are changing toward a better world. Understand that by uncovering the darkness, we are moving into the light, even though it looks like chaos during the transition.

We need forward out-of-the-box thinkers with completely new ideas, not just restacking the same blocks in a different orientation. They might look better, or at least be a change, but it's still the same old blocks. This is like shifting the chairs around on the Titanic. We need intuitive thinkers who are also courageous, because we know how "new thought" is welcomed in the world: not very well. We live in a world where many new discoveries in science, medicine, government and teaching are blocked. People are even killed for having the audacity to voice their ideas and new discoveries. This also comes from fear. Corporations fear losing money, government and politicians fear losing power, religions fear losing power and control. The media has sold its soul and is a puppet of the highest bidder. People who dare to voice new ideas are ruined, personally bullied and destroyed. When the media creates public opinion, society is disempowered. It's called social engineering. If you go against the prevailing public opinion you're ostracized. If you try to bring new ideas forward, you're destroyed.

The following chapters are an exposé of, in my experience, the out-of-control bureaucratic institutions that are contributing to the harm and death of our children and society.

Tristan's Message (10/23/18)

H*ello Mom,*

You wanted me to say something about the shift of this world—the Procession of the Equinoxes. Things are changing—all are changing. This is a time to be at your utmost awareness. Watch how things seem to be turning upside down everywhere.

I want to tell you about important facts that many people still don't know anything about. They are totally unaware. It is being kept quiet because of those in "high authority"—I call it that because even though you hear the term "Deep State" a lot it is still a mask. The Deep State are the puppets of those really in charge so we will call them the higher authority of Earth. True that we all have a "Higher Authority" which is our Divine Authority where all is love. It is not really authority in the worldly sense—it means that there is a natural order to all life, based in compassion and caring. When you are on this side it is what you want. It only changes in the lower dimensions of Earth where fear and competition for resources and survival mentality comes into play.

So back to the Earth's higher authority: they know the Earth moved into a new place in the 2012 shift. And they are fighting mad because they don't want to lose control and power. They are using all types of energy behind the scenes. Much of it is out on the Internet—some true—a lot of it is true, yet don't be afraid of it. You are considered crazy if you talk about it because fear rules the day there still. People are fearful to step out of line. You reference the book The Emperor's New Clothes *a lot and indeed that is what is going on. No one wants to be the one who says, "The king is naked!" So all goes on status quo until someone says something. Then we all have a chance to respond. I am not saying people are bad—they are fearful—but I say to you do not fear. Be aware.*

Yes, I was what is termed by some an Indigo child. Indigos came in on a vibratory rate that was stronger to combat the old energy. Yes, you use the term "Systems Busters" (haha)—that I was—and still am! But they cannot destroy me now and while they think they did I have not left, and I have a lot more to say and get done before I come back in. The Indigos (yes, the Earth's higher authorities know about this) had and still are having a difficult time. It is a noble cause on this side to take up that mantle (mission), and while it sounds good and on a soul level you are equipped fully to handle it, when you are on Earth and under the power of the veil of illusion you question why you are different. Why people are so blind. You can't fit in with most everything. You can't understand the blindness of everyone around you. We bust the systems not because we are consciously doing that, but because truly our vibrations stir the lower vibrations of the environment and kind of like throw static into the system, and the inadequacies just become apparent.

In time these new Indigo children start to wear down. They themselves become questioning of themselves. They are bored and start to investigate other things. Or they are drugged by the suggestions of the teachers and they now sit in complacency—their vibrations lowered. Very sad indeed. Let no one diminish the light of a child so he or she can sit in a chair all day—seriously. Indigos get labeled, shamed, humiliated, etc. They look rebellious—indeed they are, they are wired that way as I just explained. It is a tough mission—it's like we were the trailblazers sending a message. Of course, we know what usually happens to the messengers. But listen and behold what they are showing. Old systems must be torn down before being recreated in the light of a new day. That is the mission—it was my mission—a systems buster. But it is with love—like trying to show a child a new way. It is like I knew my mission would be short. I could have changed it but my work was done. A horrible ending but almost fitting to the end. An Indigo's mission is not easy. I unconsciously did what I came in to do. My body and spirit had had enough. There are many Indigos still on Earth. They get lost because they have this crazy vibratory rate and it gets frustrating. They have been medicated as well. They get pulled in many directions by the school and media, etc. Some get fighting mad while others are quietly making a difference by simply influencing others around them in their own communities. Some have done great things; some we know about, while we haven't been shown much of it. Everyone is confused now. This is why we are writing this book—to help explain what is happening and how to live in peace with it all in these times. Only people on Earth can make the changes—direct the thoughts and ambitions of people so they don't succumb to the dark fears manipulated by the higher authorities of Earth. It is like when you pour water on an ant hill—how they go running all over until they rebuild—do

you like that vision? [smiling] *So true--everyone is scattered, "What is happening, our home has just been dismantled?" But they do pull it together and rebuild, don't they? Be at peace—listen to your higher self—your intuition. Love even when it is difficult. Have compassion.*

It is with the greatest of love and respect that I speak to you this morning, Mom. Feel for me. I am always near with only love, Tristan.

CHAPTER 5

Our School Systems

"[There is] much higher thought needed before [the school system] gets built back up into areas of higher learning, where children are supported and loved and nurtured as unique children of God—our Divine Creator who loves all. We need to bring love through first—only love will change this."

-TRISTAN

BARBARA'S RESEARCH AND EXPERIENCE

We tried a variety of schools for our three sons. We were leaning toward private school because we had heard friends talk about issues with public schools; some had transferred their children to private schools. We looked for an overall school philosophy that would best fit our concept of what our children needed.

I am assuming most parents go through a learning curve regarding the education of their children. I naively thought that schools had their students' best interest at heart, and that it was a pretty black-and-white situation. We would get our children to school on time after a good night's sleep, nourished and dressed, with appropriate supplies for the day. They would teach the appropriate curriculum, allow for lunch breaks, give them some recess breaks, we would pick them up, and voila! It would be like a TV show from the 1950s.

We had a few great teachers and moments—and even a few good years—but the picture I painted above was only in my dreams. I didn't realize that I was going to have to supervise the schools, teachers and every aspect of what was happening with and to my children. My hat is off to young parents who understand this prior to choosing where and how they are going to educate their children. I used to make fun of the helicopter moms who were the classroom parent and practically camped out at their children's schools. Don't get me wrong—I rarely missed an open house, teacher/parent conference, school show and fair, fundraiser, meeting, PTA group, etc., but I wasn't "overly involved" like these moms. Now I look back and see that they knew something I didn't. By being so involved and present, they were able to exert a positive influence on what happened with their children. My big congratulations go to the parents who homeschool their kids, realizing the damage that our current educational system does to children—and society.

Back when our children were young, there was still a stigma surrounding homeschooled kids. Now the research shows quite a different story. I found the following information in a blog post on the National Home Education Research Institute website (www.nheri.org) dated 4/20/18.

The US Department of Education reported on data gathered from the National Household Education Surveys from 2016 and estimated that 1,689,736 students ages 5–17 were being homeschooled in the spring of 2016. This represents 3.3 percent of all school-age children that year. These government statistics most likely are not indicative of the real number of homeschooled kids in the US due to data-gathering methods. The NHERI estimates there are 2.3 million homeschooled children, growing 2–8 percent annually over the past few years. The 2014 SAT scores of college-bound homeschoolers were higher than the national average of all college-bound seniors that same year:

	Homeschooled	Schooled
Critical Reading	567	497
Math	521	513
Writing	535	487

After John Holt, an American educator, became a popular proponent of homeschooling and challenged the current thought that a formal school setting was the best environment for children to learn, homeschooling quickly gained in popularity. The religious groups took the lead. Homeschooling currently is legal in all fifty states and has grown way beyond religious groups. Sociologists Philip Q. Yang and Nihan Kayaardi propose that the homeschool population is now representative of the general population. [Kyle Greenwalt, *Home Schooling: Creating Schools That Work for Kids, Parents and Teachers*, published in 2016 by Sense Publishers.]

The home-educated typically score 15–30 percentile points above public school students on standardized academic achievement tests, regardless of their parents' levels of formal education or the family's household income.

It's important to note that families engaged in homeschooling are not dependent on public, tax-funded resources for their children's education. It's estimated that this represents $27 billion that American taxpayers do not have to spend annually, since these children are not in public schools. [https:/edwp.educ.msu.edu/new-educator/2017/faculty-viewpoint-heres-how-homeschooling-is-changing-in-america/].

Another benefit to homeschooling appears to be that homeschooled children are more tolerant of other people's beliefs. *The Journal of School Choice* published research finding that homeschoolers have "the willingness to extend civil liberties to people who hold views with which one disagrees."

Another type of alternative schooling, unschooling, is a type of homeschooling but with a different slant. Although the terms are often used interchangeably, homeschooling follows a set curriculum, but unschooling does not. The parents (or guardians) assume the role of facilitator and aid in guiding students and helping to create the learning plans. Unschooling focuses on real-world activities and tasks that are chosen by the child. This is based on the idea that children are naturally curious, and if they are allowed to follow their own interests, they will have positive learning experiences.

This trend toward alternative methods of schooling is quickly growing and my hope is that it will, by force, create the much-needed evolution in our educational system. The main benefit of taking children out of the controlled system and homeschooling or unschooling them is that they are accepted for who they are and treated as individuals. Their unique needs and desires are considered—by the people who know them best—and their education is tailored to them. They are not forced into a mold and made to conform to rigid guidelines—many of which seem designed to crush their spirit and eliminate individuality. They are not told who or what they should be or how they should act. They are not confined into the caste system created by standardized test scores and the subjective opinions of exhausted teachers.

There is a popular analogy of a frog in water; it says that if you put a frog in boiling water, it will jump out, but if you place it in cold water it will stay in, even as you slowly turn the heat up to boiling—and it will cook to death. We as a society have been placed in the cold water and have allowed ourselves, our families and our cultures to be cooked to death. The young children coming into this world are so sensitive that they feel like they have been placed directly into the boiling water. They are jumping out. They are rebelling. They are refusing to adapt to a suffocating, authoritarian system that is the antithesis to life.

A very good friend of mine, a psychologist, uses the term "same content different form." It doesn't matter how many times you change the appearance of something, it is still the same thing on the inside. That's how I would describe our experiences with private schools. Yes, the campus was smaller, the student-per-teacher ratio was smaller, etc., but as far as the contents— you know the expression "SSDD" (same stuff different day). After doing some research, I understand why. They are not independent. The education vouchers, tax credits and other government funding that non-public schools accept is a Trojan Horse carrying government control. Following is an excerpt of a letter written in 1991 by Virginia Bert Baker, a homeschool pioneer and activist who uncovered a document explaining what the government was planning by giving federal money to families to attend private schools [Iserbyt, Charlotte Thomson, *The Deliberate Dumbing Down of America*, Conscience Press, 1999, 2011]:

"Education is an emotional issue," he said, (referencing the document written by a bureaucrat in the education system.) "We're staying away from the word 'voucher' because educational choice sounds a little more palatable to parents. Educational choice is giving students and their parents a voucher—and we want to mobilize a significant number . . . to get the camel's nose under the tent . . . We've got to prepare for the long term." Prepare for what?

The Associated Press has reported that past president George Bush said, "Choice will be a critical element in education reform for years to come." This recent upsurge in support of "choice" and the voucher program is nothing new, and it deserves closer scrutiny by parents and especially by private and homeschool patrons. The truth of the matter is, once private education accepts tuition tax credits or vouchers it can no longer remain "private" because through government regulation, it will lose all independent control and will be forced to follow the same guidelines as public schools.

When one of our older sons was in the third grade, he attended a well-known non-traditional private school franchise that is designed for students to be allowed a great deal of self-direction and where sitting most of the day was not a required part of learning. However, we were told that our son probably had a learning disability, as he was "unable to focus" and was distracting other students. We took him to a private school psychologist who ran him through a battery of tests, including an IQ test. Jack and I went to see the psychologist days later, prepared for the disheartening news that would validate what the teacher thought: that our son indeed had a learning disability (which I now find a reprehensible term). The doctor sat us down and said "Well, your son is gifted." We actually argued with him, saying "No, you don't understand . . ." He spoke very distinctly: "Your son . . . is gifted . . . look at his scores . . ." We were astounded!

I now understand that teachers are trained to think that if a child doesn't fit a mold, then he or she has learning disabilities. Teachers are taught classroom management, and if a child isn't conforming then it's the child's fault. What if Jack and I did not have the means for private testing? Think of how many children fall into the snares of teachers and administrators—who may be well-meaning but are more likely focused on themselves—and are labeled, sent to low-level classes, and, as in most cases, drugged? Their entire life's potential has been severely threatened by one person's ignorance.

This is nothing new. Back in 1970, my family lived in Miami, Florida. My sisters and I went to the public school in our district. My younger sister was left-handed and was being taught to write with her right hand. The teachers would actually slap her hand if she tried to write with her left. They even put her outside of the classroom as a punishment one day. (She proceeded to walk home and surprise our mother. You would have to know my sister to see the humor in that.) But even with such a strong-willed child, they were able to break her spirit. Her frustration with the difficulties of working against her own natural ability turned into fear and dislike of school. She would have the classic belly aches and cry not to go to school.

Since she had a hard time learning how to write with her non-dominant hand, the school authorities decided she had learning difficulties. Back in those days you were labeled a slow learner. Each successive year she was placed in the slow learners' class. Even with no words said, all the children knew which classroom that was. The teachers didn't try to teach those children different ways to learn. They were just warehoused in those classes, and often the teachers themselves were not the sharpest knives in the drawer.

Fortunately, her fourth-grade teacher noticed that she was not "slow." This teacher was working on her master's degree and used my sister as part of her thesis about what happens when a child is forced to write with his or her non-dominant hand. This was my sister's ticket to freedom. She is now a gifted surgeon with a great heart, and her ambidexterity has indeed served her well in her craft. Unfortunately, most children don't have such a savior looking out for their best interest.

My takeaway from these experiences is, don't let anyone in the school system, from teachers to administration, tell you about your child. You know your child better than anyone else. And, if you listen to "authority figures" more than you listen to your child, it can severely damage the relationship between you and your child. Our son and my sister would have had completely different lives if the system had had their way and pushed them through the dysfunctional program. Luckily, our son had us as parents, and my sister had a very aware teacher. They were rescued and allowed to let their innate abilities shine.

After the testing, we realized that schools are not one-size-fits-all as we had been led to believe. We tried another, more traditional private school with a small campus and a small student-to-teacher ratio. The first year our older children excelled. We thought we had found the perfect school. And then there was Tristan. He was in three-year-old preschool and was his own man from the start. He was funny and wise beyond his years and was most likely a handful in the classroom. One day the principal of the school told us that Tristan was an amazing and talented boy, except he had one flaw: that he had too much self-confidence. Can you imagine? One of the most foundational innate traits a parent can hope to instill in their children was considered a deterrent in this school!

On another day when I picked him up from school, the teacher was standing at the front door, large and in charge, with a stack of "pink slips" in her hand. When I see this procedure now, I immediately feel that here is a teacher who should not be teaching, who has no ability to handle a room of young children—even with assistant teachers! Tristan's teacher explained to me that Tristan was getting a pink slip because he would not cooperate in yoga class. I asked her if the remaining stack of pink slips were for all the three-year-old boys who were unable to be still in yoga class. Embarrassed, she said yes. Surely, there could have been other alternatives for the little ones who were about to burst at the seams with energy that needed to be run off. Instead, they were made to feel like bad kids and shamed in front of their classmates—then had to endure humiliation in front of their parents at the end of the day, long after their little minds had forgotten about it.

The second year in our new school, our oldest son did well. Our middle son's fourth-grade class, however, had serious difficulties. Apparently, the teacher went off on her own agenda, and it came to the administration's attention quite late into the year that the children were not learning the appropriate age-level curriculum. They were seriously behind. The administration couldn't even tell us what the children had been doing. The children absolutely loved the teacher though. We never really got a clear explanation of what had happened. I wonder just how far off the teacher really was, or if she was just following the natural progress of her students. We do know that there was an awful verbal altercation between the teacher and principal, with quite colorful language, which amused the children. The teacher and principal were terminated by the board.

Because of this, the following year I signed up for the most thankless job in the entire school system: PTA president. I did this because the PTA president had a voting position on the board, and Jack and I wanted to see what was really happening in this school by planting ourselves in the center of action. That lasted one year. If you ever want to quickly disillusion yourself about any organization, join the board. If you want to stay in ignorant bliss, just continue to sit on the sidelines. I soon came to see the arrogance of the parents on the board. The game was, whoever could write the largest check got their way, and their children were treated with more concern. The teachers were exasperated because it was always those parents who won the day and valuable input from teachers was ignored. Even though Jack and I were paying three of the high-priced tuitions, we weren't given the same respect as the other parents who could write large "extra" sums on the side. I was beginning to see how things work in this world.

So then we entered into the realm of public schools—which are really government-owned monopoly schools. Tristan started kindergarten at the local public elementary school, as we figured it couldn't be any worse than what we had experienced at the high-priced private schools. We had been told by parents who had children older than ours that we should put our kids in public middle school to prepare them for the realities of high school, so we did that with Alex and Chris. Looking back now, I know the word "realities" could have been replaced by many other terms—some quite positive, but most not.

Chris was in the sixth grade. As the first school dance was approaching, I signed up to be a chaperone. I don't know who was more naïve—Chris or me! There was such a vast difference in the maturity and puberty levels of the students at the dance. There was one little boy who looked like he could still have been in fourth grade, running around playing tag in his Spider Man tee shirt. Then there were fully physically matured eighth graders who had more in mind than playing tag on their night out. When the lights went down and the music started, so did the dirty dancing. I mean really dirty dancing—I even learned a few things that night. The children would form a circle around a couple who would be grinding. The teachers would then go in and break it up. The exhausted teachers repeated this exercise in endurance all night. The cute little Spider Man stopped still in his tracks when the dancing commenced and realized that he wasn't in Kansas anymore. Needless to say, this was the last dance Chris went to that year. It was too scary!

Academically, Alex and Chris both did well. However, I could see a rather quick attitude change begin to develop. Christopher ended up getting more interested in the social life and he went down from the A student that he had been previously. Alex loved playing sports, but he was relatively small in stature. When he moved on to high school, he found that he couldn't compete with the two hundred-pound, six-foot athletes that filled the teams, and he became less interested in the school experience. Tristan had a very loving and patient teacher and had a great kindergarten year, but things deteriorated the following years. Sometimes he had good teachers but mostly they were exasperated by children who didn't follow rules. And being compelled to "teach to the test," they were unable to customize learning. The teachers either saw Tristan's heart and happy nature and absolutely fell in love with him, or considered him a total distraction and had no idea how to help him perform well. And of course, Tristan was astutely aware of each teacher's personality and how they perceived him.

After years of hit or miss in the public system, we moved Tristan to a religious-based school. Suffice it to say, it didn't go well here either. Tristan was never one to hold back. While in the ninth grade at a small private Christian school, Tristan asked the Bible teacher (and I use the term "teacher" hesitantly), "What about if there is a serial killer who accepts Jesus on his deathbed and he goes to Heaven, yet, a man in Africa, who has never heard of Jesus, but has taken good care of his family and community, ends up in Hell for eternity—why?" The annoyed teacher snapped back, "Yes, because the man in Africa could have found a missionary!" Experiences like this make me ask, "Where do they get these teachers, why are they hired and why do we accept this as being OK?"

Looking back now as an observer, I see how our school systems—private and public, religious and non-religious—are failing our children. The inexperience of many of the teachers and staff is staggering. Their behavior would be unacceptable if they were working in an adult corporate environment, so why is their behavior acceptable for our precious children?

Children who are inquisitive, independent critical thinkers, as Tristan was in his Bible class, don't do well with those kinds of absurd answers. Teachers lose their credibility and the child tunes out. What an amazing opportunity these children give, not only to the other children in the class but also to the teacher! If a self-confident child has the courage to ask a question out loud, how many other children are silently thinking something similar? That teacher had a golden opportunity to engage a student and address a question asked by so many—especially if the teacher's goal was to win another soul for the Lord. Instead, Tristan's dad, Jack, found the answer. It is in Romans 2:11–14: "For God shows no partiality. When Gentiles who do not possess the law, do instinctively what the law requires these, though not having the law, are a law to themselves. They show that what the law requires is written on their hearts, to which their own conscience also bears witness. All who have sinned apart from the law will also perish apart from the law, and all who have sinned under the law will be judged by the law. For it is not the hearers of the law who are righteous in God's sight, but the doers of the law who will be justified."

What a completely different story could have unfolded if the teacher had said, "That is a good question! In fact, many people have asked that over the generations. Tristan, can you read Romans 2:11–14 and report to the class tomorrow what that means to you? Thank you for bringing that up." Instead, this teacher was threatened by a fifteen-year-old asking questions that revealed the teacher's incompetence, as well as his insecurity about his own religious beliefs!

I could fill an entire book with the antics and stories of this little trailblazer, but here I will share just one more story. In middle school, Tristan was in science class and the lesson was on astronomy. The night prior, Tristan and I had watched a Discovery Channel show about the cosmos. (He enjoyed watching shows about real life rather than sitcoms and canned shows.) The next day, the teacher was discussing a topic related to the exact thing Tristan had seen on the television show the night before. When he told her in class that her information was incorrect, as he had just seen that scientists had proved new evidence, she sent him to the principal's office. Can you imagine the insecurity and immaturity of a teacher who cannot allow a discussion in her classroom? Again, here was a student who was being actively involved in the lesson, and instead of stimulating his natural curiosity and intellect, as well as allowing a class discussion, she shames and humiliates him. Of course, afterward we had a discussion with Tristan about how sometimes it's best to not say things—but isn't that the antithesis of learning? How can there be progress when we are not allowed to think outside of the box? This is one way we are programmed, at a young age, to give up our power. These and other experiences make me ponder the idea of "conscious parenting" and how it could also be applied to "conscious teaching."

To bolster my point, I borrow another quote from John Gatto in *The Underground History of American Education:*

> "No public school in the United States is set up to allow another George Washington to happen. Washingtons in the bud stage are screened, browbeaten, or bribed to conform to a narrow outlook on social truth. Boys like Andrew Carnegie, who begged his mother not to send him to school and was well on his way to immortality and fortune at the age of thirteen, would be referred today for psychological counseling; Thomas Edison would find himself in Special Ed until his peculiar genius had been sufficiently tamed."

Buckminster Fuller was a renowned twentieth century inventor, engineer, architect, mathematician and visionary philosopher who dedicated his life to making the world work for all of humanity. He left us with numerous brilliant quotes. Among his thoughts on schooling: "If I ran a school, I'd give the average grade to the ones who gave me all the right answers, for being good parrots. I'd give the top grades to those who made a lot of mistakes and told me about them, and then told me what they learned from them." . . . "If you want to teach people a new way of thinking, don't bother trying to teach them. Instead, give them a tool, the use of which will lead to new ways of thinking." . . . "We are deliberately designed to learn only by trial and error. We're brought up, unfortunately, to think that nobody should make mistakes. Most children get de-geniused by the love and fear of their parents—that they might make a mistake. But all my advances were made by mistakes. You uncover what is when you get rid of what isn't." . . . And lastly: "I have spent most of my life unlearning things that were proved not to be true."

This is where the current stage of my life has brought me. I am questioning all those ideas I had about our society, and discovering through research that the vast majority of what I believed is not true. I delved into the history of our school system and now understand that, not only is it currently in a state of unrepair, it was totally designed to be dysfunctional.

HISTORY OF PUBLIC SCHOOLING

Have you ever wondered why and how schools could have such a controlling force in the lives of your children and family? If you haven't, you are not alone, as most citizens today are generally unaware of the overreach of government in education. Like me, you were programmed to accept it. We have that "it's how it's always been done, it's how it's done now and how it's always going to be done" mindset. We don't think about it critically. This mindset has developed due to conditioning from the government propaganda and misinformation we are continuously exposed to. Some of these include the idea that the compulsory school system just organically evolved as parents realized they were unfit to thoroughly educate their children; that for the country's welfare there had to be a conformity of knowledge that only the government was able to supply; and that taxpayer dollars should fund this. Thus, we have free, compulsory schooling. If ever there was an oxymoron, it is "free compulsory."

How can one dispute the education of our children? Obviously, all people need education. I am not questioning that. My question is about the delivery of the information: the curriculum and the environment in which it is delivered. Even the concept of "delivery of information" is flawed, actually. Learning is more than just being force-fed information and then parroting it back. This method actually obstructs real learning. Learning involves creative thinking. We need to awaken the powers of creativity, which stimulate children to want to learn. Also, who decides the curriculum as well as the format of the delivery? As discussed in the last chapter, we don't really think about this. We accept what we were taught without critically thinking about the reality behind the belief system. Are we products of a school system that has suppressed our innate power of critical thinking? I think so.

The educational system takes over from where organized religion left off. One has to be a bit of a sleuth to follow the historical path to see who, what, why and how the school system morphed into the one we have today and to follow the money and power trail. It is hard to believe that a few people wanted to control the school system and future generations for pure greed and selfish gain—but that is what my research indicates. Let us begin . . .

As we have been taught, American history starts with Europeans discovering this New World in the late 1400s, beginning a power struggle for the control and ownership of this new land between Spain, England and France, followed by the Netherlands and the Scandinavian countries. These adventurers were looking for resources such as gold, silver, spices, and furs to bring back to their homelands and make money. By the 1600s Europeans were coming to the New World to settle and create a new home. Some came as employees, military personnel, and officials in varying capacities from their mother countries. The later years brought people who were escaping persecution for political and religious reasons. Additionally, it has been estimated that more than half of the people who came to the New World in the 1600s came as slaves, servants and indentured servants and were mainly Irish. The indentured servants came with the hope of freedom after their contract was finished—but it's estimated that only about forty percent of servants outlived their contract. And for those who did, the terms of their release were less than favorable. Vast numbers of servants were required to help run the farms, plantations and businesses in the growing New World, but another reason so many were brought over is that landowners were given extra land for each servant they had.

The Irish slave trade began with the King James I Proclamation of 1625 requiring thirty thousand Irish political prisoners be sent to the New World as slaves. From 1641 to 1652, over five hundred thousand Irish were killed by the English and another three hundred thousand were sold as slaves. During the 1650s, more than a hundred thousand Irish children between the ages of ten and fourteen were taken from their parents and sold as slaves in the West Indies, Virginia and New England. Also during this decade, fifty-two thousand Irish (mostly women and children) were sold to Barbados and Virginia. Another thirty thousand Irish men and women were also transported and sold to the highest bidder. Some may have been fortunate enough to be indentured servants but the majority were simply slaves with no hope of release.

The African slave trade was just beginning around the late 1600s as well. The reason I mention this part of history is to shine some light on the beginning of the racial divide in this country and to show that the educational system has been unsuccessful in bridging the divide since its inception in the mid-1800s. Many historians acknowledge an event called Bacon's Rebellion in 1676 as the moment when the spark was ignited to intentionally pit the races against each other. A wealthy white property owner in Virginia, Nathaniel Bacon, (who was a relative of the governor, William Berkeley) was opposed to Berkeley's handling of the raids on their colony by the surrounding Native tribes. Eventually, Bacon organized a militia consisting of white and black indentured servants and enslaved black people, who joined the militia in exchange for freedom. Bacon's militia attacked the tribes, engaging in a power struggle with the governor, the Virginia House of Burgesses, and the colony's elites. In September of 1676, after months of unrest and fighting between the two forces, Bacon's militia burned Jamestown to the ground. Bacon passed away after being sick, but there were other skirmishes by the servants and slaves as they continued to fight as a united force. The wealthy landowners and planters were fearful of this powerful alliance and realized that they had to do something about it. They permanently enslaved all Virginians of African descent, and gave all white indentured servants, slaves and farmers new rights and status. Thus, by separating these two groups, they hoped to make it less likely that they would join forces again in rebellion. This is when the government-sponsored division between black and white in our country began. In other parts of the country there were still white slaves and servants and their lot in life was certainly difficult, but they weren't held as hereditary slaves for two hundred more years like the Africans.

Much has been made of the colonies as a place of religious freedom, where those who were persecuted in Europe because of their beliefs could worship in their own way in peace. Yes, many of those who came to the New World were escaping the Church of England and were able to found new churches that were more in line with their beliefs, without the fear of persecution. Yet, was there true religious freedom within the new colonies? Only if you believed in their prevailing religious concepts. There wasn't much tolerance for those who believed differently, such as the Quakers and the Baptists. Lord help you if you were thought to be a witch! Actually, if you dissented, the Old Testament provided many examples of techniques for properly punishing dissenters. Yes, there was freedom from the overreaching church in Europe, but fear was still the predominant means of controlling colonists' new freedom.

When government took over children's education in the mid-1800s, it followed a similar path. The intolerance of the churches against dissenters was the model for the intolerance of the state against parents who resisted compulsory government schooling. Let's draw the comparisons. Tax-supported churches and ministers fostered tax-supported schools, teachers and administrators. Compulsory church attendance fostered compulsory school attendance, with truancy officers hired to enforce it. Beatings and burnings turned into fines, incarceration and children seized from their loving and functional homes. Again, fear was—and still is—the predominant means of controlling the populace.

For generations families had been doing just fine educating their children. How did we lose the right to choose how to educate our own children? How did we morph our intolerance within religion into the intolerance of those who resisted compulsory education? And out of all the many creative ways to pass on information and stimulate creativity in young minds, how did we decide on the terribly dysfunctional style of schooling that we have today? Freedom is guaranteed to us by the First Amendment. How did we lose it in this area? I'll try to answer this as briefly as possible. First, remember that history is always written by the victors. The history of the public school system as written by the public school system is insulting nonsense.

Let's begin with the premise of why we went from an organic form of education—decentralized, entrepreneurial and demand-driven by parents and communities—to a centralized, government-controlled monopoly. The primary reason was not, as has been said, to enhance learning and literacy rates. Rather, it was so the government would have control over what was taught and how it was taught. By controlling what people read, you can control what they think. and therefore, you can control their behavior. Through schools, the state can control the minds of each new generation.

Before the government got involved, learning and literacy rates were actually quite good, and steadily improving. According to *Literacy in Colonial New England* by Kenneth Lockridge, between 1650 and 1670 the literacy rate of white New England men was 60 percent. It rose to 85 percent between 1758 and 1762, and it continued to rise to 90 percent between 1787 and 1795. In Boston, the literacy rate was close to 100 percent by the end of the 1700s. Women were also well off, as half the women born around 1730 were literate. Women born around 1810 joined the ranks of 100 percent literacy. In fact, in 1800 a magazine named *The Columbian Phoenix and Boston Review* stated, "No country on the face of the earth can boast of a larger proportion of inhabitants versed in the rudiments of science, or fewer who are not able to read and write their names, than the United States of America."

Enter the government, as who is better at breaking what is not broken? Today, the U.S literacy rate is approximately 79 percent. Most of the illiterate are composed of white US-born adults. It took the government just over two hundred years to destroy our literacy rate. What do you want for our more than 700 billion dollars in tax money annually?

But why? Why did the government get involved when it was clearly unnecessary? Around the 1830s, industrial giants like J.P. Morgan and John D. Rockefeller began pushing for compulsory, tax-supported government schools because they needed a place to warehouse the children while parents worked at their new factories. Also, they wanted schooling that would conform the children, grooming them to be good workers and making them accept that this would be their lot in life. However, it took until 1852 for the first state, Massachusetts, to enforce compulsory school attendance laws. The reason it took so long was because "free common schools" were strongly resisted by the citizens. The last holdout in Massachusetts was the town of Barnstable on Cape Cod. They resisted until the 1880s, when the government sent in the militia, took the children from their homes, and marched them to school backed with artillery. By 1918 all states had adopted compulsory school attendance laws.

After successfully establishing centralized education, the government needed to create a standardized system for these schools. It found the perfect template: the Germanic Prussian model for their military state. This new system was named "The New England System," and eventually every state adopted it.

In 1837, the Massachusetts Board of Education was founded and Horace Mann was appointed as the first secretary. He visited Prussia in the 1840s and praised their school system in his Seventh Annual Report. However, the one part of his visit which was never mentioned was that when he visited the schools, they were closed for vacation. The classrooms he "observed" were empty; he "interviewed" schoolmasters who were on vacation. He claimed to have read old official reports. He especially liked their compulsory school laws in which "after a child has arrived at the legal age of attending school, whether he be the child of noble or of peasant, the only two absolute grounds of exemption from attendance are sickness and death."

Why did Mann go to Prussia and decide it was the perfect place to emulate? Why did we choose Prussia as the model and what was it about their system that made it so enticing? Let's follow the money. Mann was heavily bankrolled by very wealthy people, including New England's prominent Peabody family. If he could accomplish compulsory school attendance, he would "win" a Congressional seat. He did, and he did. Some say he was a philanthropist enhancing the education of our children. But, remember that history is written by the victors, and literacy rates were already almost one hundred percent. They had to come up with other reasons that centralized, compulsory education was necessary. Since Prussia was under compulsory school attendance law, it was the ideal place for Mann to take his arsenal of information and propaganda from. The industrialists knew that Britain and Germany had already been successful in getting compulsory school atten-dance laws passed. These countries had created the diabolical mechanism of converting large populations of free landowners to a labor class, which seems to have been the ultimate goal of the industrialists.

Why did Prussia adopt compulsory schooling? The reason goes back over two hundred years in history, to 1808 when Napoleon defeated the Prussian military at the Battle of Jena. He demanded humiliating and severe terms for Prussia. After that, Prussia wanted to create a populace that would form a strong military force to ensure that what happened with Napoleon would never happen again. They set up a massive compulsory school system to facilitate the creation of a society where people would learn to submit their personal will for the "greater good of the country," and would be willing to die in its service. The Prussians, influenced by Johann Gottlieb Fichte, learned about mass schooling through the Swiss educator John Henry Pestalozzi (father of the modern elementary school). In their schools, they divided students into three categories. One percent of the students would be earmarked as future policy makers, and 5–7 percent of students would be earmarked as future professionals. But for the majority of the students, the emphasis would be on instilling pure obedience. Therefore, according to John Taylor Gatto in *The Underground History of American Education*, the majority of students "were being bred to be obedient soldiers, obedient workers for mines, factories and farms, well-subordinated civil servants, well-subordinated clerks for industry, citizens who thought alike on most issues," creating "national uniformity in thought, word and deed." The psychological techniques they used to do this were taken from the fields of animal husbandry, equestrian training and military training. This is what our government chose to replicate in the US, encouraged and financed by the industrialists and instituted by Horace Mann.

Does it seem far-fetched that our educational system is based on methods used in equestrian training? Let's examine a striking similarity. To control the children in the classroom, "operant conditioning" has been the chosen method. It controls behavior by equating certain behaviors with consequences—both rewards and punishments. Good grades, gold stars, prime seating arrangements, awards, etc., are rewards given to the children who display the appropriate behavior. Bad grades, pink slips, detention, humiliation and shame are the punishment for those who cannot quite fit into the system for one reason or another. It is just like training an animal. If you've ever had a puppy, you recognize the method. To illustrate the comparison to equestrian training specifically, here is a quote from an old journal by the Equine Mental Health Association:

> " . . . Keep them predominantly idle, keep them apart from other
> horses, and you will create an animal that interacts with the

world in ways clearly un-natural . . . timid, crazy, undependable, bolting, bucking, avoidant, shying, etc. Keep a horse from accessing the wisdom of the herd and the wisdom of its own nature and you get a horse that doesn't know where it belongs in the world. Under such conditions well-bred horses with tremendous potentials end up living their lives as . . . consumers instead of contributors."

As an aside here: the industrialists Morgan, Rockefeller and Andrew Carnegie are historically considered to be great philanthropists. But, as always, there is more to the story. They needed to engage in philanthropy to improve their public images. Rockefeller was instrumental in pioneering tax-exempt foundations that preserved the vast fortunes of people like himself and Andrew Carnegie from income and inheritance taxes. Through their foundations they still had control of their money and were able to finance projects under the guise of philanthropy. Frederick T. Gates, a former minister, was hired by the George Pillsbury company as a public relations agent. He brilliantly came up with the "Pillsbury Formula." He cooked up the idea that if Pillsbury "gave away a dollar in donations to something, and you set in motion a citizen committee that will go out and raise money from the community, then for every dollar that's raised in the community you agree to give a dollar" . . . "Now what you have is efficiency in philanthropy. Because now you give only half as much as you would have normally, and you've got thousands and thousands of people working with you and feeling identified with you as a person because they like this project. So, it's a means of reaching a lot of people and bringing them into your team, and they think better of you because of that." Rockefeller and Carnegie later employed Gates and used him in reforming not only the public school system but also medical schools. How our medical schools were corrupted is a topic on which many people are doing a tremendous amount of investigative research.

Forced schooling's negative effects on children in the United States didn't go unnoticed by the citizens who still believed in the freedom and liberty of America. In 1918, Thomas Alexander, professor of elementary education at the George Peabody College for Teachers, wrote in his book, *The Prussian Elementary Schools*, "We believe, however, that a careful study of the Prussian school system will convince any unbiased reader that the Prussian citizen cannot be free to do and act for himself, that the Prussian is to a large measure enslaved through the medium of his school, that his learning instead of making him his own master forges the chain by which he is held in servitude, that the whole scheme of Prussian elementary education is shaped with the express purpose of making ninety-five out of every hundred citizens subservient to the ruling house and to the state." Unfortunately, protests like these were ignored.

The concept of stratification in schools and society wasn't only supported by the Prussians. Britain, France and Germany were already adept at maintaining social order by the time of our country's founding. America was new, and originally founded on the idea that all people were created equal. A country of self-supporting, independent, confident men and women was frightening and unacceptable to the elite who had become accustomed to maintaining their flocks for centuries. They needed to instill the old power structure in this country. It had to be done gradually, and the best way was through public schooling.

The Prussian structure wasn't the only one that was used in the creation of our educational system. Believe it or not, the caste system of the Hindus in India also contributed. Here's how this came about. By 1700 Great Britain had surpassed the Netherlands, France, Spain and Portugal in trade with China and the conquest of India. Tea and other products came from China through India and were sold through Britain's East India Trading Company to the civilized world. This helped to finance the industrialists in America. The Chinese, however, did not want to reciprocate and buy products from Britain, so Britain was financially suffering from a major trade imbalance with the Chinese. Their solution was to grow opium in India and smuggle it into China. Many Chinese became addicted, causing severe social and economic disruption. The Chinese government attempted to resist, confiscating and destroying tons of British opium, but Great Britain sent military forces to China and the first "opium war" ensued. Britain won that war, as well as a second one that also included France, forcing China to concede to trade demands. Britain had a monopoly on the drug market now as well. Through Britain's occupation of India, Hindu customs became known in the West.

A Scottish cleric, Andrew Bell, made his way to India and was intrigued by the structure of the Hindu caste system and how education there supported that system. The Hindu caste system has five strata. The upper five percent is divided into three categories. The Brahmins, the highest level, are the priests, followed by those trained in medicine, law, teaching and other professional occupations. The second class is the military and administrative caste. The third level is the industrial caste, such as merchants and land cultivators. The largest group, the lower ninety-five percent, formed the menial caste and were called the "pariahs" or "untouchables." This lowest ninety-five percent is what interested Bell the most.

In India, Bell secured a position as superintendent of a boys' English orphanage, which was the perfect place to experiment with implementing the Hindu system. In 1797, Bell especially liked how the Hindu system promoted memorization of information in the lower caste, enabling them to accept their lowly level in society. He saw it as an effective way to prevent critical thinking and the need to learn how to read and write. This way the lower class didn't have to think, and they willingly became humble servants. According to John Gatto in *The Underground History of American Education*, Bell's theory that schooled ignorance was more useful than unschooled stupidity and his take on the Hindu system became popular in Great Britain; it was useful in training the masses there to work in the various industries.

Top philosophical and political minds of the day also played a role in education. George Wilheim Fredrich Hegel was a nineteenth century German philosopher and a proponent of compulsory schooling. He had seen the fate of Marie Antoinette during the French revolution (she was executed by revolutionaries) and concluded that people should not be given suffrage. He proposed that they should be given enough information and freedom to give the appearance of true liberty, but dumbed down enough that they had no idea they were truly enslaved; this would prevent any ideas of rebellion. His philosophy drew a thread from Christianity during the second century— the concept of unity consciousness—but controlled by the government. He believed that under a dictator or socialist state, people would naturally form a unity consciousness to support the state, which would bring about peace.

I prefer to think of that as forced unity consciousness or indoctrination and brainwashing. "Unity consciousness" is a divine spiritual concept that we are all one, born of the Supreme Creator. Hegel's idea of serving the state as "the one" rather than God (or whatever term you like to use for a higher sacred force) goes against our innate humanity. Hegel believed that through the state all people would then unify around one allegiance.

Another of his concepts that appealed to those in power was that governments could secretly provoke crises, outside of the view of the public, thereby manipulating an artificial sense of national unity through fear, then use it to "fix" the crises. This abusive manipulation allowed the government to institute laws and policies that the populace never would have agreed to otherwise. This is how history is deliberately manipulated. Hegel's theories became known as Hegelism, a philosophy that many future tyrants found very useful.

Karl Marx was a follower of Hegel. Looking at history, it's easy to see how much death, torture and misery his concepts were responsible for. Communist uprisings in Russia, China, and several other countries were inspired by Marx's work in *The Communist Manifesto*, along with that of Friedrich Engels in *Das Kapital*. Their theories both promote the suppression of the individual. Marx's theory, "From each according to his ability, to each according to his needs," sounds lovely and humanitarian, but when put into practice, it culminates in anti-individualism and the devaluing of human life. Under real world communism, the state owns the people, their property and what they produce.

Communism is estimated to be responsible for the deaths of up to a hundred million people, and perhaps even more. From Josef Stalin's "Great Purge" and the Holodomor to Mao Zedong's famines to Pol Pot's killing fields, Marx's legacy is one of death [Freedomworks.org]. Why has communism caused famine, terror, torture, massacres and brutal deaths? Because communist governments cannot have an uprising. It is much easier to control a smaller population, so they murder their own citizens, then use the fear created by that terrorism to squelch any further uprisings. Also, when people are starving and suffering, in their desperation, they become more submissive to the wills of the government. History proves that communism did not create the Utopia that Hegelism promised.

Even though communism has caused such horrific destruction, there are those who still seek to promote it, because they want to control the citizens. In the US, the elites in charge of the educational system have removed any sense of individuality, creative thinking or self-motivation and have created division and victim groups among our children. Slowly, they have made the youth believe that socialism and communism are the cure. They glamorize communism despite all the horrors it has caused over the course of the past century—-not only millions of deaths, but the imprisonment of tens of millions more in gulags and reeducation camps from Russia and China to Vietnam, Cambodia and North Korea, and the oppression of hundreds of millions more under current regimes. None of this has dissuaded those on the modern Western left from embracing Marx's bloody legacy [https://www.nationalreview.com/2018/05/karl-marx-legacy-millions-murdered-enslaved-in-poverty/].

J.P. Morgan was also a follower of Hegel. Morgan, who was born into a wealthy banking family, became one of the largest financiers of the nineteenth century and was a founding member of the Federal Reserve System. Marx and Morgan were two sides of the same coin. Marx blatantly took people's freedoms away by force and Morgan successfully manipulated an entire population into thinking they had freedom while actually destroying individual freedom and liberty. Similar results, just different appearance and tactics. J.P. Morgan believed in a strong class system and was one of the four major creators of modern forced schooling. The other three were Andrew Carnegie, John D. Rockefeller, Sr. and Henry Ford.

Andrew Carnegie immigrated to the United States from Scotland as a child. He perhaps is best known for his creation of the steel industry. In his article "The Gospel of Wealth," he promotes the concept that the wealthy owed it to society to take over everything—in the public interest, of course. He was a proponent of Darwinism, which is based on competition for limited resources and survival of the fittest. Darwinism came at the right time in the history of the creation of the Western economy as we know it now. The competition, separation, and conflict is how our corporations were formed. To dispute the validity of Darwinism is practically forbidden, and marks the death nell of any educator. But, even Darwin questioned his own theory, saying:

> "Why does not every collection of fossil remains afford plain evidence of the gradation and mutation of the forms of life? We meet with no such evidence, and this is the most obvious and forcible of the many objections which may be urged against my theory."

The question that appears to have plagued him was that even though there is evolution within a species, he could find no evidence of evolution from one species into another. In fact, the 1933 Nobel Prize winner in physiology and medicine, Thomas H. Morgan, wrote in his book *Evolution and Adaptation*, "Within the period of human history we do not know of a single instance of the transformation of one species into another."

Since Darwin's time DNA studies have proven that humans did not descend from Neanderthals. Humans are a unique species that appeared on Earth around two hundred thousand years ago with an advanced brain and nervous system not found in any species already in existence. According to Gregg Braden in his book *Human by Design,* "An honest scientist, who is not bound by the constraints of academia, politics, or religion, can no longer discount the new evidence about our human origins and still remain credible." The reason why I include this information in a discussion of the school system is to show you that the authorities support this outdated theory because it serves their agenda. Darwinism puts forth the idea that humanity was just lucky to rise to the top of the food chain, that we are not unique, just evolved from a single cell somewhere in the very distant past rather than unique souls empowered by the light of our Creator, Divine Source. Through Darwinism, industrialists such as Carnegie were able to validate—to themselves perhaps, but definitely to others—that some people are born superior, and the rest should just accept that they are not as evolved and should be grateful for the scraps fed to them by those superiors.

Carnegie also firmly supported a planned economy and society. He donated vast sums of money to create schools and universities. This philanthropy sounds wonderful, yet to look beyond the facade one must delve deeper into who was in control and what was taught. Since his time, these institutions have imposed their objectives from a center of operations hidden from the public. These institutions are staffed by self-proclaimed experts and elites of social engineering.

One man who helped establish social control, thanks to funding from Carnegie, was William Torrey Harris. He was the US Commissioner of Education for sixteen years, from 1889 to 1906, and was supported and influenced by Carnegie. Don't be fooled by accounts that he was responsible for high academic standards. He was of the mind that parents and local traditions shouldn't play a role in children's lives. His mission was to standardize and

Germanize our schools. Here are two quotes of his taken from *The Philosophy of Education*, published in 1906:

> "Ninety-nine [students] out of a hundred are automata, careful to walk in prescribed paths, careful to follow the prescribed custom. This is not an accident but the result of substantial education, which, scientifically defined, is the subsumption of the individual."

> "The great purpose of school can be realized better in dark, airless, ugly places . . . It is to master the physical self, to transcend the beauty of nature. School should develop the power to withdraw from the external world."

Harris adhered strictly to Hegelism. He also believed that children were property and were therefore instruments of the state, and he supported the stratified caste system. To understand what Hegel and Harris were about is to comprehend that to divide and conquer is at the foundation of the school system. It supports alienation from one's family, friends, and neighbors, as well as from nature, beauty, traditions, and religion. The goal of this alienation is total loyal obedience to a central government instead. From the earliest grade, children are divided from those who could help them mature and learn, such as older children, parents, and community members. Also, rather than support each other, programs are geared to make the children exist in a competitive environment. Harris agreed with the idea that alienation was the best way to a successful industrial society.

Under people like Harris, the goals of schooling descended from critical thinking, creative problem solving, ingenuity and high moral values to molding children into future human resources to support businesses and governments. In 1909 Woodrow Wilson, who was president of Princeton University at the time, gave a speech to the New York City School Teachers' Association, saying:

"We want one class to have a liberal education. We want another class, a very much larger class of necessity, to forgo the privilege of a liberal education and fit themselves to perform specific difficult manual tasks."

In the early 1900s a self-appointed group of "experts" called themselves "the education trust." They sought to control all major school administrative jobs. In 1917 there is a record of their first meeting, and as expected, both Carnegie and the Rockefellers had representatives attend. Also, by 1915, a small group of industrialists and financiers had formed charitable foundations with which they subsidized university chairs and researchers, school administrators, and of course, forced schooling initiatives. Carnegie and Rockefeller, once again, were heavy contributors.

If you are still not so sure about the school system and these "charitable foundations" having diabolical intentions, then you may have a change of heart after reading the following. It is an excerpt from the first mission statement of Rockefeller's General Education Board, from the Occasional Letter Number One written by Frederick T. Gates, Director of Charity for John D. Rockefeller's Southern Education Board (SEB):

"Is there aught of remedy for this neglect of rural life? Let us, at least, yield ourselves to the ratifications of a beautiful dream that there is. In our dream, we have limitless resources, and the people yield themselves with perfect docility to our molding hand. The present educational conventions fade from our minds, and, unhampered by tradition, we work our own good will upon a grateful and responsive rural folk. We shall not try to make these people or any of their children into philosophers or men of learning or of science. We are not to raise up from among them authors, orators, poets, or men of letters. We shall not search for embryo great artists, painters, musicians. Nor will we cherish even the humbler ambition to raise up from among them lawyers, doctors, preachers, politicians, statesmen, of whom we now have ample supply. The task we set before ourselves is very simple . . . we will organize children . . . and teach them to do in a perfect way the things their fathers and mothers are doing in an imperfect way."

Several years later Edward Thorndike of Columbia Teachers College said that school should create conditions for "selective breeding before the masses take things into their own hands." In 1920, H.H. Goddard, head of the Psychology Department at Princeton, said in his book *Human Efficiency* that government schooling was about "the perfect organization of the hive." He wanted standardized testing to be used as a way to make lower classes recognize their own inferiority.

On April 11, 1933, Max Mason, president of the Rockefeller Foundation, announced that a comprehensive national program was underway regarding "the control of human behavior." Rockefeller was very interested in Hermann Muller's work in genetics. Muller was a European geneticist interested in planned breeding. Muller convinced Rockefeller to invest in control of human evolution. (He won the Nobel Prize, if that tells you anything.) Muller said that the state must prepare to consciously guide human sexual selection, and it would be the school's responsibility to separate worthwhile breeders from those whose genes were less than desirable. The National Education Association announced that their organization planned "to accomplish by education what dictators in Europe are seeking to do by compulsion and force."

This human breeding idea was heavily funded by not only the government but also academia and the military. Hitler took notice and began his own aggressive program. Those in charge of America's sinister program moved underground so as not to seem aligned with Hitler's program. (By the way, did you know that after World War II, the CIA instigated Operation Paperclip, a secret program in which more than sixteen hundred German scientists, engineers and technicians were taken from Germany and hired by the US for government employment, primarily between 1945 and 1959? Many were former leaders of the Nazi Party. The narrative at the time was that most of the Nazi offenders were convicted in the Nuremberg Trials. However, only ten were hanged and only seven went to jail. They had way too much knowledge to go to waste. Adolf Heusinger, Hitler's Chief of Staff, was hired to be Chairman of the NATO Military Committee. Werner VonBraun, who was a Nazi rocket engineer, was hired as the Director of the Marshall Space Flight Center and Chief Architect of the Saturn V Rocket for NASA. And, of course, many were employed in academia. Many went to South America as well.)

To see how the forced schooling program has worked, we can look at literacy rates. Remember that by 1800 we had literacy rates of close to 100 percent. The millions of men who took academic tests in 1942–1944 to join the military during WWII had a literacy rate of 96 percent. Ten years prior to that, the rate was 98 percent. The Korean War began six short years after WWII was over, in 1945. By then, the literacy rate was only 81 percent. (Keep in mind that only a fourth-grade level reading level was necessary to be considered literate.) The difference was that the men who tested for WWII were schooled in the 1930s, and most of the men in the Korean War were schooled in the 1940s. By the time of the Vietnam War, our literacy rate had fallen to 73 percent. These were people who had been in school in the 1950s. This doesn't say much about the effectiveness of the public school "experts."

Moving into the years of 1967–1974, there was a concerted effort led by the US Office of Education plus private foundations (of course), select universities and think tanks, certain government agencies and large global corporations to impose radical changes to teacher training. Three programs were launched: Designing Education for the Future, The Behavioral Science Teacher Education Project and Benjamin Bloom's massive Taxonomy of Education Objectives. These gargantuan programs led to a massive increase of central control of our school system. The US Office of Education redefined education as "a means to achieve important economic and social goals of a national character." (Note—they say nothing about education or personal achievement.)

Also, the state education agencies were ordered to act as on-site federal enforcers, making sure local schools complied with central directives. The state education departments were told to relinquish "independent identity as well as authority" or they would be charged with financial penalties for noncompliance! In fact, between 1960 and 1998 the nonteaching bureaucracy of public schools increased by 500 percent. Yet with this burgeoning bureaucracy, the number of school districts with elected boards shrank from 40,520 in 1960 to 15,000 in 1998. Who are these nonteaching bureaucrats, what positions do they fill and how much money do they take from the education budget?

The Behavioral Science Teacher Education Project promoted "impersonal manipulation" through schooling in which "few will be able to maintain control over their opinions." The project also proposed that "each individual receives at birth a multi-purpose identification number" to enable employers and other controllers to track individuals and planned to institute "chemical experimentation" on minors as normal procedure. (This preceded the massive Ritalin prescribing that has become part and parcel of forced government schooling).

Bloom's new taxonomy directives allowed schools to experiment with testing and data collection without any public notice and used testing to give each child an official rating on a scale. His program also featured new behavioral psychology that would force children to learn "proper" thoughts, feelings and actions while "improper" ones brought from home were "remediated."

Also, in the mid-1960s a man named Ralph Tyler of Carnegie Endowments secretively instigated the collection of students' personal information and created computer codes to enhance cross-referencing. Tyler's justification was that it was "the moral right of institutions." These programs gave useful information for social engineers to further control the minds of the young.

Around the late 1960s another charitable organization, the Ford Foundation, introduced and funded an idea that actually escalated the chaos and destruction in schools and children's lives. Of course, it was sold to us as an idea that would be helpful to the school environment. The Ford Foundation and other outside agencies claimed the right to supervise whether or not the "children's rights" were being supported. On the surface, who can argue that? (They always make their devious plans sound so philanthropical.) But basically, they took away teachers' and administrators' rights to control discipline in the classroom and school grounds. Instead of being able to handle issues as they arose, the school had to imitate the court system's due process. Therefore, since nothing could be handled in the moment of necessity, chaos and horrible behavior ensued. Staff and teachers were stripped of all authority, and of course, the students knew it. But according to the Ford Foundation's and other agencies' "experts," this was necessary to prevent low self-esteem in those who were having difficulties.

This opened the door for yet more creation of agencies and expert groups to research how and why we have such trouble in our schools (and also laid the groundwork for the "school to prison pipeline" (which will be explained shortly). Many of these agencies are nonprofits whose existence depends on government grants (your tax dollars). It's the Hegelist philosophy: secretly create a problem, then come in with the solution. The modus operandi of these foundations has been to create the problem, then have the government and other people contribute to your charitable organization to figure out how to fix it. We pay out financially on both ends, yet the true cost is the loss of our children.

The story continues with each consecutive decade and administration. I would like to say that it has evolved, but unfortunately more money, experts and programs just continue to move the chairs on the Titanic. This ship has sunk. It's going to take a complete overhaul to fix our educational system. But I have come to believe it isn't broken as much as it's exactly where it was designed to be. It is so top heavy, with so much money in so many hands—the unions; foundations; textbook, test creation and computer companies; contractors; lobby groups; and universities. And that's nationally, before we even get down to the local districts. Unfortunately, at the bottom of the pile are the crumbs that get spent in the actual classroom. Most of the money given to the education system is to support the system and keep it breathing—not to educate the children. Our evolution has been slowed down by these self-proclaimed experts. The problem is not the children. The problem is this insane, dysfunctional system, intentionally designed, maintained and perpetuated by a bureaucratic machine where everyone is making money and the needs of the global elite are the only thing that matters, not the future of this amazing planet: our beautiful children.

We all know that the system is not working. Everyone points fingers at everyone else. The teachers point at parents, and parents point at teachers and administrators. The administration points to the local boards and they reflexively point back. Yet, does anyone know who really is in charge of this system? As I stated above, there are universities, special foundations, expert groups, nonprofit agencies too numerous to count, social welfare groups, lobbying groups, teachers' unions, the National Board of Education, etc. It is sad when only an average of 50 percent of new teachers are able to survive teaching in the public school system for three years. They have all the accountability but no authority, due, in part, to the due process program. It's such a dysfunctional system that many teachers give up on their dream of teaching children.

The parents are blamed for not actively taking part in their child's education. That may be partially true; I'm sure teachers have seen their share of frustrating and heartbreaking cases. But as we have learned, the system was designed to distance children from their family's traditions, cultures and "inferior world views." It was designed to brainwash children to create a more uniform herd of employees and to mindlessly hand over taxes to an ever-growing government. Parents have been pushed out of contributing to their children's education from the beginning. We have no control over the cost, the curriculum, who our child's teacher is, where they will be sent to school, how the day is to be organized and on and on. We may have a small degree of input but never the final say. There are vast amounts of homework and projects that come home with children, and parents are expected to make sure that they are doing their homework and doing it well. If not, they are expected to find additional resources. There are special programs, fundraisers, etc., and it's expected for the families to attend, usually after a day spent at their jobs. There is little to no time for children to create and explore, to have quality time as a family, or to enjoy individual interests. It is exhausting and demoralizing for both children and parents.

Going back to the Hindu caste system and how it inspired the stratification of children, we can see how that plays out in today's school system. Depending on the district, there can be any combination of categories such as highly gifted, gifted, honors, mainstream and special education. In the course of my research, I have learned that the special education camp has spawned an untold number of experts, agencies, and non-profits, as well as impacting welfare assistance. It has created a large part of the social service empire we have today. A school will get much more financial assistance for this unfortunate group. Not that they are truly unfortunate; they are unfortunate in that they must endure the imprisonment of this system that uses them to increase its bank accounts.

We know that children are as unique as their thumbprints, and each learns in their own way in their own time. Their interests, genetic inheritance, home environment and so much more goes into their individual learning style and pace, as well as their readiness to learn. But schools pigeon-hole them, strap them into their little desks and tell them what, when, and how to learn. And once a child is classified, they are expected to live up or down to it. It matters not if the classification is inaccurate (because it usually is—recall the story of my son when we were told he had learning problems); this classification (or label) will stick and affect the rest of their life. Being placed in a "lower" level degrades children's abilities and demoralizes them.

Obviously, there are children with true physical and mental challenges who need extra care, but those sweet children form a much smaller group. All children are forced into a category because the system says that all children must be part of the stratification process. Many children are labeled "special ed" because they don't meet the standards, which continually change. Children endure an insane amount of testing with norms that also continually change, as well as subjective teacher assessments. These assessments are not fair and impartial, and yet they are regularly used to change children's lives dramatically—often for the worse. It's not that I don't believe that we need programs for special needs children. They do exist, and I'm thankful there are amazing therapists and teachers, as well as programs, to help. What I protest is the corruption and abuse of the system, and how many hands are in the till taking money that should be going to the children and families who need help. For example, it is painfully obvious how arrogant the leaders in the school system are when in October 2015, the president of the National Education Association, Lily Eskelsen Garcia, made this statement regarding students with disabilities during a Campaign for America's Future:

> "We diversify our curriculum instruction to meet the personal individual needs of all of our students, the blind, the hearing impaired, the physically challenged, the gifted and talented, the chronically tarded and the medically annoying."

With over three million members, made up of teachers paying hundreds of dollars each in dues, the NEA is the largest union in the United States. As its head, Garcia got a salary of approximately a half million dollars—when the teachers she "represents" can't get enough money for simple supplies for the children in their classrooms. Maybe it is time to reevaluate the necessity for such a large institution.

I have an acquaintance who is a vice principal of a middle school. She was approached by a mother regarding the grades of her daughter. She was very concerned that her daughter was earning a C grade. When the vice principal attempted to console the mother that the reason her daughter didn't make a higher grade was due to her performance, the response was completely different from what the vice principal expected. The mother didn't want her daughter to make a C because it was too good. As long as she was failing, the mother received approximately $600.00 a month in welfare. I am not aware of what assistance they were on or all the details, but this particular vice principal was shocked this was actually happening, and to have a mother brazenly ask for her daughter to fail. We have a broken system when failure is rewarded.

Curriculum

The government continues its overreach into our children's lives at earlier and earlier ages. For instance, Bobby Jindal, past governor of Louisiana, enacted reforms there related to early childhood education. One of the new rules stated this: "Establish performance targets for children under the age of three and academic standards for kindergarten readiness for three-and four-year-old children to be used in publicly funded early childhood education programs." These reforms were enacted despite ADHD now being diagnosed in children as young as three, especially in "academically oriented" preschools, and some of them being medicated with stimulants! Children this young learn best by playing, not being forced to sit still in rigid school environments.

In my research I found a study by two researchers, Dr. George Land and Beth Jarman. They were contacted by NASA to develop a highly specialized test to effectively measure the creative potential of their scientists and engineers. Land and Jarman created this test to assess the ability to look at a particular problem and propose multiple solutions. This has been termed the process of "divergent thinking." During the course of creating this test, these two researchers wanted to understand the source of creativity. They wanted to find out if it was nature, or nurture, or something else.

The test Land and Jarman created for NASA was quite simple, so they were able to give it to all age groups. They gave the test to sixteen hundred four- and five-year-old children. To their surprise, 98 percent of the children scored at the genius level! They decided to turn it into a longitudinal study. Five years later they tested the same group of children, who were now around nine and ten. Sadly, their performance had declined to 30 percent! Five years in school had resulted in a reduction of 68 percent. After another five years, they tested the same group, now in high school. A mere 12 percent scored at the genius level. This is the result of ten years of "education."

Even though the researchers were quite dismayed, Land continued giving the same test to adults aged twenty-five and up (with an average age of thirty-one). He gave this test multiple times, and on average a lowly 2 percent of adults scored at the creative genius level. These results have been replicated more than a million times for accuracy. Personally, I would like to know more about these 2 percenters—were they homeschooled, what was their home environment like, where did they live and what are the similarities among them?

These findings are perhaps not too difficult to understand now that we know the intentions of the creators of the school system and the exponential growth of those in power who maintain it. It is designed to cripple our ability to think for ourselves. We have been intentionally manipulated to serve the powerful elite—to be consumers of the goods they have led us to believe we need, rather than self-empowered producers. Still not sure this is being done intentionally? Let's look at who is currently constructing the curriculum of today. A company called Lifetime Learning Systems told their corporate clients, "School is the ideal time to influence attitudes, build long-term loyalties, introduce new products, test-market, promote sampling and trial usage and—above all—generate immediate sales."

Recall that back in the 1960s the power of the local school districts was stripped and they became local administrators of state (and federal) requirements and policies. They have essentially no significant say in policy, curriculum selection, student attendance, total hours in the school year, etc. They give the community the false illusion that parents have a say in their children's welfare, but really local districts just carry out the dictates of the state. This leads us to ask, where does the state get its ideas about what must be taught and how?

State governments are tailoring curricula to meet their agendas, and textbook companies are helping. An investigation by the *New York Times* uncovered vast differences between the textbooks that students in California were issued versus the textbooks students in Texas were issued—by the same publisher! The publishing company in this case was McGraw Hill. The politicians, left- and right-leaning policy makers, and centralized state panels decide how they want our children to think and will distort historical events and steer the narrative to ensure their intended results. For instance, the author of this investigation compared eight different textbooks, and found they had substantially different viewpoints on current issues such as sexuality, immigration, race relations, self-defense rights and economics. California textbooks leaned left and instilled a more socialistic ideal, explaining how there is a massive gap between the haves and have-nots and the distribution of wealth concept. Texas policy makers required high school economic books to stress the benefits of a free enterprise system.

Even textbooks that claim to be completely objective use clever, albeit manipulative, language to control the intended perceptions of the students. Textbooks are a foundational tool used to educate and, therefore, have an authority and power that most students wouldn't even think of questioning.

And since success in school is test-driven, students must memorize the information to do well. The textbook writers' ultimate goal is to sell books; therefore, they must appease the policy makers' goals to shape the views of history, society and democracy in young impressionable minds.

Now, let's look at the recent debacle of the curriculum called Common Core. The main groups who decided this process were the Bill and Melinda Gates Foundation, the Department of Education and well-paid testing companies such as Pearson Education, a British-owned education publishing and assessment service to schools and corporations. Common Core was an initiative launched in 2009 by the government (this should immediately give rise for concern) that was supposed to improve public education by creating and implementing standards defining what students should learn in math and English language arts from kindergarten through twelfth grade. Common Core replaced states' varying guidelines with one set of federally supported standards, plus stringent assessment and accountability systems. It ties teacher evaluations to test scores, causing most of them to "teach to the test" rather than have individual approaches based on their students. It also penalized schools for doing poorly on the tests, causing enormous pressure on administrations and teachers—which filtered down to students. The methods of teaching and learning for both teachers and students changed greatly. The curriculum even completely leaves out cursive writing.

As Alfe Kohn, educator and author, asked in *Education Week* on January 14, 2010,

> "What's the purpose of demanding that every kid in every school in every state must be able to do the same thing in the same year, with teachers pressured to align their instruction to a master curriculum and a standardized test? . . . I know of no evidence that students in countries as diverse as ours with national standards or curricula engage in unusually deep thinking or are particularly excited about learning. Even

standardized test results, such as the Trends in International Mathematics and Science Study (TIMSS), provide no support for the nationalizers. On eighth-grade math and science tests, eight of the ten top-scoring countries had centralized education systems, but so did nine of the ten lowest-scoring countries in math and eight of the ten lowest-scoring countries in science . . . a prescription for uniform, specific, rigorous standards is made to order for those whose chief concern is to pump up the American economy and make sure that we triumph over people who live in other countries."

These "standards" are damaging to the spirit and psyche of our children. Again, I quote Alfe Kohn. He writes in *Educational Leadership,* September 2005,

"Has there ever been a wider, or more offensive, gap between educational rhetoric and reality than that which defines the current accountability fad? The stirring sound bites waft through the air: higher expectations . . . world-class standards . . . raising the bar . . . no child left behind. Meanwhile, educators and students down on the ground are under excruciating pressure to improve test results, often at the expense of meaningful learning, and more low-income and minority students are dropping out. The current version of school reform is changing what we value. If the sole goal is to raise achievement (in the narrowest sense of that word), then we may end up ignoring other kinds of learning beyond the academic. It's exceedingly difficult to teach the whole child when people are held accountable only for raising reading and math scores. Moreover, when some capabilities are privileged over others, and a broader approach to education is sacrificed, we begin to look at students differently. We come to lose sight of children 'except as they distribute themselves across deciles' (Hogan, 1974, p. iii). That means that some kids—namely, the high scorers—are prized more than others by the adults. One Florida superintendent observed that 'when a low-performing child walks into a classroom, instead of being seen as a challenge, or an opportunity for improvement, for the first time since I've been in education, teachers are seeing [him or her] as a liability' (Wilgoren, 2000). A diminution in *what* we value, then, may affect *whom* we value. But the damage isn't limited to those students who fail to measure up—that is, by conventional standards. If some children matter more to us than others, then all children are valued only conditionally. Regardless of the criteria we happen to be using, or the number of students who meet those criteria, every student gets the message that our acceptance is never a sure thing. They learn that their worth hinges on their performance ... All of us want our students to be successful learners, but there is a thin line that separates valuing excellence (a good thing) from leading students to believe that they matter only to the extent they meet our standards (not a good thing). Some people elevate abstractions like Achievement or Excellence above the needs of flesh-and-blood children. Thus, by steering extra resources to, or heaping public recognition on, students who succeed, we're not only ignoring the counterproductive effects of extrinsic motivators (Kohn, 1993), but possibly sending a message to all students—those who have been recognized and those who, conspicuously, have not—that only those who do well count. . . . Sometimes the conditions placed on acceptance have more to do with compliance than with success. A case in point: temporarily ejecting a student from a class activity—or even from school— for misbehaving. This practice is sometimes rationalized on the grounds that it isn't fair to the others if one student is allowed to act badly. But those other students, the ones in whose name we are allegedly taking this action, are being told, in effect, that everyone is part of this community only conditionally. That creates an uneasy, uncertain, and ultimately unsafe climate."

Adele Faber and Elaine Mazlish, authors of *How to Talk So Kids Can Learn—at Home and in School*, 1995, ask us to put ourselves in the place of a child who has been subjected to this temporary ejection (otherwise known as time-out):

> "As an adult you can imagine how resentful and humiliated you would feel if someone forced you into isolation for something you said or did. For a child, however, it is even worse, since she may come to believe that there is something so wrong with her that she has to be removed from society. Teaching in this way is not just a matter of how we respond to children after they do something wrong, of course. It's about the countless gestures that let them know we're glad to see them, that we trust and respect them, that we care what happens to them. It's about the real (and unconditional) respect we show by asking all students what *they* think about how things are going, and how we might do things differently, not the selective reinforcement we offer to some students when they please us."

On a personal note, my family attended many school night awards banquets. The kids would be excited to go to the function and see all their schoolmates outside of the classroom, especially with the school hyping the evening up for weeks in advance. We would usually bring a dessert and everyone would socialize before the awards portion began. A few dozen children would get awards or acknowledgements of some sort, but the vast majority of the children present would get no recognition whatsoever. It is an exercise in humiliation for those children. Again, this is an example of the operant conditioning being used to lower our children's self-perception and self-esteem. I believe it is archaic and destructive. Surely every child could be made to feel good about themselves in some manner at events like this. Or just do away with them. I am not referring to a "participation trophy" in Little League, where you win or lose as a competitive team. I am talking about where the children spend the majority of their day with their peers and with authorities who have a major impact and influence on their lives. As John Holt, known as the father of homeschooling, so perfectly states, "We destroy the love of learning in children, which is so strong when they are small, by encouraging and compelling them to work for petty and contemptible rewards, gold stars, or papers marked one hundred and tacked to the wall, or As on report cards, or honor rolls, or dean's lists, or Phi Beta Kappa Keys, in short, for the ignoble satisfaction of feeling that they are better than someone else."

Our educational system is a means of mass indoctrination. One can get no better understanding of how than from Charlotte Iserbyt's research and firsthand accounts of working in the US Department of Education, as detailed in her two books. The first is *Back to Basics Reform or OBE Skinnerian International Curriculum*, where she documents her experiences as a senior policy advisor. In this position she was informed about past and future plans to restructure American education from traditional academics to values clarification (changing from traditional moral values to humanist values) and global workforce training, using tax-funded private education, charter schools without elected boards, and the Skinnerian master learning outcomes-based methodology in conjunction with computers. The learning outcome methodology is defined as a way to determine exact end-behavior. For example, in chapter 1.3 of its 2009 report, the European Association for Quality Assurance in Higher Education (ENQA) set as a standard for higher education in Europe that "students should be assessed using published criteria, regulations and procedures that are applied consistently . . . student assessment procedures are expected to be designed to measure the achievement of the intended learning outcomes and other programme objectives." I previously mentioned Alfe Kohn's, Adele Faber's and Elaine Mazlish's insights regarding the detriments of this approach. Her second book, *The Deliberate*

Dumbing Down of America, is a massive seven hundred-page chronological record starting in the 1800s of the deliberate dumbing down of not just America but of the world.

Most of the research in both of these books is regarding the expenditure of hundreds of millions of US tax dollars a year on academic programs to change student's attitudes, values, and beliefs from those taught in the home and by the church. She has uncovered a major tax-exempt foundation project titled the Goodlad Study. She found that the goal of the Goodlad Study, which was made available to all fifty state commissioners of education, was/is to change United States education in order to merge it into the global education system. Iserbyt later came across a federally-funded grant titled Better Education Skills through Technology (Project BEST). Having served as a local school board member, she was shocked by one page marked CONFIDENTIAL that stated, "What we [the US Dept. of Education] can control and manipulate at the local level," which listed the selection of members of task force, content of curriculum, etc. Iserbyt leaked the entire grant to *Human Events*, a D.C. weekly journal, but not before she had removed all other controversial anti-family/anti-American curriculum plans and documents from her office to her apartment. Many of these confidential documents are included in her two books listed above.

Iserbyt was subsequently removed from her position in the Department of Education and returned to Maine. She considers the Carnegie Corporation to be the primary tax-exempt foundation involved in changing the USA from a capitalist economy to a planned economy. In her Internet interviews, Iserbyt reads from Carnegie's Conclusions and Recommendations for the Social Studies, 1934 (page 264 in the PDF of her book), which details how education would be used to bring about not only a planned economy for the United States, but also the necessity of, in some cases, the seizing of private property for public use.

Iserbyt is also the author of "Soviets in the Classroom . . . America's Latest Education Fad," 1989, which exposes the US-USSR Education and Cultural Agreements signed by President Reagan and President Gorbachev, as well as the Carnegie-Soviet Academy of Science Agreement (both negotiated in 1985 and still in effect as of 2017).

In another interview, in 2011, concerning secret societies and the elite agenda, she disclosed that in the early 1980s she had a chance to meet with Norman Dodd, who was the chief investigator for the United States House Select Committee to Investigate Tax-Exempt Foundations and Comparable Organizations (commonly known as the B. Carroll Reece Committee). She quotes Dodd regarding the "network" of individuals and foundations, including Carnegie, whose goal was/is to bring about world peace by means of **war and rapid changes in society**. She mentions Dodd's "off-the-record" discussions in 1953 with the late Rowan Gaither, president of the Ford Foundation, during which Gaither stated:

> *"Mr. Dodd, all of us here at the policy making level of the foundation have at one time or another served in the OSS (the Office of Strategic Services, the forerunner of the CIA) or the European Economic Administration, operating under directives from the White House. We operate under those same directives . . . The substance of the directives under which we operate is that we shall use our grant making power to so alter life in the United States so that we can be comfortably merged with the Soviet Union."*

School Is the New Religion

The notion that school would become society's new religion gained footing quite early on with the ideology of state-forced schooling. Edward A. Ross, a sociologist at the University of Wisconsin, wrote in his 1901 book *Social Control*, "Plans are underway to replace community, family and church with propaganda, education, and mass media . . . the State shakes loose from Church, reaches out to School . . . People are only little plastic lumps of human dough." His book caused huge effects in social and political science, economics and psychology. It also influenced genetics, eugenics, psychobiology and the beginnings of molecular biology.

The idea that public school is becoming a state religion has been noticed by many. In his 1971 book, *Deschooling Society,* Ivan Illich commented:

> "School has become the world religion of a modernized proletariat and makes futile promises of salvation to the poor of the technological age. The nation-state has adopted it, drafting all citizens into a graded curriculum leading to sequential diplomas not unlike the initiation rituals and hieratic promotions of former times. The modern state has assumed the duty of enforcing the judgment of its educators through well-meant truant officers and job requirements, much as did the Spanish kings who enforced the judgments of their theologians through the conquistadors and the Inquisition.
>
> Children are protected by neither the First nor the Fifth Amendment when they stand before that secular priest, the teacher. The child must confront a man who wears an invisible triple crown, like the papal tiara, the symbol of triple authority combined in one person. For the child, the teacher pontificates as pastor, prophet, and priest—he is at once guide, teacher, and administrator of a sacred ritual. He combines the claims of medieval popes in a society [ostensibly] constituted under the guarantee that these claims shall never be exercised together by one established and obligatory institution—church or state.
>
> Schoolteachers and ministers are the only professionals who feel entitled to pry into the private affairs of their clients at the same time as they preach to a captive audience."

President Obama's comments about education in a State of the Union speech made me wonder what else the government has up its sleeves for our children and the future of this country:

> "We all know that young people will be more successful if they have a strong moral and ethical foundation. So tonight, I am proposing that every state—every state—require that all students be taught ethics and morality each year until they graduate or turn eighteen. Since all children must receive this specialized training and to ensure fairness and access for all, we will require each state to create non-sectarian tax-supported state institutions that I'm calling Centers of Ethics and Morality. A new federal cabinet position called the Secretary of Ethics and Morality will be established to ensure that each state establishes centers meeting federal guidelines.

> This new institution will incorporate what our experts, guided by the latest scientific research, deem to be the best of the ethical and moral teachings of all religions. By having the government provide this instruction we will remove all sectarian competition and strife that has characterized religious movements and belief systems of the past. My plan will, over time, eliminate the wasteful duplication of hundreds of thousands of obsolete and unnecessary traditional churches competing for attendees. By bringing economies of scale and utilizing existing school buildings that are empty on the weekends, we can save religious Americans billions of dollars. Plus I will promote the conversion of thousands of tax-exempt private church buildings to productive uses that will now generate tax revenues to help support our local communities.

> I suppose that some folks will contend that that this action violates the First Amendment to the Constitution. However, the

government is simply teaching ethics and morality, not religion. Don't forget that public schools have been teaching children what they must think and know since the nineteenth century with the support of the Supreme Court. If you find the idea of government teaching ethics and morality objectionable from a freedom of conscience perspective, then you will just have to get over it. You live in the twenty-first century now so it's time to leave behind the thinking of the past and rely on our experts to teach your children the best, most scientifically advanced ethics and morality available in the world today."

I must ask, which "experts" must we "rely" on and what research will determine the best moral and ethics of ALL religions? Would it be the same self-proclaimed experts who currently determine our educational standards? I don't know about you, but that above speech gives me the shivers—the scary kind! (Maybe I should just "get over it.")

A current example of what happens to a state-supported religion can be found with Catholicism in China. Chinese Bishop John Fang Xingyao, who presides over the government-sanctioned Catholic ecclesial association, said, "Love for the homeland must be greater than the love for the Church and the law of the country is above Canon law." His job is to bring the teachings of the Catholic Church into line with the communist doctrine. China insists the Catholic Church must adapt to the requirements of the Communist government and thereby produce "a religious ideological system with Chinese characteristics in line with the demands of the times." Another bishop, Peter Fan Jianping, said a year prior, "We, as citizens of the country, should first be a citizen and then have religion and beliefs."

Why would they put Christ's teachings second to that of the government? Because in China priests and bishops of the Catholic Church who have refused to recognize the authority of government have been tortured, imprisoned, and executed. China requires the Vatican to get government approval prior to appointing bishops to Chinese dioceses. Bishops and priests must register with the Communist authorities; failure to do so results in persecution. Bishop Vincent Guo Xijin refused to register with the government and was detained by the police. Fortunately, he was able to flee custody and went into hiding. There is no freedom and critical thinking in unity consciousness when it's controlled by the state. Once you have given over your power to the state, there is no stopping the human rights violations. China is a good example of this as they engage in practices still fortunately condemned by the West, including compulsory abortion, imprisonment in concentration camps (especially of Muslims) and squelching free speech and freedom of religion.

EDUCATIONAL SYSTEM INTO THE CRIMINAL JUSTICE SYSTEM

One of the difficulties in writing this book was determining whether a topic belonged in the chapter on schools or the chapter on criminal justice (which to date is an oxymoron.) Sadly—and shamefully—there is an overlap between the educational and criminal justice systems. When a child doesn't fit into the mold the educational system lays out for them, rather than the system coming to the child's aid, they shunt him or her right into the next system . . . the criminal justice system. To me there really isn't much distinction between where public school leaves off and the criminal justice system begins. Actually, as you will see, they truly are one institution for many of our youth.

As explained in an article in the American Bar Association's *Human Rights Magazine*, Fall 2005, "The Human Rights of Students in Public Schools: Principles and Trends" by Aaron H. Caplan:

> "American public schools proudly teach students that our system of government protects human rights, including the freedom of religion and conscience; freedom of expression; freedom from arbitrary detentions, unreasonable searches, and

cruel punishments; and fair governmental procedures before curtailing any important rights. Yet in these classrooms students are subject to more direct and palpable government control than any adult who is not enlisted in the military, incarcerated, or civilly committed. They are not free to leave the room without permission. Teachers decide when students may speak or be silent and which subjects they must speak about. Rules for proper conduct go far beyond the ordinary obligations imposed by civil and criminal law, and punishments for misconduct are imposed without the protections of a civil or criminal trial . . . court decisions considering the rights of public school students sometimes uncomfortably resemble court decisions about the rights of prisoners. The asserted right will be found to exist, but in a weakened form that must yield to the essential needs of the institution."

As you are aware, all states have compulsory education laws requiring some amount of formal education. They claim this is because the societal benefits of government-approved formal education outweigh the choice of ignorance. You can see a logical fallacy in the last statement: is the choice only between government-approved "formal education" or "ignorance"? Have we completely been conditioned into an erroneous notion that unless we are trained by the government, we are ignorant?

Many districts and states are fining and incarcerating parents if their children miss school or are tardy for an unacceptable amount of days. Even if at first if you think that the state must have a good reason, perhaps we should take a step back and look at the larger picture. We have already learned that your children's minds are the most valuable resource the government has, and school districts are rewarded with a great deal of money to make sure that "no child is left behind." Here is a reprint of part of a letter that Orange County, California, District Attorney Tony Rauckauckas sent out to all parents there:

"Law enforcement, Deputy District Attorneys and District Attorney investigators, along with school staff, monitor school attendance, tardies and truancies and conduct Truancy Sweeps and Curfew Sweeps throughout the school year. Students are not allowed to have more than three unexcused absences or excessive tardies. The fourth unexcused absence rises to the level of a crime and as the parent or guardian you can be prosecuted and charged with a crime."

So here it is: law enforcement and the criminal justice system tracking children and getting involved in families. And why? Because they care about you? No. The letter also notes, "One of the many benefits that come with improved attendance is increased school funding through the Average Daily Attendance funding from the state."

One of the main components of the Orange County Gang Reduction and Intervention Partnership (OC-GRIP) "focuses on student school attendance," Rauchauckas also states in his letter. According to spokesperson Michelle Van Der Linden, "The Orange County District Attorney's Office (OCDA) is in the process of sending out the attached letter to all the schools benefitting from the OC GRIP program, as we have done for the past eleven years. In addition to academics, social and emotional relationships also deteriorate when a student is absent. When children miss school they are more likely to become victims of gang crime or fall into gang activity." Here, again, we see the manipulation devised by Hegel. Remember, they create the problem behind the scenes, then come to the rescue to correct the problem. This allows them to put in the agenda they want, which no one would have agreed to if there had not been the fabricated crisis.

According to the California Legislative Analyst's Office, "the department uses attendance data to allocate state funding for various programs." If the schools meet a certain quota, they get the complete allocated amount of money. But an "increase in the number of students who were chronically absent cost the district $45 million in state revenue that year," reported The

74, an education news site, about the LA Unified School District in 2017. During the 2009–2010 term, traditional public schools in San Diego County lost out on at least $102 million in state funding because of absences. That's a lot of money to hold your kids hostage! This is how the federal government controls the state, which controls the local school systems.

It's not just Orange County that is taking its cues from the *Communist Manifesto* and enjoying its overreach into your private life. *The Sacramento Bee* reported in 2017, "A student only needs to be thirty minutes late for school three times to be labeled a truant and have a letter sent home threatening their parents with prosecution . . . Being tagged a chronic truant—after missing 10 percent or more of the school year—could mean up to a $2,000 fine and jail time for parents or the student."

And California is not the only place that employs bullying to ensure funding. Jacksonville, Florida is quite aggressive to the parents of truant kids. Parents with a child who has more than five unexcused absences in a month can face up to sixty days in jail. There are many publicized instances of parents serving that time. Then there is the incident of Eileen DiNino, who died in her cell at Pennsylvania's Berks County Prison in 2014 after being sentenced there "because she owed the local courts more than $20,000 in fines and fees related to the truancy of two of her teenage sons." Berks County jailed more than sixteen hundred parents between the years 2000 and 2015. The Marshall Project, a nonpartisan, nonprofit news organization that seeks to create and sustain a sense of national urgency about the US criminal justice system, reports that there are more than 150,000 such incarcerations annually. Just because it hasn't happened to you or someone you know, and hasn't been publicized by the mainstream media, doesn't mean it doesn't exist. In case you're wondering, no, this isn't in the Constitution. To me, it's completely unconstitutional that we are mandated to report to the government where our children are or get imprisoned!

Unfortunately, it's the poor who are most susceptible to this overreach. Once incarcerated, if a parent can't pay the fine, then usually they stay in jail, accumulating daily fees that are added to the fine. Certainly, excessive school absences are not good. But if the bureaucrats use police to arrest and the court systems to jail and fine, do you think that will cause children to love school?

A report from December 2010 titled "Texas' School-to-Prison Pipeline, Ticketing, Arrest & Use of Force in Schools" highlighted some disturbing statistics:

- A conservative estimate of more than 275,000 non-traffic tickets are issued to juveniles in Texas each year, based on information from the Texas Office of Court Administration. These are mainly issued for offenses that used to be simply school-related misbehavior such as disruption of class, disorderly conduct, disruption of transportation, truancy and simple assaults related to student fights.

- There is no age minimum; students as young as six have been ticketed at school. Can we seriously criminalize six-year-old children for not listening in school?

- School-based arrest of students is not as common, but does occur—and often without prior notice to parents, or a lawyer being present during initial questioning of the student.

- Ticketing of students in Texas public schools has increased substantially over a two- to five-year period—consistent with a growing law enforcement presence in schools, but in sharp contrast to a reported overall drop in juvenile crime.

- Most Class C misdemeanor tickets written by school police officers are for low level, non-violent misbehavior—but ticketing of students can have far-reaching financial and legal impacts [$60 to more than $500 per ticket].

- School district police departments are arming police officers with force that includes pepper spray, tasers, "stun bags," guns and canines—and some of these weapons are being used on students, despite the risks they pose.

When you send your dear children to school, you don't think that physical harm from "law enforcement"—or incarceration—could be part of the package. I didn't think that children's education could lead to incarceration.

As I have pointed out, the majority of these cases resulting in arrests of juveniles at school simply involve bad behavior, not criminal activity. Students are routinely arrested on disorderly conduct charges for talking back to teachers, skipping class, spitting spitballs, etc.

There are many reasons why students are being arrested in school but certainly the most obvious is the increase in the number of police officers, or School Resource Officers (SRO), employed on school campuses. In New York City there are a greater number of arrests of students on Wednesday. It's not that students are committing most of their "crimes" on Wednesdays—it's when the NYPD is the highest staffed. That information was uncovered by Paul Butler, former federal prosecutor, in his book *Chokehold*.

The Student Resource Officer program started in the late 1990s as part of a "zero tolerance" policy for misbehavior. After twenty years of data to analyze, studies have found that having police officers in schools has been counterproductive. In his study "School Resource Officers and the Criminalization of Student Behavior," University of Tennessee sociology professor Matthew Theriot found that students in schools with Student Resource Officers (SROs) were nearly five times more likely to be arrested for disorderly conduct—such as classroom disruption—which obviously is not criminal behavior.

In one elementary school, an incident was recorded on video in which a student refused to leave class. While she was still sitting in her desk, the SRO flipped her desk, slammed her to the ground, and threw her across the floor.

Her classmate Niya Kenny spoke up, saying "Isn't anyone going to help her? Y'all cannot do this!" The same SRO arrested Niya for disorderly conduct as well. Interestingly, the officer was fired by the school, yet not charged with a crime.

In 2017, *Education Week* published an extensive statistical analysis of the school-to-prison pipeline to date and found that nearly seventy thousand students were arrested during the 2013–2014 school year. The main commonality in the arrests was the presence of an SRO on campus. They also found that black students were taken into custody in a greater percentage in 43 states and the District of Columbia.

I am not in favor of less police, nor do I think that all police are dysfunctional and do a bad job. Recall that this was a maneuver set up by the Ford Foundation's "experts." They institutionalized due process in schools. It always sounds good when they introduce their agenda with their slick sales pitch, but look at how they increased the prison population with innocent young people. This is the descending spiral of these charitable foundations.

In 2012, the Department of Justice accused the city of Meridian, Mississippi, of operating a school-to-prison pipeline. There, the police department's standard policy was that all students faced arrest if they were referred to the police by the school, regardless of the pettiness of the offense. This was in direct violation of the Fourth Amendment, since there was usually insufficient evidence to support the claim of a crime.

Disturbingly, 67 percent of youths in the Meridian detention center were sent from the school system. They were routinely detained for more than forty-eight hours without receiving a probable cause hearing and were often interrogated without being informed of their Miranda rights. Even after leaving jail, the injustice continued, because every minor act of misbehavior at school was a potential probation violation.

The DOJ eventually reached a settlement agreement with Meridian in 2015. The city agreed to no longer commit any violations and not to initiate arrests for offenses that should be handled only by the school. The DOJ extended its investigation to the Walnut Grove Youth Correctional Facility, the largest juvenile detention center in the country, located sixty miles south of Meridian. They found that conditions there were incredibly violent. Correctional officers often forced inmates to fight for their entertainment. Many of the officers had gang affiliations and knowingly allowed certain inmates to possess deadly weapons. Female staff members had sex with male inmates frequently.

There is also the case of a hard-working student in Texas who was academically successful but was jailed for truancy. The young woman, Diane Tran, was an eleventh grade honor student who was working two jobs to help support her family. She apparently violated Texas truancy law and was jailed. The judge's comment to the press is perfectly consistent with an authoritarian regime: "If you let one run loose, what are you going to do with the rest of them? Let them go, too?"

This quest for power and money and lack of concern for our youth happens daily across the country and causes a lifetime of trauma and difficulty for those who are unfortunate enough to be caught in its snare. Some begin a life of crime, while others drop out of school and suffer the life-long repercussions of that. With a criminal record, it's difficult to get a loan, get into college, get financial aid or be gainfully employed.

We had an unfortunate but eye-opening incident with zero tolerance ourselves, with Tristan at a local public high school. He had decided that the Honors Biology class he was put into in the eleventh grade was going to be too much homework, so he changed his class to regular Biology. On his first day in the class he sat in the back of the room. (By the way, I have to include the race of the students in Tristan's situation because it has much to do with the story.) Tristan took a seat behind an African American student, who was sitting diagonally back behind a white student. The white student handed the black student a bag of marijuana, and the black student turned back and handed it to Tristan and asked him if he wanted to smell it. (I could not believe this was all going on in class behind the teacher's back! I guess she was just overwhelmed.)

Tristan wanted to go into law enforcement and start at the police academy after graduation. When the class was over, Tristan asked the young man who had handed him the bag of marijuana if he had anything else he wanted to sell, thinking he would act like a cop on a sting. The student said yes and sold him two pills for twenty dollars. (They turned out to be vitamins, so the young man was both a little drug dealer and crook.) Tristan immediately went to the School Resource Officer to report that he had found a drug dealer at school and showed him the evidence. The School Resource Officer told Tristan that Tristan was going to be the one charged since he had bought the drugs. Tristan was immediately suspended from school, and nothing happened to either the student who sold Tristan the drugs nor the student who was walking around campus with a bag of marijuana.

It doesn't end there. We had to go to a trial at the school where the principal, the school board attorney, the SRO who Tristan had erroneously trusted, and three vice principals pulled from other schools sat as jurors. Tristan told his story, then we went home and awaited the verdict. They decided to recommend to the school board that they expel Tristan from the public school system. The only place that would be available to him, if he was expelled, would be a "school" called Camelot. We had never heard of this "school."

After this school "trial" my husband received a phone call from one of the school board members. He told Jack that in the nine years he had sat on the board, this was only the second time he had called a student's parent. He was incredulous and disturbed about what had happened to Tristan. He explained that the NAACP was keeping on a close eye on the school system and was making sure that for every black child that was expelled there were the same number of white children. He said that there was even a girl of Asian descent who had a 4.0 GPA who had done one thing wrong, and they were expelling her as well because they needed to fill a diversity quota. He said he was going to leave the school board because he just couldn't stand it anymore.

All the names of the students who had been recommended for expulsion went to the school board members. During their meeting, they are to decide whether or not each student should be expelled. One would think, as I did, that it was a fair process based on the situation of each individual student. Actually, all the records were in one envelope, and they voted "yay" or "nay" on the entire group of names in the envelope. Of course, it was nay. This school board member told Jack that he was telling the other members of the board Tristan's story at the board meeting, but he purposely reversed the races of the boys to see how people would respond. They all said that the white student who had the drugs (vitamins) should be expelled. But when he told them the races had been reversed, they changed their minds and said that the white student who purchased the drugs (vitamins) and brought them to the SRO officer should be expelled. It is apparent that the facts of the case were not as important as the "diversity quota."

Fortunately, the school board member who had called Jack was able to contact the local college and explain to them the injustice that had happened to Tristan, so he was able to go to the adult high school at the community college rather than going to Camelot.

After learning more about that "school," we would never have sent Tristan. Camelot Education is a privately owned company based out of Austin, Texas. This is a for-profit company that is contracted by individual school districts to come in and take the reins of the students that are not able to fit into the structure of the regular classroom. On their website they say:

> "Camelot's services include a full range of solutions tailored to
> the varying needs of our district partners. Our solutions include
> setting up and running high-performing schools for our district
> partners, setting up and running classrooms or programs

embedded in the district's existing schools, embedding key staff to help districts address acute challenges, and providing comprehensive professional learning solutions to help the district's existing staff develop a stronger school culture of connection, belonging, engagement, and academic achievement for their most challenged students.

"Camelot Education partners with school districts and other local education agencies across the country to provide targeted and effective alternative school programs that are specifically designed to serve students with various needs…"

At the time of this writing only six states have contracted with Camelot, for about forty schools in total. In Florida, only two cities have contracted with Camelot: the neighboring cities of Pensacola and Pace in the western Panhandle, which is surprising considering the much larger cities such as Miami, Tampa and Orlando in the state. On the Camelot website you will find very favorable reports from students about how Camelot Academy helped them turn their lives around so they could graduate high school and become successful adults. I would imagine that there have been and are such success stories. On the Camelot Academy in Escambia County, there are mixed reviews. Perhaps the hiring of this for-profit management firm has been a positive adjunct to many school districts. It may come with a price, though.

In 2017 in Philadelphia, a Camelot Academy caught the attention of local councilwoman Helen Gym. She investigated this alternative school, including their disciplinary practices, due to alleged physical abuse of students by the Camelot staff. The Philadelphia school district was paying Camelot almost ten million dollars a year to run four schools. According to Gym, "There is almost zero public data about these schools. These are very vulnerable young people who end up in these programs where a lot of information about them drops off the books." Camelot schools in New Orleans,

Pennsylvania and Pensacola have had complaints of physical beatings and aggression as well as verbal abuse.

These seem to be very expensive institutions that school boards vote to spend local tax money on—for questionable results. They appear to be the last stop before the criminal justice system for many our youth who have not been able to fit into the system for one reason or another, be it poverty, no family support system, learning disabilities, drugs, etc.

Something needs to change to end the horrible atrocity of the school-to-prison pipeline. Since the Ford Foundation changed schools from teachers being able to discipline at the moment of necessity to forcing a due process, chaos and destruction have resulted. Unfortunately, due to mass shootings at schools, people have demanded more police on campuses—and that is completely understandable. Yet, as statistics show, it comes at a cost. In the Justice Policy Institute's published report "Education Under Arrest," it was concluded that the presence of a school resource officer was counterproductive and there was no correlation with school safety. The chief judge with the Clayton County Juvenile Court in Georgia, Steven Teske, testified before Congress that he had personally observed the damaging effect of zero-tolerance policies. Teske helped put into action a program that was already in existence called the Juvenile Detention Alternative Initiative. It is a coordination between police and school officials to do away with criminal charges for minor offenses and develop alternative approaches to current disciplinary actions. The statistics are very favorable: arrests at the schools there decreased by 67 percent, there was a remarkable 73 percent decrease in the number of weapons on campus, and as a result the graduation rate increased. This program also has a proven track record in a number of other cities. The only unfortunate part of this program is that it is underreported and ignored.

CURRENT TIMES

It is difficult for many people to comprehend that there is a human rights issue with a compulsory government-controlled school system. After going through years of government indoctrination ourselves, it may be hard to even notice the violation of freedom of conscience that exists due to the state's overreach. But it is a violation forcing us to submit to arbitrary demands and regulations on who teaches, what the curriculum will be, what perception of history and social ideals will be supported, what type of discipline is enforced, how your child's day will be planned and how all the information will be delivered. Should we, as sovereign citizens, entrust our government—any government—with such an all-important task as shaping our children's minds, and therefore, our planet's future?

John Holt, educator, author and advocate for home education, says that the school system leads us to believe in what he calls the "Divine Right of Experts": ranking us in school by subjective means causes self-worth issues, and absolute control of teachers makes us think we don't know as much as others do. It causes us to believe that someone outside ourselves needs to tell us what to do next. Holt thinks that this is one reason people are reflexively obedient to government even when it is unreasonable, unconstitutional or unlawful. He calls it a "devilishly clever self-perpetuation system. Once government seized the patently unconstitutional power to rule over our children's intellectual development, its system of indoctrination ensured that it would be unlikely that their subjects would care or even notice the violation of the basic human rights." He observed the contradiction of government schools teaching the liberties guaranteed by the Bill of Rights but at the same time violating those rights every day. He claims that compulsory schooling is a tyranny and crime against the human spirit and says we would all do well to escape it any way we can.

We have been witnessing the decline of educational quality, the gargantuan growth of industries that have been created to support the school system, increasing intrusion into our lives, and the devastating effects it has had on the youth of our country. They are being failed by the system that is supposed to educate them. A group called Project Baltimore analyzed Maryland state testing data from 2017 and found that one-third of the thirty-nine high schools in Baltimore had zero students proficient in math. Another six high schools had only one percent of students who tested proficient. Out of 3,804 students who took the state test, only fourteen were proficient in math. To top it off, nine out of ten black students in Baltimore were not reading at grade level. This has gone on for far too long.

We learned quite a bit during the Covid-19 pandemic when schools were shut down and children had to stay home and be taught online. There were many revelations during this time. Many parents saw a positive change in their children's behavior. Some families chose to stay home with their children and take advantage of increased time together. But then parents began reporting from around the country that the schools were requiring that parents not be in the same room while their child was in online class. Some even had to sign a contract agreeing to this suspicious requirement. It became clear that political and social agendas, inappropriate for young minds, were going to be taught with increased vigor, and schools feared staunch resistance from parents. Remember, from the beginning of compulsory government schooling, one of the goals has been to separate children from their parents' belief systems.

ECONOMIC IMPACTS

Jen Gresham is a high-performance coach and business strategist. On her podcast, "Learning to Learn," she discusses the deficiencies of our educational system in meeting the needs of today's economy. She explains that the working class jobs—those in manufacturing, transportation, construction, etc.—used to comprise 60 percent of America's workforce but are now down to just over 20 percent. The service class jobs—such as massage therapists, food servers, tourism and hospitality—comprise roughly 50 percent and are the fastest growing segment of the workforce. The creative class (tech workers) makes up the balance. We have a massive income inequality, as the top 10 percent of earners' income has been steadily increasing while the lower 90 percent have remained flat for around ninety years! This is the shrinking middle class.

Our country used to run on these service jobs. For instance, my husband's grandfather immigrated to America from Italy in the early 1900s. He was the only income earner in the family and was able to support five people as a house painter. Jack's other grandfather, who also immigrated from Italy roughly around the same time, owned his own fruit and vegetable delivery service. He was able to buy a small truck and would go down to the port in Boston early each morning, then deliver the orders to his community north of Boston. He also was the sole income earner for his family of four, and they lived quite comfortably as well. Many families at the time lived on one income and thrived on their earnings from the service industry.

Gresham points out that education pigeonholes students into jobs of specialization. It's not that we don't need specialists, but they are usually not the ones who can solve complex problems for which there is no obvious solution. These are out-of-the-box thinkers—she uses the term "Agilists." Agilists are those who can step back and see the big picture. They can define what the actual problem is and come up with multi-faceted approaches to solving it. With so many changes in today's environment of warp speed growth in technology, ecology, economy, the health field, etc., it is the Agilists who will be able to direct the specialists. Gresham makes the case that Agilists are not the product of a liberal arts college education. In fact, the goal of college is to make sure that you graduate and get a good job. Never once when I was in college were we given opportunities to take classes in becoming entrepreneurs in our given field.

In fact, James Flynn, a famous academic most known for his studies on intelligence, tested college seniors on critical thinking in a variety of different majors. He asked them to take abstract ideas from various areas of the physical and social sciences, logic, philosophy, and economics and apply them to real world problems. He had two big findings. The first is that there is absolutely no correlation between critical thinking ability and grade point average (GPA). Second, he found that English and Biology majors did not score well in anything other than what was related to their field. None of the majors, including Psychology, understood social science methods. Science students essentially did not understand the scientific method and Business majors scored very poorly across the board, including in economics. He summed this up by saying that there is no sign that any college department attempts to develop anything other than narrow and critical competence. In summary, he also found that our education system produces specialists and is not addressing the need for agile thinking.

Industries today are top heavy with specialists such as human resources, IT, finance, marketing, etc. They have the current educational pool of specialists to choose from and of course, the managers are educated as specialists as well and are not aware of the need for Agilists. That is, until they realize that they have to hire expensive consultants when they have complex problems. The people we need most are those who are creative and have ideas, knowledge and skills for which we have no measures. I often wonder if we had had a different type of schooling based on curiosity, socializing and play, whether Tristan would have had a different outcome. If he had had a curriculum based on those three things, I think he would have flourished, as he was curious, social and playful.

When I think about children like Tristan, who are smart, curious and energetic, trying their best to sit at a desk for hours while focusing on one subject, I realize that these are most likely the Agilists. Their brain needs a different type of stimulus. They are beyond bored; their brain is wired to be looking at many things at once, but they are in an environment that discourages that. It's a set-up for failure and discipline problems. Our system is failing these children. Instead of redirecting their approaches, they medicate, stigmatize and basically abandon this group of children who have vast potentials. Many of them do not finish school because they learn to dislike the containment of its physical and mental processes. Many of them can only find low-paying jobs in service industries. If they were acknowledged for their strengths and were supplied with the right environment and learning methods, they would have highly paid, sustainable jobs. These types of children have the potential to help solve this world's complex problems and hopefully close the gap in income levels.

Gresham points out that our country is missing out on the rich untapped creativity, intelligence and complex problem-solving ability in these potential Agilists. This is a real disgrace. Imagine how it could be if they were supported in schools and sought after by employers. What could our world look like?

Hope for the Future

When people think of education they normally think about sitting in a classroom at school, or behind a computer at a desk. We have come to believe that schooling is the responsibility of adults to force certain ideas, principles and facts into children's minds. It is the tabula rasa theory— that we are born with an empty slate and the only way to keep the children from going wild is to subdue and civilize these little minds. As Peter Gray, psychology research professor as Boston College and author of *Free to Learn: Why Unleashing the Instinct to Play Will Make Our Children Happier, More Self-Reliant, and Better Students for Life,* explains, "Children come into the world with instinctive drives to eat and drink what they must learn to survive, they come into the world with instinctive drives to educate themselves—what they must to become effective members of the culture around them and thereby to survive. Those instinctive drives, broadly construed, are curiosity, playfulness, and sociability."

Curiosity drives a person to want to learn. Studies have shown that very young children are quite capable of very sophisticated reasoning. There have been many studies regarding this subject. For instance, if a small child is given a toy and left on their own to learn how to use it, they are very curious and will spend time figuring it out. On the other hand, if a child is shown how to use the toy so they no longer need to use any reasoning, they soon lose interest in it.

This is how schools currently inhibit children's curiosity. A teacher shows a math problem and exactly how to solve it, leaving no room for students to exercise their brains. This reminds me of when Tristan was in seventh grade in a private non-traditional school. He was able to figure out a pretty complex math problem. The teacher told him that he did it wrong, even though he got the right answer. She said, "Tristan, this is not how we do it." Tristan said, "But this is how I do it and I can get the right answers." That story was told to me by a friend of mine who knew this teacher. The teacher was unaware of his passing, and when she saw Tristan's photo on my friend's home altar, she told her story and said that Tristan was always one of her favorites because of this type of autonomy and drive.

Mind you, many teachers did not share in her opinion. Most don't want children who think out of the box. As Peter Gray says, children are usually not given alternative ways to solve a problem and "they therefore fail to learn all the dimensions of the problem or the full power of arithmetic operations. Ultimately they are deprived of the joy of discovery in the realm of numbers and learn not to go beyond what was taught." In essence, they are dumbed down.

Once a child is curious, their next instinct is to play. Playfulness drives them to practice new skills and allows them to develop their creativity. Karl Groos, a German philosopher and naturalist, studied play and presented his findings in two books: *The Play of Animals* (1898) and *The Play of Man* (1901). He noted that children in every culture have play activities that are essentially universal to everyone, but also play activities that are specific to their culture. They also desire to learn new things, especially things that are on the cutting edge of society. According to Gray, we can see an example of this in how children typically learn to use new technology faster than their parents. (This is very interesting when we apply it to what Tristan says about the new children—that their souls have come in for greater things, and the curriculum is not matching the missions they have come to Earth for.) British psychologists Miranda Hughes and Corrine Hutt studied the physiological responses of children when in an exploratory mode versus a playful mode. When two-year-old children were given a new toy, they went into an exploratory mode, exhibited by a serious face and focused concentration mixed with momentary expressions of surprise and happiness. Their heart rate was slow and steady. When they became comfortable with the toy, they moved into play mode and their facial expression relaxed and their heart rate became more variable (representative of a more relaxed attitude). They also became more willing to interact with others. Our schools, then, with such little room for play, are extremely unnatural learning environments. We can imagine the stress that causes children, and what harm it is doing to their physical, mental and emotional health.

Play is defined as an expression of freedom—doing what you want instead of doing what someone else wants. If learning is best done in a playful environment, then school is the complete antithesis of it. In one research study, kindergartners identified as "play" only those activities that were voluntary—the things they did during recess. What they identified as "work" was everything else—even things that were meant to be enjoyable, like finger painting, running relay races and listening to stories. Gray describes players as free agents, not pawns in someone else's game. They can choose to play or not and they also direct their own actions during play. Free play is how children—let's say the human race—learn to make friends, solve their own problems, overcome fears and take control of their own lives. This concept is not new. Paracelsus, a man who lived during the Renaissance period, was a physician, surgeon, botanist, astrologer, and alchemist. He is considered the founder of toxicology and the famous phrase *"The dose makes the poison."* Paracelsus believed in Hermetic philosophy (which I write about in Chapter 9). He also believed that the final arbiter for a theory should be experience, and that humility and diligent labor is necessary. When children are playing, they are experiencing and learning. Experience cannot be found in a textbook.

Humans are social beings. Research has shown that children exploring in pairs were more apt to solve a problem than children working alone. As children learn, they show a natural inclination to demonstrate their knowledge to others around them. They have no fear of competition or sense of lack until it is taught to them. (Remember the Darwin theory of competition for resources?)

Even though many parents realize the shortcomings of the school system, most allow it to continue as is. This could be because they're overwhelmed by work schedules and other obligations, or perhaps they're not really aware of how destructive the system is. After all, the majority of parents went through the same system and survived. We hope for the best when we send our own little ones off. But since the Covid-19 pandemic, there has been somewhat of an education revolution. After having to do school at home via remote classes produced by the schools for the remainder of the 2019–2020 year, parents got a taste of the current educational world, and many didn't like what they saw. Plus, according to the *Wall Street Journal*, most parents felt that remote schooling just didn't work. And with some districts continuing remote classes, they are looking for other ideas. The time is ripe for alternative solutions to conventional schooling.

Homeschooling has been the main alternative to traditional schooling, but now, out of necessity, parents are getting creative. (When you don't have anyone telling you what to do, it's amazing how creative you can get. Perhaps there are some agile thinkers available, sorting through all the possible ways to educate!) Ideas that were once marginalized are now being looked at with renewed vigor by the mainstream. Some of these are microschools, which look like a modern version of a one-room school-house; learning pods where parents pool their money and resources to hire teachers and tutors as well as share in the teaching; and unschooling. Parents are facing the hard truth that traditional schools aren't completely in their children's best interests; they don't want to replicate an oppressive system that doesn't work. We have entered the age of DIY schooling. More power to them! Educational experts in alternative schooling knew that we would one day reach a tipping point, and I believe it is here.

Many states have seen a surge in children being withdrawn from the school system in favor of some type of homeschooling. North Carolina's website for families who were signing up for homeschooling crashed in the beginning of July 2020 "due to an overwhelming submission of Notices of Intent." Homeschool filings in Nebraska were up 20 percent in late July 2020, and Vermont had a 75 percent increase over the same time in 2019. The Texas Homeschool Coalition maintains an online tool for families to notify their school districts that they are withdrawing their children in order to homeschool. They saw fifteen times the number of public school withdrawals compared to July 2019.

There will most likely be continued reshuffling and more alternative school ideas as time goes on. But the scales have tipped, and those who are able to are pulling their children out. It will be very interesting to see how this will shift not only the economy but also the entire welfare of our communities as creative thinking gets a chance to flourish. Imagine the increased chance of happiness and fulfillment in life for future generations who are no longer force-fed their education, as well as of inventions, artwork and new ideas that will truly change the world!

This chapter was so disheartening to write; it took me a long time to get through the vast amount of material. It took me by surprise. I knew the school system's difficulties and inadequacies, but I was unprepared to uncover so much information about it. I was only able to fit a small amount into this book, because it's more about Tristan's story and about how the systems, as they are, are hurting our children. I encourage you to investigate this more.

TRISTAN ON SCHOOL (10/19/18, ALMOST SIX MONTHS AFTER HE PASSED)

M*y story continues here, Mom—thanks.*

Be at peace as you write this—this is a human story—my human story—to aid and help humanity, not to make you sad but to help bring or should I say continue my work that I was doing while on Earth. I am still on Earth in a way but differently—in spirit seeing from a broader sense of what my soul mission was then, and still is, with greater understanding—which is to help you, Dad and my brothers understand my story and to heal but also to heal and create the new Earth. One where selfish greed does not win the day—a new Earth that outgrows that limiting mindset into a greater understanding of your soul's evolvement while in embodiment. Better ways—dissolving the old and bringing that new understanding to light. New children—as I was—cannot exist in those low vibrations. Some can still play the game and cooperate but truly, in their hearts, they know there is more. Even those who have been brainwashed by the system know in their hearts—they are angry but it is displaced anger. They are missing that piece of their soul that has been shut out. I couldn't go there. Most children and young people just go their own way. It seems rebellious, but truly, their soul just can't meld with the old energies. They are given drugs, humiliated, scolded in so many other ways and they take it rather than to be brainwashed. They get sick and some give up and die—cross over as I—because it is too harsh for our hearts. It's like we have come in with higher love frequencies and ideals and the pressure of the old ways makes it impossible. Many persist, as I will again. These children need our help—a better way. We will be one more unified voice to lift up new ideas—to throw cold water in the face, so to speak, of parents of children. To wake up and see the destructive forces that are hurting their beloveds. Family is first. That is how it always should be. Keep the dark out with the unified and group force of love from your family. Yes, school is terrible. I couldn't play the game—as you well know. LOL lots of conferences! I didn't know then that it was my high sense or knowing coming from my soul that I had difficulties in school. I thought I was just kind of like a bad kid, but yet I knew I wasn't bad. I just couldn't care less. I was bored and just couldn't work and exist in such a dark system. All the kids around me were not truly happy—like caged animals in that environment. That is sadly the case of our schools—yes public and private alike—like prisoners in an environment they can't escape so they either roll over and buy the "shit" of the system and get "dumbed down" as in the book you are reading or they give up and fail or they rebel. Not such lovely choices as childhood and youth should be.

I loved my life, but it became increasingly difficult. I chose rebellion—it was more fun—dignified. I had a strong foundation of myself—thanks to you and Dad as well—and courage from my Akash to go that way instead of roll over or do drugs. Drugs came much later, as you know, only to dull the pain of horror and physical pain because I was ready to shut down—it was too much.

I didn't want to play in that game or arena—the dark won that. It was like game, set, but they will never win the match! Because the Earth is evolving with each new embodiment, or essence—I liked that one [referring to the expression of a lifetime's incarnation]. *We all come back stronger—more light and more love, especially in these times. The recalcitrant souls (the really bad ones) won't be allowed to come back. Yes, we have karma but we are not "bad" you know. The Earth holds more light daily and the old school system will be slowly dismantled—not in a day as there are too many greedy, money-hungry people involved, but the children will actually change it from the inside. Because it's not working. Parents have to step up and pull out. Money talks and the schools will lose money with each child removed. The children will become the teachers—people will listen to them with new ears—so much chaos, there will be a need to hear fresh insights from the newly-from-spirit. I will cherish that time to return—as you will be one of the new children when that time comes. We continue, you know, to work—not only while in embodiment but from this side—we get a lot done over on this side. I like your busy joke (hear my laugh). I want to see you laugh more—it doesn't mean you don't love me or miss me anymore. Enjoy your time on Earth—I haven't gone anywhere. I'm working on sending you stronger thoughts of me, my voice, smells, what I look like—it's coming.*

Back to school . . . they suck essentially! Take my example . . . when the principal told you when I was three years old that my problem was that I had too much confidence. Or the red popsicle sticks, yelled at, isolation, sitting by yourself in the room or at the lunch table—who learns from that? I know teachers have to discipline, so it is almost a completely futile system for the teachers because the kids can't focus, so the teachers are shoveling sand against the tide. They do their best in a system where their hands are tied. Oh,

I gave them a ride indeed—my poor teachers (lol). The children are in an impossible situation with this curriculum. They could learn so much faster in a different environment. It is like taking a racehorse who wants to run free and making him walk around in circles inside of a pen. The children are crawling out of their skin and the environment is so stale and not a happy vibratory rate to be in day after day. I knew that my teachers were not basically happy. They are exasperated. So I, like any good rebel, took advantage of that. Yes, it is wrong to gloat over that, but really, my job was to say "this isn't working," but no one listens to the children. That's not their job. Mom, you did the best you could with your options, but I could have done better in a very different situation. But truly there wasn't one readily available. Guys need to be out and active—discovering life—how it works and putting it all together— creating, discovering, inventing, etc. Yes, with direction, of course, but we need to have way more self-direction than we are allowed to now. No, the kind of stuff—the extras like football (boy, was that humiliation—I didn't like to get run over and hurt) or all the balls, etc. Yes, some of it is fun and lots of kids like it but not when it is forced on them. They need to find their level. Yes, they need to be introduced to things, but if we were allowed to investigate and discover, the children would show you where our interests and talents lie.

So best is to keep kids out of the system—find like-minded people to help you teach and raise them. Farms are good for that! But don't farm your kids out to someone else in the system. New curriculums will be made but there is a transition—and it is now. The more people leave the system, the sooner it will break down and change by necessity. Much higher thought needed before it gets built back up into areas of higher learning, where children are supported and loved and nurtured as unique children of God—our Divine

Creator who loves all. We need to bring love through first—only love will change this.

I love you, Mom--more to come--keep your antenna up. *T*

In June of 2019, Tristan mentioned school again and said, *"By some standards I would have been called an Indigo child. Those spirits have a difficult time with their extreme sensitivity and gifts. I always felt bombarded by judgment. On this side, you are here to love each other. There is no judgment."*

And after witnessing his evolving spirit over the nearly two years since he crossed, I asked him to give me an updated message on schools in March 2020.

TRISTAN:

T*his is going to be heavy . . . The time has long passed to help our children through the education—if we can use that phrase—system. Its usefulness and purpose has come to an end. Yes, of course, we need to train and educate the youth. That is not the issue at hand. The issue is in the how and what, etc. The school buildings are built and intact, but they are not—at least the majority of them—exciting and happy places. The frequencies are quite low. The little children are showing and telling the truth in that they are not thriving and some are quite unhappy spending their lives in these cramped environments. Their souls have come in for greater things and the curriculum is not matching their missions or their life's work that they have come to Earth for. The knowledge is so insignificant to the grandness of their missions. Yes, teach them to read, write and understand the true sciences and math. But so much of the sciences and histories are false and misleading. Some of it just downright lies. Would it be appropriate to use the buildings and schools and send your children to* *school—of course. No one is denying this. But a building is just a building. The entire system needs redesigning and reimplementing. The powers-that-be need to be flushed out but it is not a thing to be accomplished in a day. Not only is the monstrosity devouring our children but also our resources in money, time, and space! Many industries are trying to figure out what can be fixed and what is broken. I say just about all of it is broken. Not only those thoroughly entrenched in this governance of this insane system— those funding it to remain in power—but most parents and regular community members won't believe it. They are such believers in the system and to say it needs to have a complete overhaul is too overwhelming. So there is that.*

First comes an awareness, change, or shift before any true enlightenment can occur. In the meantime, the poor kids are being shelved and warehoused and stripped of their identity—conformed to old standards and beliefs that are not anywhere congruent with the new energies and truths of this age. The kids will let you know—just look at the breakdown of the system. These are old souls coming in and declaring that they have greater knowledge in their Akashic remembrance than what is droned into them. They know the teachers know that it is a failing system. Change happens—it can and will happen as time progresses. It is just a matter of how easy and smooth it can be or do we have to wait for it to completely implode on itself? It partly depends on the greed and egos of those who are benefiting from keeping higher knowledge and true freedom from gaining a foothold in the populace.

Awareness is growing, the consciousness of this planet is increasing, and the Wizard behind the curtain will be exposed when the curtain is drawn open. Those who have eyes to see—open them now so you won't be caught unaware—dragged into the implosion.

So much is happening in all areas. Life on Earth is changing. The children now will be the ones who will be in charge of the new higher thought. The more you help, the easier it will be when you incarnate as their children or grandchildren. You will be living in the environment you are creating now! Lift the light—lift the veil! The schools will one day be used for higher thought and inventions, but not to brainwash and warehouse these little people. For now, keep close watch on your children if you have to send them to school. Very close watch. Those who don't want the system to change are fighting back, and they have great resources to use and they are also masters of illusion. They will, like a narcissist, cause you to doubt yourself. They are skilled at manipulation and false premises. The more you can dismantle them the better.

If you can, keep your children out of the system. The more who do this, the more the system will have to change. Homeschool or group homeschools will let these souls discover their strengths and talents. It is a huge transition, but it can be done. Just as forced schooling was created, it can be uncreated. Strength comes by numbers of people searching for truth and standing in their power. Don't let the children's spirits get dampened and their light put out.

It is YOU who have to say NO. It takes courage but the time is now. The time has passed to wait for someone else. You are all powerful. Take the lid off of your light and power—look up—make the change smoother. The sooner, the better. It will be rough for a while. But life on Earth at this time is not for the faint hearted. As they say, you signed up for this. Don't lose heart now. Prepare your hearts and move forward on this path of truth with your shield and swords of light. It can be done. The support of the heavens is behind you. We are all cheering you on and are here to assist from this side.

Much love, guidance, and support are yours for the asking. We want to help—after all we will be coming back in too! Haha.

With love and encouragement,

Tristan

CHAPTER 6

Our Religious Systems

"Love is all there is—no book, no religion, no creed, no organization, can contain or explain this all-encompassing power. One must feel it in their own heart. One must live it."

-TRISTAN

BARBARA'S RESEARCH AND EXPERIENCE

I was raised in the Catholic church. What I love about this religion is its inclusion of Mother Mary, archangels, angels and saints, a spiritual hierarchy that is always here to support and love us and support the loving message of Jesus and the belief in God. But as a young child, I remember thinking to myself that there was something wrong about what the church was telling me. In second-grade Sunday school, the teacher was explaining what happens to our soul when we die, and how all souls will wait in some sort of limbo until Jesus comes back to open the gate to Heaven. I remember thinking, these people have it all wrong! They don't know what they are talking about. Intuitively, I never felt comfortable professing myself as a sinner. I used to make things up to tell the priest in the confessional just to get out of that scary dark box as quickly as I could. It was so freaky that I had to tell a man everything I did wrong, who not only hid behind a curtain but also supposedly had control of my soul! I remember being in that black box shortly after my first communion, shaking uncontrollably and wetting my pants. I often wonder what they thought when they found the remnants of my visit! This was not the loving Spirit that I intuitively knew and craved, both back then and now.

Once I got my driver's license I would tell my mom that I was going to the early mass by myself, but I would stay in the car in the parking lot and read. Books like *Life and Teachings of the Masters of the Far East* and the *Aquarian Gospel of Jesus the Christ* brought meaning and understanding to the life and works of Jesus, as well as a deeper understanding of God. I felt that I wasn't lying about going to church, but I just couldn't bring myself to go to what seemed so dry and repetitive. The only part I loved was the statues of Mary and the saints. I could barely look at Christ suffering on the cross. I much preferred the pictures of him in life or of his resurrected spiritual body. I felt then as I do now, that I had a much closer relationship and communication with him personally than the church could supply.

As our children grew, Jack and I wanted them to have a religious education as well. Since I had studied esoterics, mysticism and spiritual teachings of the East and West, I wanted my children to have a more conventional understanding of the Bible as a foundation so they would be able to create their own relationships and beliefs as they grew. We began with a Unity Church and liked it as adults, but there wasn't enough support for young children. After that we attended a Methodist Church, as we felt it matched in our philosophy of service to others. I didn't then and still don't believe in the doctrine that all you must do is believe in Jesus Christ as your savior and you are good to go for all eternity. I believe the evolution of our soul is not that simple. We felt that the Methodist Church taught a message of love and service to mankind, based on the teachings of Jesus. It was a good fit when the children were young, but as they grew older and had natural curiosity and questions, the church wasn't able to answer them fully. Tristan and I would have very deep conversations—he was a critical thinker. He would tell me that he did not believe that a loving God would leave his children in a pit of boiling sulfur with gnashing of teeth—at least not for all of eternity! He said that the only thing in the Bible that had meaning to him were the words in red print (Jesus's words) and even then they were suspect because of the years, interpretation and editing that has occurred.

Christianity is based on the life and teachings of Jesus Christ—but in its current form, is it really? Yeshua bar Yosef (Yeshua, son of Joseph) is the original Aramaic name for Jesus. His friends, family and disciples called him by that name. Since his death, his name has gone through many changes. The name Jesus is a distortion due to the translation from the Greek Iesous (ee-ay-SUS) to the Latin Iesus. In Latin, it was pronounced (ee-ay-SUS) as well because the letter "j" did not appear in the English language until the middle of the 1600s. Even the King James Bible, which was written at the beginning of the 1600s, used the name Iesous without the "J."

The church created the image of Jesus the Christ that we know today. We most likely would find a different Jesus—the one I yearned for and communicated with—if we look at his life and teachings, and not at what the church has creatively packaged and sold to us over the years. The church doesn't own Jesus's story, or have the sole right to interpret his messages. In fact, I would go so far as to say they have created much damage over the centuries with wars, inquisitions, judgments and fear—all in his name. Jesus's message was given without a church. He spoke of love, compassion, acceptance of others, forgiveness, and the brotherhood of man, and healed many people and performed miracles. His profound wisdom came from beyond, and yet is so simple a child could understand it. However, it can be difficult for adults who try to rationalize and intellectually fit it into their preconceived ideas. But his example was and still is an inspiration meant for everyone.

Following the death of Jesus around AD 30, as his followers awaited his return, organizations of small groups called churches were created. Violence ensued rather quickly. The apostles were waiting for Jesus's return to set up a kingdom of Israel. Luke asked him about this when he appeared and ate with the apostles after his death. Jesus told them that Heaven was already here, that "the kingdom of the father is spread out upon the Earth, and men do not see it." He also said that the Kingdom of God was within man, not externally found in any one person or in the land. I believe he wanted his disciples to embody the Kingdom of God in themselves when he said to be born again (John 3:3). The disciples wanted to defeat the Romans, and felt that Moses' words were true—that everyone who does not obey their Prophet (Jesus) will be cut off from his people altogether (Acts 3:23). But Jesus said to pray for and forgive your enemies.

The Jerusalem church had separated into two factions. One was the Hebrew Christians and the other was the Grecian Christians or Hellenists. There was a Grecian Christian named Stephen who did many wonderful things. Luke refers to him in Acts 6:5 as one who received much blessing and power from God. Some Hebrew Christians disagreed with Stephen. According to Acts 6:5–7:60, they paid some people to say, "We have heard him [Stephen] say wrong things about Moses and God." Stephen was caught and taken to court. They brought in his accusers, who said, "This man is always saying wrong things about this holy place and the laws. We have heard him say that this Jesus of Nazareth will break down this place and that he will change the law that Moses gave us." Stephen admonished them about being deaf to the truth and said how throughout history all the prophets were killed, even Jesus. The members of the court took Stephen out and stoned him to death. Stephen became the first martyr.

This leads us to Apostle Paul, who wrote about half of the Bible's Second Testament. He had been known as Saul of Tarsus and was involved with persecuting Christians, including Stephen. After Jesus's death, Saul was struck down by a large flash of light while traveling. He and his companions heard Jesus say, "Saul, Saul, why do you persecute me?" He was blinded for three days, during which he converted his beliefs and became referred to as Paul. Paul believed that Jesus was returning soon, so his mission was to convert as many people into believing Christ's teachings as quickly as possible. In doing that, he concentrated on the belief that Jesus was the only son of God and would save the world. I believe Paul did this to try to convert as many people as he could to the truth of Christ. He also wrote extensively about the love of God and salvation for your soul, and his many experiences give testament to his faith.

The writers of the Bible, especially Paul and John, stressed that if you believed in Jesus, you and your household would be saved. But nowhere in the churches' creeds do they mention Jesus's central message of internal soul growth to bring forth the Kingdom of God within. Under church leadership it became all external. Jesus's teachings were substituted with church dogma, and as in most other religions, they preached that theirs was the one and only way to save your soul. Most of this planet's worst atrocities have been rationalized without remorse by this belief, which is far from the true teachings of Jesus. Jesus's teaching was "I give you a new law. That law is, 'Love each other as I have loved you, so you also love each other. This is how all people will know that you are my disciples'" (John 13:34–36).

Today the creeds of the Church are about rules and what is an acceptable belief doctrine. For instance, my husband's grandmother told me when she was in her nineties that a priest had told her she was not going to go to Heaven because she used birth control (whatever it was in those days). This was back in the 1920s, during the Great Depression, when she and her husband agreed they couldn't afford to raise a larger family. Imagine her fear, her entire adult life, believing that she was going to spend eternity in Hell—all because of an egotistical priest. My mother was never allowed to take communion because she chose to marry a divorced man. I guess the church forgot about Jesus forgiving the prostitute in Luke 7:36–7:50 or the adulteress in John 8:2–8:11. Not putting my grandmother-in-law or my mother in these categories, of course, but Jesus's lesson in love and forgiveness would certainly cover a woman using birth control and another marrying a man whom she loved who had been legally divorced. This is the control of the people by the Church, using fear, judgment, and shame, that I have witnessed.

How did we get to where we are today? Around the years AD 110–200 there was disagreement and violence among the various groups regarding the true message of Jesus, which apostle had greater spiritual understanding, and what the official message of a Christian philosophy should be. Some groups borrowed from other traditions, while other groups were taking out vast information from Christian sources. Some leaders hated Christians and demanded they denounce their faith, while other leaders wanted only a certain message and would not accept any deviation. Either way, the fate of those who didn't conform remained the same: burnt alive at the stake, imprisoned, beheaded, strangled, hung—or for entertainment of the villagers, one could be torn apart by wild animals. Despite the chaos and potential for torture and execution, Christianity was spreading throughout many countries.

A young Bishop of Lyons, Irenaeus, was witness to all the hostilities and division between the Christian groups. His hope was that Christians would unite under a single church they called "catholic," which means "universal," and he wrote up guidelines for this. It seems to me that he initially had good intentions. He wanted to unify Christianity and stop the bloodshed and violence, and he believed that he practiced true Christianity because his mentor, Polycarp, had told him that he personally knew John the true apostle.

Irenaeus developed creeds, which established beliefs he put forth as the true word of God. At the time there were many gospels and factions who claimed their own version of Jesus's message, but Irenaeus declared that only Matthew, Mark, Luke and John were to be included in the whole gospel. Irenaeus's quandary was how could he "tell the difference between the word of God and mere human words?" If one believed anything other than the orthodox (right opinion) set out by Irenaeus, he would be considered a heretic. As a matter of fact, Irenaeus claimed that if anyone even deviated from his interpretation of a belief, they would be considered a heretic.

Irenaeus' ego seems to have taken control when he warns that one's eternal salvation depends on being aware of which priests in the Christian church are genuine and which are not; he says it's necessary to "obey the priests who are in the church" and who have also received "the certain gift of truth" but to hold in suspicion those who stand apart from the primary line of succession and "who gather in any place whatsoever," and to regard them "either as heretics with evil intentions or schismatics, puffed up with themselves, or as hypocrites." He ends his five-volume *A Refutation and Subversion of Knowledge Falsely So Called* encouraging his fellow believers to judge and excommunicate heretics!

Ireneaus's canon of texts were complete by the end of the second century, and still flourished over one hundred years later. In AD 325 , The Council of Nicea, a group of approximately 300 bishops from more established churches, was called by Emperor Constantine to settle the issue of who Jesus was and to put Jesus's official message in a neat package. The Council of Nicea created their own rules, beliefs, structures and policies, becoming the infallible absolute owners of the power of God and thereby, the owners of your soul. Jesus's message now had an official religion and name—Christianity—and by the end of the fourth century it became the state religion of the Roman Empire. At that time the Nicene Creed was adopted, which refers to one "holy catholic and apostolic church."

In AD 367 the Bishop of Alexandria, Athanasius, wrote the Thirty-Ninth Festal Letter, which starts out, "But since we have made mention of heretics as dead, but of ourselves as possessing the divine Scriptures for salvation; and since I fear lest, as Paul wrote to the Corinthians, some few of the simple should be beguiled from their simplicity and purity, by the subtlety of certain men, and should afterward read other books—those called apocryphal—led astray by the similarity of their names with the true books; I beseech you to bear patiently, if I also write, by way of remembrance, of matters with which you are acquainted, influenced by the need and advantage of the Church. . . . to reduce into order for themselves the books termed apocryphal, and to mix them up with the divinely inspired Scripture, concerning which we have been fully persuaded, . . . to the end that anyone who has fallen into error may correct those who have led him astray; and that he who continues steadfast in purity, may again rejoice, having those things brought to his remembrance." He then goes on to list the literature which is designated as acceptable, authoritative, and divine. In this way, Athanasius condemned as heretical all books that were not on his list. In fact, one could not even have "evil interpretations" of the accepted books. [This type of censorship is still used by those in "authority" to this day, as we are now witnessing Big Tech and Mainstream Media censoring and manipulating any information not consistent with their preferred narrative. Not much has changed.]

Monks in Egypt who received this letter were in possession of the "other" writings, the apocryphal ones that were of the same era as Matthew, Mark, Luke, and John but had been considered heresy and "secret writings" by Ireneaus and didn't make the cut into what became the Bible. These writings were from the Gnostics, whose interpretation of God and the life of Jesus was different from the apostles chosen as the four pillars. Their understanding was that of the "living Jesus." "Gnostic" means "to know." They believed in knowing yourself first and foremost, and to knowing yourself as a spiritual being. They were not denigrating Jesus; rather, they felt they were embodying his true message. They were concerned not with the "universal catholic church," but with their God inside. They didn't want the church to be the middle-man between them and their Divine Source, as they wanted to have a relationship and alignment with the true Light.

When you read the apocryphal texts, it becomes apparent why the Church didn't want the people to read them—they would undermine the Church authority. There are a total of fifty-one texts. The monks had transcribed the writings onto strips of papyrus, bound in books which contained between two and eight works per book. Wanting to protect these spiritual writings from destruction, they placed them in a large earthenware jar about six feet in height and buried it at the bottom of a cliff in the sand. There the books rested until one day in 1945, when two Egyptian men digging for bird lime came across the unearthed jar. The texts went through many hands as they were interpreted and preserved.

Some of the fifty-one texts include The Gospel of Thomas, The Gospel of Truth, Prayer of Apostle Paul, The Gospel of Phillip, The Acts of Peter and the Twelve Apostles, The Gospel of The Apocryphon (Secret Book) of John, and the Dialogue of the Savior. By the way, no one knows who actually wrote the gospels. It has been discussed that a more appropriate word than "writer" could be "compilers" as there were probably many people who collected the stories and sayings and wrote them down. The Gospel of John (written AD 90–100) and the Gospel of Thomas (written AD 120-130) look at the story and teachings of Jesus differently, but have many similarities as well. Neither starts at the beginning of Jesus's life as do the gospels of Mark (written AD 68–70), Matthew and Luke (both AD 80–90), as we find in the Bible, and John starts with the beginning of the Universe, followed by Jesus's baptism, followed by the wedding at Cana in Galilee.

The Gospel of Thomas has 114 statements by Jesus. In this Gospel Jesus says, "The Kingdom is inside you, and outside you. When you come to know yourselves, then you will be known, and you will see that it is you who are the children of the living father. But if you will not know yourselves, you dwell in poverty, and it is you who are the poverty." He speaks of the light inherent within man: "There is light within a man of light, and lights up the whole world. If he does not shine, he is darkness." Thomas's Jesus tell his disciples that not only does he come forth from the light, but so do we all: "If they say to you, 'Where did you come from?' say to them, 'We came from the light, the place where the light came into being by itself, and was revealed through their image.' If they say to you, 'Who are you?' say, "We are its children, the chosen of the living father.'" Jesus speaks to Thomas about the symbolic meaning of his name, meaning twin, and a message to all: "Since you are my twin and my true companion, examine yourself, and learn who you are . . . Since you will be called my (twin)…although you do not understand it yet … you will be called the one who knows himself. For whoever has not known himself knows nothing, but whoever has known himself has simultaneously come to know the depth of all things."

The statements from Jesus in the Gospel of Thomas impart to us that we are responsible for our own behavior, actions, thoughts, words and beliefs. It is not enough to believe in the message of Jesus; we must embody it, understand it with our greatest capacity to do so, and live it. Carl Gustav Jung (1875–1961), recognized as one of the most influential psychiatrists of all time, was among the first to explore the religious nature behind human psychology. He posited that there was more than empirical evidence behind psychological or scientific truths, and that the soul plays a key role in the psyche. The translator for the first part of the Gnostic texts knew Jung and showed him the translation. Jung is quoted as having said, "I have worked all my life to know the psyche—and these people knew already."

Much of our current Christian belief system and religion has ventured far from the original beauty and depth of Jesus's teachings. In the Gospel of Thomas, Jesus mentions how the spiritual truth has been kept and censored from people. Saying 39 states, "Jesus said, 'The Pharisees and the Scribes have taken the keys of knowledge and hidden them: they have not entered and neither have they permitted entry to those who wished to enter. But you, be shrewd as serpents and innocent as doves.'" The truth of it has been suppressed for almost two thousand years. Do Christians love Jesus because of his message and teachings, or do they love him because having "a relationship" with him guarantees eternal salvation? We would certainly benefit if we could strip away the dogma and embrace and incorporate the simple yet profound love, compassion and acceptance of this master soul.

My favorite book on the life of Jesus, *The Aquarian Gospel of Jesus, the Christ*, gives an account of the "lost years" of Jesus—those that were left out of our Bible. It says that Jesus went to India where he sat with Vidyapati, the wisest of the Indian sages. Here it describes their discussion (Chapter 35):

"1 The Indian sage and Jesus often met and talked about the needs of nations and of men; about the sacred doctrines, forms and rites best suited to the coming age.

"2 One day they sat together in a mountain pass, and Jesus said, The coming age will surely not require priests, and shrines and sacrifice of life.

"3 There is no power in sacrifice of beast, or bird, to help a man to holy life.

"4 And Vidyapati said, All forms and rites are symbols of the things that men must do within the temple of the soul.

"5 The Holy One requires man to give his life in willing sacrifice for men, and all the so-called offerings on altars and on shrines that have been made since time began, were made to teach man how to give himself to save his brother man; for man can never save himself except he lose his life in saving other men.

"6 The perfect age will not require forms and rites and carnal sacrifice. The coming age is not the perfect age, and men will call for object lessons and symbolic rites.

"7 And in the great religion you shall introduce to men, some simple rites of washings and remembrances will be required; but cruel sacrifice of animals, and birds the gods require not.

"8 And Jesus said, Our God must loathe the tinseled show of priests and priestly things.

"9 When men array themselves in showy garbs to indicate that they are servants of the gods, and strut about like gaudy birds to be admired by men, because of piety or any other thing, the Holy One must surely turn away in sheer disgust.

"10 All people are alike the servants of our Father-God, are kings and priests.

"11 Will not the coming age demand complete destruction of the priestly caste, as well as every other caste and inequality among the sons of men?

"12 And Vidyapati said, The coming age is not the age of spirit life and men will pride themselves in wearing priestly robes, and chanting pious chants to advertise themselves as saints.

"13 The simple rites that you will introduce will be extolled by those who follow you, until the sacred service of the age will far outshine in gorgeousness the priestly service of the Brahmic age.

"14 This is a problem men must solve.

"15 The perfect age will come when every man will be a priest and men will not array themselves in special garb to advertise their piety.

Jesus was born at the beginning of the Piscean Age and we are now at the beginning of the Aquarian Age. As I interpret this, Vidyapati is saying that the Piscean Age was not the age of "spirit life," so men would need things such as rites, rules, dogmas and other external means of acknowledging God. And this has been the truth for the last two thousand years. But in the Aquarian Age, which just began, we will live the way Jesus taught—internally embodying the spark of the Sacred Divinity of God. This is what I feel the shifting of consciousness refers to.

Jesus gave us the blueprints for spiritual growth and the evolution of our soul. He tells us that belief is not sufficient, and spiritual growth is necessary: "Not everyone who says to me, 'Lord, Lord,' will enter the kingdom of Heaven, but only he who does the will of my Father who is in Heaven. Many will say to me on that day, 'Lord, Lord, did we not prophesy in your name, and in your name drive out demons and perform many miracles?' Then I will tell them plainly 'I never knew you. Away from me, you evildoers!'" (Matthew 7:21–23). He also said, "And now I give you a new commandment: love one another. As I have loved you, so you must love one another" *(John 13:34).* One of his followers, an expert in the law, tested him with this question: "Teacher, which is the greatest commandment in the Law?" Jesus replied: "You must love the Lord your God with all your heart, with all your soul and with all your mind. This is the first and greatest commandment. A second is equally important: Love your neighbor as yourself. All the other commandments and all the demands of the prophets are based on these two commandments" (Matthew 37–40).

Paul stressed that believing in Jesus was the only way to eternal salvation, and promoted doctrines and rules, but he also had the heart of love. In Romans 8:38–39 he writes, "And I am convinced that nothing can ever separate us from his love. Death can't and life can't. The angels can't and the demons can't. Our fears for today, our worries about tomorrow, and even the power of Hell cannot keep God's love away. Whether we are high above the sky or in the deepest ocean, nothing in all creation will ever be able to separate us from the love of God that is revealed in Christ Jesus our Lord." Even with Paul's teachings of love, however, the Church's interpretations used his doctrines as a way to encourage hatred, intolerance, judgment and arrogance. It is my belief that if we had lived the last two thousand years with the true, unedited teachings of Jesus and no church rules or dogma, we would have a much more tolerant, caring, compassionate, loving world. In fact, Jesus mentions rewards and punishments, but never eternal suffering. If eternal Hell was real, I believe Jesus would have emphasized it during the Sermon on the Mount. But eternal Hell was a fabricated myth, concocted by the church and in full force by the 1600s when the King James Bible was written. Eternal Hell is more in alignment with the church leaders of the time, who were tormentors and evildoers, than with a Loving Creator. As we hear from Tristan, there is a balancing of energies, of karma, if you will. All thoughts, words and deeds are known and you do have to atone for them, but it's not burning in a pit of sulfur for eternity. Through all my studies and channelings, I believe that we each will have to feel—first person—everything we have ever done to another. Tristan calls this life review the Good, the Bad and the Ugly!

Allow me to interject here that I am fully aware of the many contributions to communities and people in need that churches perform. I believe the people belonging to churches have and continue to come to the aid of millions of people across the planet, not only in physical and financial help but also in prayer. This is the heart of the people, serving their fellow man. I am referring to the philosophies of the establishments when I am referring to the destructive dogma.

As we discussed, after Jesus's death there were opposing Christian philosophies—one Hebrew and one Grecian. Understand that Paul's intentions were good. He felt, along with the disciples, that Jesus would return soon, perhaps in months, and he felt that he needed to convert as many people as possible so the world would be ready for salvation. He wanted all people not to perish, but to have eternal life. To convert the pagans, Paul needed to appeal to them. Many pagans believed in an ancient god named Mithras, the prominent figure in a mystery religion called Mithraism that was accepted in Persia, India, Greece and the Roman Empire. Mithras's followers were already promised eternal life, so Paul had to make a few changes to Jesus's life story so the pagans would be more amenable to convert from Mithra's eternal life to Jesus's eternal life. Paul wove the story of Mithras into Jesus's story—we can find many similarities. I'm not saying that Jesus's story is false, but there is quite a comparative analysis.

Mithras, or Mitra (from Vedic Sanskrit) was a major figure in the religion known as Zoroastrianism, which originated in ancient Persia (Iran). Mitra was the god of friendship and the sun and served as one of the judges of the dead. Mitra's other role was that of the god of war. Originally worshipped by outsiders of the Roman state, such as thieves and slaves, Mithras was adopted by the Roman soldiers, and his cult spread throughout the Roman Empire. There were hundreds of temples and sanctuaries dedicated to

Mithras. The Roman legionnaires merged elements of the cult with "Deis Sol Invictus," which means "Unconquered Sun God." Mithras artifacts have been found under the Vatican Hill. Here are some of many similarities between Mithras and Jesus:

Mithras was born of a virgin who was given the title "Mother of God."

Mithras was born on December 25. Before Emperor Constantine (a follower of Mithras) changed the date, the birth date of Jesus that his followers observed was January 6. However, Jesus's actual birth, based on the descriptions, would most likely have been in the spring.

- Mithras was born in a cave (as many other gods were) and his birth was attended by shepherds bearing gifts.

- Mithras was considered a great traveling teacher and master.

- Mithras had twelve companions or disciples (some believe this represents the sun and twelve astrological signs).

- Mithras performed miracles.

- Mithras' followers were baptized.

- Mithras suffered to bring salvation to a sin-cursed humankind.

- Mithras was buried in a tomb and rose after three days.

- Mithras' resurrection was celebrated every year.

- Mithras ascended into Heaven after finishing his deeds.

- Mithras' followers were promised immortality.

- Mithras was called "the good shepherd" and identified with both the lamb and the lion.

- Mithras was called the way, the truth and the light, Logos, word, redeemer, savior and messiah.

- On the Judgment Day, Mithras would use the keys of Heaven to unlock the gates of Paradise to receive the faithful. All the unbaptized living and dead would perish.

- Mithras's sacred day was Sunday, called the "Lord's Day" because Mithra was a sun god. Jesus's sacred day was changed from the Jewish Sabbath, Saturday, to match Mithras' day.

- Mithras had his principal festival on the day that was later to become Easter for Christians.

- Mithras' religion had a Eucharist or "Lord's Supper" at which Mithras said, "He who shall not eat of my body nor drink of my blood so that he may be one with me and I with him, shall not be saved."

- On a final day of judgment, the dead would resurrect and in a final conflict, the existing order would be destroyed and light would triumph over darkness.

There are many parallels to Jesus's story and other religions, as throughout time and through many religions, we hear similar stories—the birth of a great teacher who is afterward called savior. They are usually born in mysterious circumstances. Some say that these teachers and saviors come to Earth to show how people can evolve their souls. It is interesting to follow history to see the origins of religions and the interconnectedness of them all. Maybe this will lead you to further research if you are interested. My intent is to address the areas that affected our lives and to underscore the message of Christ, not the dogma that has evolved around Christ. I wish for people to look for universal truths, feel the love and compassion for each and every soul, and understand what life brings to them. It is time to stop trying to fit this love and compassion into a mold that was formulated thousands of years ago. We are moving into an era in which we will be required to feel and live from our hearts rather than just from our intellect. Tristan's messages throughout the book help us to have a clearer understanding of God's Kingdom and his many mansions.

It has been human nature—albeit not a very good trait—to judge others. Many religious groups take this to the extreme in claiming that they can determine what will happen to someone's soul after they die! Is it enough just to say you have accepted the Lord Jesus Christ as your personal savior? Can you then be selfish, judgmental, greedy, violent, envious, gossipy, vain, intolerant, hateful and other non-Christ-like attributes without consequences? This is extreme hypocrisy. The time has come to embrace the true living message of Christ, not the message that has been packaged by established religion. Too many people have suffered through the millennia at the hands of zealots from many different religions. It is time to end this hypocrisy. It is time to become and embody the real truths of our Creator that Jesus came to teach and manifest in this world.

We experienced this hypocrisy first-hand when the local religious community were the ones to throw the first stones, metaphorically speaking, at Tristan. Since his friend Van's family was well known in the Christian community, as soon as the sheriff's investigator told the father that they were going to treat this case as a murder/suicide attempt (remember this was within one hour, despite absolutely no evidence, medical examiners or CSI), Van's family told everyone that Tristan had "murdered" Van, and the metaphorical stoning began. There was an outpouring of vindictive emotion. There was much anguish over this difficult and tragic event on both sides. But there was no mercy or compassion. There was no patience to wait on evidence. Van's family never once took any responsibility for letting teenagers play with loaded guns. Van's father went immediately into self-preservation mode, moving evidence and setting out to pin it all on Tristan. The mother's sole goal in life seemed to be to see Tristan suffer rather than to search for truth. We were told to stay away from the family by the sheriff's investigator, so we were unable to offer any type of condolence or have any discussions with them.

No more evolved than when Saul convinced the crowd to stone Stephen, these "Christians" espoused their love of and faith in Jesus, yet they immediately judged and turned against Tristan without proof. They told all of the boys' friends that Tristan had killed Van, and most of them turned against Tristan when they heard this lie. In his darkest hour—an hour that most people could never imagine in their worst nightmares—when he needed compassion the most, he was betrayed and shunned. It was horrible.

In times like these, human nature, judgment, or perhaps some sort of fear, takes over; there is no compassion or logic. How could there be no compassion toward a devastated young man, who they knew to be a good person? How could there not even be a thought that they should wait to hear the entire story? Where was their "God inside," their "Christian heart," their "Heart of Jesus"? Without God inside, there is no compassion. How surprising to see these individuals who go to church and call themselves Christians have no feelings of empathy at all, to be so heartless and cruel.

We all have free choice, whether you are "born again" or not, whatever man-created religion you believe in. It is in all the daily moments—each thought, each action—that you have free will, to create with, or accept or reject. Love and compassion are not always automatic (obviously). They must be chosen. Just because someone has intelligence and adheres to a certain religion does not mean they have love, compassion and emotional maturity. It is God-given, yet we don't always live and embody it. One of my wise teachers once told me, "We recite The Lord's Prayer, sing The Lord's Prayer, shout The Lord's Prayer—everything but live The Lord's Prayer."

Where is the greater love and compassion? It is in every heart of every person. It is not in any religious system. A man-made system does not make one person better than another. The only true system is God's system in the hearts and minds of each individual. Consciousness is not just in the brain—it is also in the heart and, I believe, in each cell. Where is the sacred? I had expectations of a higher baseline, a higher consciousness. We are given opportunities to raise our consciousness—to act from our heart. I believe that this community failed to do that.

There is a relationship between what we believe and how we react to life's situations. How we respond to circumstances is a window into our subconscious—our true belief system. We are presented with opportunities to awaken into a humanity who doesn't war on all levels. Morals and values should remain constant no matter what religion you accept or how one worships God. Masters came, prophets came, they performed miracles, and they taught love, but many were killed or done away with. Same with Tristan—a higher thinking old soul—one who told me he shot himself when the accident occurred because he didn't want Van to cross over alone. Is there a greater friend? I believe Tristan came in to this life because those around him needed a push—to cause us to look at ourselves and our systems. Yes, I'm angry about how they reacted. But I must be careful not to judge the people and systems who judged Tristan. That would make me the same as them. I must not fight dark with dark, but simply turn the light on. What does that look like?

Two days before his death, one of Tristan's brothers, Chris, and I were sitting at the kitchen table. Tristan was under unfathomable stress with his trial coming up in a week. Chris and I were complaining about Van's parents, for not taking responsibility for the gun accident and for all the lies that were in the father's deposition. Tristan, who was standing at the kitchen sink, turned to us (with his deformed face) and said, "No, they were told that I killed their son, and until they hear my story from me I can't and won't pass judgment on them." I had never witnessed such Christ-like consciousness. This, from a young man who was enduring such torment, pain and a grim future—especially about people who were falsely accusing him. What a lesson that old soul taught me that day. The lesson to love unconditionally, to help others, to listen to others without judgment, to look beyond your own ego and to not put yourself on a higher pedestal than anyone else. Let's teach our children these simple truths without creating divisions and a sense of superiority and without categorizing and judging each other.

TRISTAN ON RELIGION (10/30/19)

D*ear Mom,*

It is our honor to each other that this book is written together. Well, the much-anticipated chapter that we've been working on. I know that you have been disillusioned by the state of the religions on this planet but take heart—they are all in balance created by the level of consciousness that has been in existence. They are changing as people are awakening and becoming aware of the inconsistencies inherent in them all. With the advent of new technology—along with all its negative uses, it has been uniting mankind since its inception. Yes, there are lies and untruths, yet it is up to each person to use their discretion to choose the higher light in all they read, see and witness.

Religions have caused calamities of all sorts as they have been interpreted through man's egos. However, light shines forth as those who choose to follow its path see the wisdom and beauty of God and express it and live it. There has been a dark cloak casting a shadow over the purity and simpleness of the truth and love of our Creator. No longer are those who have been allowed to bend the truth to fit their personal needs going to be allowed to continue. As it has been said, let those who have ears to hear—hear and those who have eyes to see—see.

Just imagine a world where all metaphorically unite and hold hands in love and acceptance. It is like that on this side. No one uses our Creator's force to compete or lift themselves up higher than anyone else. We acknowledge the uniqueness of each, yet know that we are all of the same force or love of our Creator.

Nowhere has it been truly said by any master to kill, maim or injure another person or soul because your God is all knowing and gives you the power to kill, maim or torture. This has been man's interpretation. Sometimes incorrect interpretation, but sometimes there is no mistaken interpretation—it is made to entirely to support their agenda. This has been a rough planet.

People feel the love of God for their friends, family, nature, yet it gets skewed to having to fit a presubscribed set of beliefs that they are taught. It doesn't matter what you believe. I know that may be a shocker but when you are back in spirit—all the Earth's stories fall away—all the illusions of beliefs fall away and you are left with the truths. So if you were a Catholic, let's say, when you come here you can still be a Catholic. There are beautiful churches here, yet all that is not true dissolves and you are free to love your God with all your heart, all your mind and all your soul with no fear or attachments of anyone telling you to do it one way or another. It is so beautiful. Wait till you get here—no hurry—lol! We are writing this book to help bring this truth so people can get closer to living this freedom and truth while on Earth and to raise the vibrations and consciousness of this planet.

As you know, I wasn't much of a church-goer. I knew in my heart that people were, let's say, missing the mark. But what's a young person to do? They have to "play the game" of their elders to get by and not be ostracized by their church, or worse, told they will burn in Hell. Newsflash—there is no eternal Hell. Oh yes—there is restitution, if you will, or want to call it that, but it is within your own soul. Hell is within your own mind. All the wrongs that you have ever done—even the thoughts—yes, the ethers are that fine and are registered in space, we shall say, and you have to feel all of it—all of it. Oh you get to experience all the good you've ever done as well—as I have told you before, it is The Good, The Bad and The Ugly when you go through your life review and evolve back to your heart over here. It takes some souls who have done a lot of damage quite some time to evolve and move through the horrors of the negativity that they have done to others or anything on Earth. They are trapped within their own hell for long periods of time. There is no time over here but it is according to Earth time. They stay "in rehab" as you call it and cannot move on. But there is no hell "place." Everything is in your soul—the love you feel and misgivings you are learning to move through. God created us all—everything is one—of the One Love. No one is left out. Yet we leave ourselves out by our own free will or choices. Some souls take a long time—a very long time.

There is a hierarchy. We just don't float around over here. Remember I told you we just don't sit on clouds playing harps with profound knowledge of the Universe when we come home. Yes, we eventually shed the old and discover the truths that we have been learning from the time of our soul's creation. But it is an evolution, not an instant awakening. The masters like Jesus—there are no words to speak of on Earth to explain his love and magnificence— are here. He comes and goes as his love is needed or requested. The bliss is real! You can't package the immenseness of this love in any package—you can't stuff this love in any box or book. It just can't be contained. Don't try to even find it in the Scriptures. They can't even write in words the love of our Father and Mother God. Yes—Mother, Divine Love. The Light of the Father—the Creative Source—and the Love of the Mother—the incubator of the light through which all is made manifest. That one may be difficult for many to still accept but it is the truth. The Mother was taken out of the picture and as you know referred to as the Holy Spirit—our Mother—Divine Mother has many names. Jesus could represent the Father's light and Mary could represent the Mother's love as these great souls choose to embody the magnificent Creator in their incarnations and personifications to us. Their love is indescribable. They came to raise this planet into a Golden Light which is how much love these souls are.

Every religion has its source from the One—the truth from those great souls who take on the mission to bring light, truth and true education to Earth. It depends on the era and the location on the planet how they "packaged" their message so to speak. It doesn't make it better or worse than any other—just different for the different levels of consciousness that were in that place and that era. It gets, shall we say, diluted and even disassembled and gets reassembled in a converted pattern. Then others that follow try to fit their lives into that convoluted package.

So, reincarnation--yes, of course! Thank God for that benevolent act of love. Can you imagine getting only one chance in all of eternity to get it right? Then you are stuck in that place—those vibrations—for all time? Who comes up with this stuff? That is why children don't readily buy into this message much anymore. We get disillusioned, as I have said. As the souls come back for another lifetime they are fresh from the truth of Spirit and know that those truths that they know are not what is being taught to them in school or by religious teachers! Now to come back in another life—you get many opportunities. We have chosen to come to Earth. It is our mission at this time. It is a challenging planet—so much beauty and love, yet so much hate and evil. Love will always win the day. We come back to right our wrongs, so to speak, and also to experience life. To love and enjoy this big beautiful Earth with all its flavors and emotions, and to be with our loved ones. We come in to learn, experience and sometimes to help someone through a particular lesson or experience they must or choose to learn. It is not that we are different souls—we come in again and again with our loved ones in our soul group. We evolve our souls. That is the plan. We can make bad choices too. Choices that do not evolve our souls. We have free will on this planet and truly through all of God's universe. But if you hurt someone or do damage, then you have to experience that yourself. You may have to sit in your vibrations and live them over and over again on this side until you are allowed to have another chance for a life on Earth. Sometimes you are sent right back in to clear it up but there are some recalcitrant souls (good term) that just are stubborn and keep hurting others—not allowing themselves to feel the love of God through the love of others. They are not allowed to return and must go to another dimension where they can feel all the negativity they have done.

God is pure love and joy—it is only through our own choices that we choose to live in love or not. Love is all there is—no book, no religion, no creed, no organization can contain or explain this all-encompassing power. One must feel it in their own heart. One must live it. Many can point the way and guide but each trailblazer only walks the path alone—and truly we are all our own trailblazers. No one ever walks the same trail. We all blaze our own trails to the beautiful light at the top of the mountain. Rays of light beckon us on. We meet each other there, and when the time is appropriate we see another mountain—more joy and love and light—and we begin our ascent again. Always in respect of each other and acknowledgment of the one God. All paths lead to the One Light.

I love your light, Mom. Tristan

CHAPTER 7

Government and the Criminal Injustice System

"There are many over here, Mom, that are working on this as this is the biggest situation that is happening on Earth now—cleaning up of all the corruption and those responsible for it."

-TRISTAN

Injustice: To harm others by applying unequal rules and damaging another's inalienable rights and dignity.

BARBARA'S RESEARCH AND EXPERIENCE

"What the hell just happened?" Have you ever said that after something devastating and incredible, that you never expected in your wildest nightmares, occurred? When something so outside the realm of your beliefs and expectations happens that shocks you to your core, that leaves you empty inside, searching for a place to ground yourself? When your foundation is pulled out from under you and you realize that everything you believed in was a farce? This is what we felt when Tristan was accused of manslaughter and later changed to murder after the horrible accident. And our shock and disbelief grew as we watched the subsequent actions of the prosecuting attorney, the sheriff's investigator, the judge and the District Attorney not dismissing the case when all the evidence clearly pointed to accidental discharge. You never know what is really happening in our public and private institutions until you live through it yourself. When someone you love is going through absolute torture and there is nothing you can do about it—when you witness the systems that you believed were there to support and protect you actually do the opposite—it's completely traumatic. Your lifelong assumptions prove to be naïve and an illusion. Multiply this exponentially when it is happening to your child.

Like I did with the education and religious systems, I felt I had to do some research to educate myself on this aspect of our society. Call it naiveté, but I had a utopic picture of our legal system—just as I did with the others. As with the school system, I needed to go back and follow the trail as close as I could to the beginnings of our legal system. We now know that our school system does the best it can to leave students unprepared for the real world, without the skill of critical thinking. This makes it very difficult for people to engage in intellectual dialogue on important subjects. (This has never been so apparent as on social media!) Writing this book, I realized that I went through high school and college without one course in civics! It showed up in bits and pieces through history classes, but teachers never really emphasized how civics is the foundation of our lives as citizens of the United States of America, and indeed of the world. It must have been an elective that I elected not to sign up for—but why would civics be an elective, when it is integral to how we live and experience this world? I believe this is intentional, so that we are left with an abysmally inaccurate understanding of our constitutional rights and responsibilities and how our government and legal system work. Without such an understanding, we accept laws and regulations that chisel away at our constitutional and inalienable rights. As Thomas Jefferson, in his wisdom, wrote, "Convinced that the people are the only safe depositories of their own liberty, and that they are not safe unless enlightened to a certain degree, I have looked on our present state of liberty as a short-lived possession unless the mass of people could be informed to a certain degree." (Taken from a letter to Littleton Waller Tazewell in 1805.)

Now that we have looked at the history of our education system, we can be certain that we have been purposely misinformed and badly educated. Censorship of the truth and the spread of misinformation is rampant, and poses a threat to our liberty these days. We can see how right this founding father was. If you are well-versed in civics and our legal system, you can skip ahead, as I am going to do a cursory explanation to lay some groundwork for those of you who, like myself, had little understanding of this important part of our lives.

GOVERNMENT

Knowing the histories and designs of various types of government gives us an understanding of the different ways we can live with one another within larger communities and societies, as well as what we want to avoid. This will be an evolving topic as we move into a new expanded consciousness on Earth. Historically, there have been several types of governance, with many subsets within each one. The main ones are oligarchy, aristocracy, monarchy, socialism, communism, fascism and democracy. There is also one that is so vast and devious that we don't really know that we are existing within its grasp, and that is technocracy.

An oligarchy is when a society is ruled by a few people, usually the wealthiest. They use their power and influence to benefit themselves and enhance their financial status. Aristocracy is a form of oligarchy.

An aristocracy is when a country is ruled by the minority upper class, usually nobility. The difference between an aristocracy and an oligarchy is that aristocrats derive their power from their family lineage, or bloodline. Power has been held by their families for many generations, and they give themselves titles such as earls or dukes. It was the favored form of government in Europe (working together with monarchy) until most of those countries became constitutional monarchies during the eighteenth century.

A monarchy is when a society is ruled by a king, queen, or emperor who rules by "divine right." Monarchy is one of the oldest forms of government, going back to the ancient times of tribalism, when the chief was the ruler. (There are still forms of tribalism today, such as in Afghanistan.) Like an aristocrat, a monarch inherits his or her title. In an absolute monarchy, the monarch exercises total control over all aspects of the government. In contrast, in a constitutional monarchy, like in the United Kingdom, the monarch's powers are mediated by the government. The degree of power the monarch retains varies from country to country. Today a person who rules with the power of an absolute monarch is called a dictator. Saudi Arabia is currently an absolute monarchy.

Plutocrats differ from aristocrats in that they need not come from noble or wealthy families. Nonetheless, they are the country's ultra-rich, and their wealth gives them power that they use to continue to increase their own wealth. A country does not designate itself a "plutocracy" in the same way it might designate itself a monarchy. The term is used as a pejorative when the wealthy class is effectively ruling the country no matter what the official form of government is.

Fascism is defined as a governmental system led by a dictator who has complete power, forcibly and usually violently suppresses opposition and criticism, and regiments all industry and commerce. This type of regime uses an aggressive nationalism and often racism. It is most known in the twentieth century as the political movement established by Benito Mussolini in Italy from 1922–1943, Adolf Hitler in Germany from 1934–1945 and Francisco Franco in Spain from the 1930s–1975. These dictators used a great deal of violence in establishing and maintaining control while attempting to expand their reach. Hitler's attempt caused World War II, resulting in a horrific number of tragedies and deaths under Hitler—approximately twenty-five million deaths. That number most likely would have been higher if Hitler had won the war.

As we briefly covered in the chapter on our education system, communism is the philosophical belief in a socioeconomic order based on common ownership of the means of production and the abolishment of social classes. It advocates a classless society and rejects religion or any acknowledgement of a Divine Source other than the state. There is no working class or capitalist class—everyone gives according to his ability and takes according to his need. In its pure form, it is idealistic and utopic, and the selling points can be quite alluring. But in reality, the dream turns into a nightmare as promises evaporate and all that remains is the residue of dictatorship.

Communism/Marxism/Leninism has caused an estimated hundred million deaths worldwide. It has never worked on a national level; with human nature being what it is, there are those who will always seek to rise to the top and lead through force. The symbols of communism often include the hammer and sickle. The hammer represents industrial labor and the sickle represents the peasants. The Union of Soviet Socialist Republics, or "Soviet Union," had a communist form of government. After its fall, the government changed to an oligarchy as those in charge were immensely wealthy and owned most of the country's resources. China is still a communist government, and there we see the tight controls the people exist under.

Socialism is basically a less intense form of communism. In my opinion, it's a slippery slope, with the end of the slide landing you into the belly of the beast of communism. Webster's dictionary defines socialism as "any of various economic and political theories advocating collective or governmental ownership and administration of the means of production and distribution of goods." In other words, everyone pays taxes and trusts that the central government will fairly and equitably redistribute the money and resources to its citizens. Socialism takes away the liberty to decide how you wish to spend your money; it presumes you are not smart enough to decide what you need. Instead, the government provides what they think you need. The same goes for your healthcare, your education, and where and how you live. The system will tell you what you need to know. With the government controlling all and any means of production and distribution, there is no driving force for ingenuity and competition. Without competition and a free market (which makes businesses have to control resources, as they focus on marketability and profit), socialist governments can run inefficiently with minimal checks and balances. They only answer to themselves.

Economist Walter Williams has this to say about the morality of socialism:

> "Can a moral case be made for taking the rightful property of one American and giving it to another to whom it does not belong? I think not. That's why socialism is evil. It uses evil means (coercion) to achieve what are seen as good ends (helping people). We might also note that an act that is inherently evil does not become moral simply because there's a majority consensus."

Can we compare communism and fascism and say one is more or less evil than the other? They have basically the same goal, of total control over society, and employ aggressive and violent means such as persecution and eventual extermination of who they define as adversaries. And they define as adversaries anyone who doesn't agree with the ruling ideology. They use humiliation, shame and all types of dehumanizing barbaric behaviors on their victims. Both types of government are the creations of the super elite, who view the common people as degenerates and deplorables. They are used only as resources until they are no longer needed; then they are just considered parasites. Communism and fascism are like heads and tails of the same coin. They look different and say different statements, but ultimately they are the same coin with the same purchasing power.

A democracy is a system of government where a society is ruled by the people or by representatives of the people. To exercise this power, a system of voting is used in which the people choose elected representatives to serve in government. There are different forms of democracies. In a pure or direct democracy, all citizens who are eligible to vote take an equal part in the process of making the laws that govern them directly at the ballot box. Laws are therefore made by the voting majority. Since the majority has almost unlimited power to make laws, this leaves the rights of the minority largely unprotected.

The United States of America is a republic. In a republic, the citizens elect representatives to make the laws and an executive to enforce those laws. While the majority still rules in the selection of representatives, an official charter lists and protects the inalienable rights of its citizens, which protects the minority from the will of the majority. The senators and representatives are the elected lawmakers, the president is the elected executive, and the Constitution is the official charter. The United States really functions as a representative democracy.

Even in 1787, during the United States Constitutional Convention, the delegates were themselves unsure about the meaning of the terms "republic" and "democracy," because prior to the American Revolution the British government, which was a monarchy, maintained that the American colonists were still subjects of the crown. The colonists were creating a brand new "by the people" government. James Madison, one of America's founding fathers who helped write our Constitution as well as the Bill of Rights, described the difference he saw between a democracy and a republic:

> "It [the difference] is that in a democracy, the people meet and exercise the government in person; in a republic, they assemble and administer it by their representatives and agents. A democracy, consequently, must be confined to a small spot. A republic may be extended over a large region."

There was a lot of debate among the founders of the US as to what form of government would be best. Alexander Hamilton's letter of May 19,

1777 to Gouverneur Morris—who was a founding father, sat in the legislature as well as the Continental Congress, and wrote the preamble to the Constitution—explains his belief that the United States of America should be a representative democracy rather than a pure democracy:

> "But a representative democracy, where the right of election is well secured and regulated & the exercise of the legislative, executive and judiciary authorities, is vested in select persons, chosen really and not nominally by the people, will in my opinion be most likely to be happy, regular and durable."

In the United States, the citizens are sovereign. While there are many branches of government, the power behind each branch ultimately lies with the citizens. Many of our founding fathers realized the fragility of our republic due to human nature. They knew the Constitution was only as good as the people who govern it and abide by it. They spent a great amount of time and effort speaking and writing about the virtues necessary in maintaining our representative form of government. In his autobiography, Benjamin Franklin listed thirteen virtues that he recommended people work on mastering one at a time in order to support the American dream. These virtues are temperance, silence, order, resolution, frugality, industry, sincerity, justice, moderation, cleanliness, tranquility, chastity and humility.

Before I did this research, I believed—as I think many Americans do—that certain standards supporting these values were in the Constitution and protected our way of life. But it turns out that this isn't the case. We have been complacent because we thought our government had a more solid foundation. Politicians and other leaders with questionable motives can get away with a lot when the populace is asleep at the wheel.

A better understanding of how those who founded the US knew that a major factor in how our country survived would be human behavior (virtues) can be found by examining the writings of our first president and other brave men and women who ingeniously created a brand new form of government:

George Washington's First Inaugural Address, April 30, 1789:

"There exists in the economy and course of nature, an indissoluble union between virtue and happiness; between duty and advantage; between the genuine maxims of an honest and magnanimous policy, and the solid rewards of public prosperity and felicity; since we ought to be no less persuaded that the propitious smiles of Heaven can never be expected on a nation that disregards the eternal rules of order and right, which Heaven itself has ordained."

George Washington's Farewell Address, September 19, 1796:

"'Tis substantially true, that virtue or morality is a necessary spring of popular government. The rule indeed extends with more or less force to every species of free Government."

America's second president, John Adams:

"The only foundation of a free Constitution is pure Virtue, and if this cannot be inspired into our People, in a great Measure, than they have it now, They may change their rulers, and the forms of Government, but they will not obtain a lasting Liberty."

Here Adams combines the importance of virtues with term limits:

"Elections, especially of representatives and counselors, should be annual, there not being in the whole circle of the sciences a maxim more infallible than this, 'where annual elections end, there slavery begins.' These great men…should be [chosen] once a year—like bubbles on the sea of matter bourne, they rise, they break, and to the sea return. This will teach them the great political virtues of humility, patience, and moderation, without which every man in power becomes a ravenous beast of prey."

James Madison, the fourth president of the US, "Father" of the Constitution, and sponsor of the Bill of Rights, in his speech at the Virginia Ratifying Convention, June 20, 1788:

> "Is there no virtue among us? If there be not, we are in a wretched situation. No theoretical checks—no form of government—can render us secure. To suppose that any form of government will secure liberty or happiness without any virtue in the people, is a chimerical idea, if there be sufficient virtue and intelligence in the community, it will be exercised in the selection of these men. So that we do not depend on their virtue, or put confidence in our rulers, but in the people who are to choose them."

Thomas Paine, an English-born American political activist, philosopher, political theorist and revolutionary, in his pamphlet, *Common Sense*, which inspired the rebels in 1776 to declare independence from Britain:

> "When we are planning for posterity, we ought to remember that virtue is not hereditary."

Samuel Adams, Founding Father, member of the Continental Congress, signer of the Declaration of Independence and four-term Governor of Massachusetts, in a letter to James Warren, November 4, 1775:

> "Since private and publick Vices, are in Reality, though not always apparently, so nearly connected, of how much Importance, how necessary is it, that the utmost Pains be taken by the Publick, to have the Principles of Virtue early inculcated on the Minds even of children, and the moral Sense kept alive, and that the wise institutions of our Ancestors for these great Purposes be encouraged by the Government. For no people will tamely surrender their Liberties, nor can any be easily subdued, when knowledge is diffused and Virtue is preserved. On the Contrary, when People are universally ignorant, and debauched

in their Manners, they will sink under their own weight without the Aid of foreign Invaders."

These quotes are more applicable today than they were centuries ago!

GOVERNMENT AND "SCIENCE" MEET

Before I go into the branches of the United States government, I feel there is an urgent need to explain one more system of government—actually, control—termed "technocracy." Basically, it is an insidious form of social engineering as it infiltrates every system: healthcare, politics, finance, education, etc. We are so immersed in the program—or should I say being programmed by the system—that we don't even know we are in it. It's like the frog I wrote about earlier, that doesn't jump out of the boiling water because he was put into the pot when the water was cold and the heat was turned up so gradually, he wasn't aware of his impending doom. There was no big announcement about this, because no one in their right mind would agree to giving up their individuality and freedom in exchange for being socially engineered. That is the whole point. The only thing standing in the way of becoming a full technocracy is our Constitution. Let's examine what technocracy is and how we got here.

Technocracy is an economic system or form of government wherein decision-makers are chosen for office based on their technical expertise and background. The government controls society and industry through these unelected elite technical experts. Technocracy reared its head in the 1930s during the Great Depression, when scientists and engineers convened to come up with solutions to the economic crisis. (Remember, Hegelism is when the government manufactures a crisis, then steps in to claim it has the solution—which is usually a solution no would have agreed to prior to the crisis.) It looked like capitalism and free enterprise were going to die, so they decided to invent a new economic system from scratch. They invented a resource-based economic system rather than a price-based or supply-and-demand-based system. "Technocracy is the science of social engineering. The scientific operation of the entire social mechanism, to produce and distribute goods and services to the entire population of this continent." *(Technocrat Newsmagazine, 1938)*

Technocracy is an economic system rather than a political system. In fact, the technocrats hated politicians; they wanted to do away with the entire political structure and simply manage the economy through their social engineering. The underlying premise of this system is that companies would be told what resources they can use, when, and for what, and consumers would be told what, when, and how much to buy. Religion has to be marginalized, ridiculed and finally removed, as technocracy does not consider humans anything other than a biological sack of chemicals without a soul. Communism and fascism are stepping-stones into technocracy.

A very rosy picture can be painted, as if for a glossy sales brochure, by those who are working on bringing in the technocratic era to lure the public into agreeing that this is advantageous for the entire world. Technocracy may sound enticing, because who among us can say that politicians rate among our most favorite and highly regarded people? However, consider that technocracy requires the total dismantling of the current political system, including the Constitution of the United States. Its unelected leaders will dictate essentially everything to do with our lives (based on science, of course)—think of Silicon Valley. These people will impose their authority as to which resources companies will be allowed to use to make products, and will direct consumers as to which products they will be allowed to buy and use. It will take away our free will. The only ones who benefit from this system are those in authority.

Current technocratic figures look like Anthony Fauci, director of the National Institute of Allergy and Infectious Diseases and the chief medical advisor to the US president during the Covid-19 pandemic. His dictates were not about the virus—they were about his social engineering plan. There are many people like that, such as doctors, researchers and scientists, who tell us that they have the only answer and you don't know anything so you have to listen to them. And if you do not believe in their science, if you find other valid researchers and scientists with different explanations and theories, you will be punished by social shaming and humiliation from those who have given up their free will and critical thinking. If public humiliation doesn't stop a dissenter, there can be fines, incarceration (quarantine, anyone?), having your children removed from your home, and so on. Bill Gates is a master technocrat. This is something in an entirely different league than the only system we have known—free market capitalism.

Technocrats think that algorithms should run everything. Political figures aren't needed. The algorithms will put you in a category, and you will not be able to deviate outside of that category. If you do vary outside of it, you will be notified of your infraction and penalized. If that sounds like science fiction and something that would never happen in your lifetime, then look to present-day China. They have what is called a Social Credit Score. If you break a rule, let's say by jay walking, you are notified the same day that you have been fined and the money has been taken from your bank account (you are tracked by facial recognition cameras, which register any infraction). You won't have your day in court; you are not innocent until proven guilty. You can also lose the privilege of living in your current apartment because your Social Credit Score has fallen below an acceptable level. Other "privileges" such as grocery shopping can be usurped. An algorithm keeps track of your profile, which includes every single thing you do, including all your "inappropriate" and "acceptable" actions. Chinese citizens are being controlled by an algorithm. There is no court system or committee to appeal to. Once the algorithm is in place, it rules you. Technocracy imprisons you in a scientific dictatorship. The only reason technocracy has not completely taken over in the United States is because of our Constitution, but they have gotten dangerously close. Is the push for a digital vaccine records system meant to move us closer to complete worldwide technocracy? I believe this is the reason that the Constitution has been chipped away at for generations. Like the frog, we have not noticed how hot the water is getting.

Technocracy's purpose is to create an economic system, not a political system. In fact, its designers regarded politics and politicians as unnecessary and actually an obstacle to its implementation. Instead of a Senate and Congress, there would be an organizational chart with a president and vice president at the top, followed by directors of all the departments. Therefore, there is no more need for representative government (though really the people haven't had the representatives represent us at all). Without representative government, the Constitution becomes null and void and we are no longer are a republic. We have seen the government fail not because the design of our republic is flawed, but because of the politicians' egos, greed and desire for control. Our beautiful form of government is powerful and almost perfect in design, but it must be supported by the virtues that were discussed by the founding fathers. Without those virtues, they knew the system would eventually fail. The downfall of our government has been human error (and the capricious whims of our representatives and the majority).

To gain an understanding how materialistic technocrats think, let me introduce you to Yuval Noah Harari, a well-known Israeli Professor and historian. He has spoken about imbedding technologies in humans to create artificial intelligence. He has predicted that humans could achieve a sort of divine state through biological manipulation or genetic engineering . . . "Humans are very likely to be upgraded into gods within a century or two at most. Yet the same technology that may upgrade humans to gods, may also make them useless . . . The rise of AI, which dispenses with organic components and seeks to create completely non-organic beings, is a particularly important and extremely worrying development . . . AI will make most humans useless . . . It is very unlikely that computers will develop anything even close to human consciousness, but to replace humans in the economy, computers don't need consciousness. They just need intelligence . . . But intelligence is now decoupling from consciousness . . . When the economy has to choose between intelligence and consciousness, the economy will choose intelligence . . . Humans have basically just two types of skills . . . physical and cognitive . . . and if computers outperform us in both, they might outperform us in the new jobs as well . . . What will we do with billions of economically useless humans? . . . Humans are now hackable animals. The whole idea that humans have this 'soul' or 'spirit', and nobody knows what's happening inside them, and they have free will, that's over."

Robert F. Kennedy, Jr., nephew of President John Kennedy, summed up technocracy when he discussed the recent coronavirus pandemic, "Every part of our lives will be subject to control. This virus is about training us for submission, training us to do what we're told. To not go to the beach unless we're told, to not kiss our girlfriend without their permission. They're turning us into production units and consuming entities. They are going to rob us not only of our democracy and our liberties, but our souls. They are going to inject us with the medicines they want and they're going to charge us for the diseases they give us. They are going to control every part of our lives. What we are doing at Children's Health Defense is using the last instruments of democracy we have left—the courts—to fight them. We are in the last battle. We are in the apocalypse. We are fighting for the salvation of humanity. We all knew this was coming, though I never believed it would come in my lifetime. But here it is."

There is a life span of organizations, countries and civilizations; human nature being what it is, they become dysfunctional and those in charge of these institutions often destroy the spirit in which they were created. It becomes the sole function of the organization to sustain life support of the organization, rather than achieve the goals it was created to achieve. I believe this is what we are witnessing now. We need to go into the dark and clean up the corruption and outdated ways of thinking. Those who are perpetuating governments, programs and regulations that are putting a stranglehold on people while eroding their liberties will not want to change. They want to stay in that mindset and keep their power and authority. It will take the citizens demanding a new way and taking away the power of those in charge, removing them from their lofty positions. The time is now to create different systems and programs. It would be wise to prepare ourselves to live in a future world that we never expected. It is time for out-of-the-box brainstorming by forward thinkers to envision a new, more positive world. (We need Agilists!)

And we need to know our true history—where we really come from—to know how to plan for this new future, one that is based on cooperation rather than on the division and separation we have been conditioned to accept as normal. As you read the statements from Yuval Noah Harari, technocracy dismisses the divinity of humanity, and the virtues espoused by our founding fathers. It ignores that we are intelligent, emotional and spiritual beings. It creates automatons out of its subjects. The Constitution is one lock on the door to full technocracy. There are also scientists who have evidence that contradicts mainstream science ideology, which echoes and supports technocracy by stating that life is completely materialistic—just what we see. Mainstream scientists say that consciousness has no place in science; anyone who claims it does is denounced. Dr. Roger Penrose is an English mathematical physicist, philosopher of science, and recipient of the Nobel Laureate in Physics as well as many other prizes and awards including the 1988 Wolf Prize in Physics, which he shared with Stephen Hawking for the discovery that black hole formation is a robust prediction of the general theory of relativity. He has written books on the connection between fundamental physics and human (or animal) consciousness. In *The Emperor's New Mind* (1989), he argues that known laws of physics are inadequate to explain the phenomenon of consciousness. He states, "Consciousness has been considered a taboo in traditional scientific theory! A scientific world view that does not profoundly come to terms with consciousness can have no serious pretensions of completeness." Penrose goes against the grain of scientists who work with artificial intelligence and believe that human thought can be calculated algorithmically. He argues that computers today are unable to have intelligence because they are algorithmically deterministic systems.

He postulates that the nature of consciousness suggests that it does not exist in the brain but is rather a quantum process that emerges from the cellular level within and beyond the cytoskeletal structures.

Another scientist, whom I first became aware of in 1986, is Rupert Sheldrake. I attended one of his lectures after he wrote *A New Science of Life* detailing his theories and experiments on what he terms "Formative Causation." Sheldrake studied natural sciences at Cambridge and philosophy at Harvard, earned a PhD in biochemistry at Cambridge, and was a Fellow of Clare College, Cambridge. He has authored several books and more than fifty scientific papers and has developed a theory named "morphogenic resonance." His hypothesis proposes that the form, development and behavior of living organisms are shaped and maintained by morphogenetic fields. He believes these fields are molded by the form and behavior of past organisms of the same species through direct connections across both space and time. In his book he states, "The more I thought about the unsolved problems of biology, the more convinced I became that the conventional approach is unnecessarily restrictive." In his latest book, *Science Set Free,* Sheldrake categorizes what he has quantified as the ten dogmas of science. The first of those is that nature is mechanical—that we are all just machines controlled by genetically programmed, computer-like brains. This thought has dominated traditional science since the seventeenth century. Another dogma is the belief that matter is unconscious and that the Universe is made up of unconscious matter. Somehow, unexplainedly, this matter mysteriously becomes conscious in human and animal brains. How does unconscious matter become conscious? Traditional science can't answer that, and labels someone who tries as crazy and a fraud. Another dogma is that the mind is in the brain. If this were true, it would mean all your intellectual ability is only brain activity with no divine input. Traditional science wants you to believe that telepathy and other psychic phenomena are an illusion and cannot really happen because, of course, everything is only inside your head. According to mainstream scientists, if anyone believes in psychic phenomena they are stupid and naïve; smart people know this is impossible.

Sheldrake suggests turning the dogmas into questions such as "Is the mind inside the brain?" He believes that when we turn these assumptions into questions, we can move beyond materialism and make all kinds of new science possible—still using the scientific method, but not bound by old notions that are holding back new concepts and discoveries. However, most traditional scientists are not even aware they have these dogmatic assumptions. They are staunch in their belief system in materialistic science, just like people have staunch religious beliefs—and they treat anyone who says differently much like religious zealots have treated those they consider to be heretics. Have we come no further than witches being burned at the stake? Now a scientist's reputation and life's work can be dismantled and ruined by traditional science zealots.

Materialism-based theory leads to an assault on any type of religious or spiritual belief. These scientists say that there is no such thing as a conscious source, and that everything is as it is because of evolution. This has caused spiritual and religious communities to push back, creating far more of a problem than there needs to be. Has the rise of the "religious right" happened because they feel their way of life is being trivialized, ridiculed and jeopardized? The same happens with those who believe in alternative sciences like parapsychology, and the many people who are able to provide proof of life after death with evidential mediumship, as Tristan does with me. I and others have helped the grieving with messages that no one else would know, proving their loved ones are still alive in another space, time or dimension that we have called Heaven. There is a battle happening between the science community trying to hold on to their cherished belief systems, and a growing group who know that they are too limited.

I believe that science is being highjacked and manipulated because it is useful to current political and economic leaders. How could the technocrats control and manipulate us if it was common knowledge that we are not automatons? That there is a higher consciousness within our DNA that can be measured in the new quantum sciences? That our existence cannot be programmed and analyzed using computer algorithms? It would slow the technocratic machine to a halt. This is one reason that evolution, Darwinism and funded science in materialism has such a strong powerful grip on this country and indeed the world. Thankfully, we have courageous scientists and researchers such as Penrose, Sheldrake and many more who keep going despite being labeled frauds and heretics, and continue to prove evidence of consciousness outside of our brains, as well as of the many branches of the quantum sciences. I believe that they are mediators who will bring together the "new science," what is true in the materialistic science and in spirituality. We must understand that it is not a winner-takes-all situation. There is room for additional information, and a consensus among the fields that would create healthier, more advanced societies, relationships and new types of governance.

Beyond the Brain is the world's premier conference series exploring a wide range of topics on the frontier of consciousness research. They present new information about whether and how consciousness and the mind extend beyond the physical brain and body. This conference was initiated at St John's College, Cambridge in 1995 by the Scientific and Medical Network (SMN) with the Institute of Noetic Sciences (IONS). Their intentions are to explore science and spiritual practices, the boundary between neuroscience and mystical experience, transpersonal psychology, psychedelics and the brain, after-death communication, and consciousness in relation to the brain and the Universe as well as the power of intention, lucid dreaming and out-of-body experiences. These meetings bring leading scientists, scholars and researchers together. At the 2020 conference they concluded that the evidence shows the mind is not just in the brain, and that the assumptions of materialistic science are wrong and have been limiting our advancement in all areas of life.

Acknowledging that we have been manipulated and controlled with deceptive and, at best, antiquated science is the first step. If you are not aware of what's happening, then your elected and non-elected government officials can give consent for you—as they represent you—to be controlled by these false or limited dogmas. Over the years, there have been voices in the scientific and spiritual communities who have been marginalized because they tried to bring the truth of new advanced technology and consciousness discoveries. Besides being marginalized, they have also been ridiculed. And in many cases, they have met with suspicious untimely deaths. This is not a world in which our children can exist with full freedom and happiness. I am very grateful to the scientists I have mentioned for having had the courage to present their discoveries against the onslaught of negativity from the mainstream. I believe they are heroes and warriors pulling us forward. I pray for the quantum leap in science and spirituality. I feel as Albert Einstein did; he said, "The more I study science, the more I believe in God."

It has been interesting to observe these scientists prove the existence of a quantum world and higher consciousness—God, if you will—while our government is working on erasing religion, calling Christians terrorists, and rolling their eyes at those who follow their own brand of spiritual beliefs— while at the same time telling us to "follow the science." Which science? Only the one they choose as correct. You couldn't make this up if you wanted to

Let's look at the foundation of our government's structure; this will help show how we have been led to follow the dictates of the ruling elite, who claim that all of their control and manipulation is for our best interest and the greater good. The government has a much easier time manipulating people when schools and religions lay the foundation for people to be easily swayed.

THE UNITED STATES OF AMERICA'S GOVERNMENT
STRUCTURE
FEDERAL LEVEL

In the United States of America, our government has three main branches: the executive, legislative and judicial. Our Constitution mandates that the United States must have a president and a vice president. The President and the Vice president, as well as the people who work for them, belong to the executive branch. The President runs the federal government, sees that the laws of our country are enforced, and is the Commander-in-Chief of our military. Much of the work in the executive branch is done by federal agencies, departments, committees and other groups. There are more than four million people employed by the executive branch, including the Department of Defense.

The legislative branch creates the laws that are enforced by the executive branch and interpreted by the judicial branch. The legislative branch consists of the Congress, which includes the House of Representatives, the Senate, and special agencies and offices that provide support services to the Congress. It also includes the fifty state legislatures. Their purpose is to propose laws that supposedly represent the needs and interests of their constituents. Under the United States' system of checks and balances, the President can approve a bill or refuse to sign it into law by vetoing the bill. The legislature can then vote to override the veto. The Congress also confirms or rejects presidential nominations for heads of federal agencies, federal judges and the Supreme Court, and has the authority to declare war. Other checks and balances include legislative powers to impeach public officials and vote on appropriations (budget and funding). The US House of Representatives has 435 voting members who are elected to two-year terms. The entire House of Representatives is up for reelection every even-numbered year. The US Senate has one hundred members who are elected to six-year terms. Senators are divided equally into three classes so that every two years, one-third of the Senate is up for reelection. There are about thirty-one thousand congressional staffers within the legislative branch. Approximately 12,500 legislative branch employees work directly for the members of Congress in their personal offices and 6,000 more work on committee staffs, with the remainder working at the Library of Congress and the Government Accountability Office.

The judicial branch is the third constitutional branch of government. Unlike the members of the executive and legislative branches, who are elected by the people, members of the judicial branch are appointed by the President and confirmed by the Senate. There are ninety-four district courts, which are organized into twelve circuits, or regions. Each circuit has its own Court of Appeals that reviews cases decided in US District Courts within the circuit. The US Court of Appeals for the Federal Circuit brings the number of federal appellate courts to thirteen. This court takes cases from across the nation, but only particular types of cases. At a trial in a US District Court, witnesses give testimony and a judge or jury decides who is guilty or not guilty—or who is liable or not liable. The appellate courts do not retry cases or hear new evidence. They do not hear witnesses testify. There is no jury. Appellate courts review the procedures and the decisions in the trial court to make sure that the proceedings were fair and that the proper law was applied correctly.

The Supreme Court of the United States is the highest court in the land and the only part of the federal judiciary specifically required by the Constitution. However, the Constitution does not specify the number of Supreme Court Justices. Congress is given this authority. Since 1869 there have been nine Justices which includes the Chief Justice. Prior to that there were six. All Justices are nominated by the President as needed, followed by a confirmation in the Senate. They remain in office until they resign, die, or are impeached or convicted. They never have to run for reelection, since they are tenured for life. Supposedly this keeps them inoculated from political pressure. The Supreme Court is mainly an appellate court and is the final arbiter of US federal law. The Justices also hear cases between states or cases involving diplomats.

STATE LEVEL

Each state has its own written constitution, and these documents are often far more elaborate than their federal counterpart. All state governments are modeled after the federal government and consist of three branches: executive, legislative, and judicial. The US Constitution mandates that all states uphold a "republican form" of government, although the three-branch structure is not required.

In every state, the executive branch is headed by a governor who is directly elected by the people. In most states, other leaders in the executive branch are also directly elected, including the lieutenant governor, the attorney general, the secretary of state, auditors and commissioners. States reserve the right to organize in any way, so they often vary greatly with regard to executive structure.

All fifty states have legislatures made up of elected representatives, who consider matters brought forth by the governor or introduced by its members to create legislation that becomes law. The legislature also approves a state's budget and initiates tax legislation and articles of impeachment. The latter is part of a system of checks and balances among the three branches of government that mirrors the federal system and prevents any branch from abusing its power.

Except for one state, Nebraska, all states have a bicameral legislature made up of two chambers: a smaller upper house and a larger lower house. Together the two chambers make state laws and fulfill other governing responsibilities.

FLORIDA'S JUDICIAL STRUCTURE

In Florida, whereas the executive and legislative branches are elected by the people, members of the judicial branch—the supreme court, each district court of appeal, and each judicial circuit court for all trial courts within the circuit—are appointed by a judicial nominating commission that is established by general law. County court judge seats are filled by election within their respective jurisdiction/county.

According to Article 5, Section 1 of Florida's Constitution, "The judicial power shall be vested in a supreme court, district courts of appeal, circuit courts and county courts. No other courts may be established by the state, any political subdivision or any municipality. The legislature shall, by general law, divide the state into appellate court districts and judicial circuits following county lines. Commissions established by law, or administrative officers or bodies may be granted quasi-judicial power in matters connected with the functions of their offices. The legislature may establish by general law a civil traffic hearing officer system for the purpose of hearing civil traffic infractions. The legislature may, by general law, authorize a military court-martial to be conducted by military judges of the Florida National Guard, with direct appeal of a decision to the District Court of Appeal, First District."

The Florida circuit courts are trial courts of general jurisdiction. Circuit courts hear a wide variety of cases including criminal felonies, family law, civil cases concerning more than fifteen thousand dollars, probate issues, juvenile cases and appeals from county courts. There are twenty judicial circuit courts.

The Florida county courts handle misdemeanors, civil matters involving not more than thirty thousand dollars, and violations of municipal and county ordinances. There is one court in each of the state's sixty-seven counties.

The judges on the circuit and county courts are elected via nonpartisan elections to six-year terms. The seven justices of the Florida Supreme Court and the sixty justices of the Florida District Courts of Appeal are selected by the governor. A judicial nominating commission screens potential judicial candidates and submits a list of three to six nominees to the governor. The governor must appoint a judge from this list. Newly appointed judges serve for at least one year, after which they appear in a yes/no retention election held during the next general election. If retained, judges serve six-year terms.

Now, I ask you, how many people, when they vote in a general election, know anything about the judges? As far as I know, most people skip these or just pick an option with no particular knowledge of the judge or the system at large. Does this seem like a good way to decide who fills these hugely powerful positions? Judges can literally hold the power of life and death. What criteria should be established to determine the qualities necessary for these positions? How can this criteria—along with the judges' past actions—be communicated to the citizens?

CRIMINAL JUSTICE SYSTEM

Our system sounds wonderful and many insist it is the best in the world. It could work exceptionally well. In theory, it guarantees every criminal defendant an impartial judge, a fair jury and a defense lawyer at public expense for those who can't afford one. The prosecution must prove guilt beyond a reasonable doubt and is required to do so in a speedy public trial. There are rules of governing the collection and presentation of evidence to ensure that justice is done in every case. But as Michael Adams states in his introduction to *Licensed to Lie: Exposing Corruption in the Department of Justice* by Sidney Powell, "The greatest human ideal of justice is only as good as the character of those who administer it, existing only if its guardians are devotees to integrity and fairness." This sounds very similar to our founding fathers' emphasis on virtues. As Thomas Jefferson wrote, "The most sacred of the duties of government [is] to do equal and impartial justice to all its citizens."

Common Law and Civil Law

Let's look at the origins of our American legal system. The American legal system maintains the common law tradition brought to the North American colonies from England. Common law emerged in England in the Middle Ages and is based on case law and precedent rather than codified law. Common law is generally uncodified, meaning that there is no comprehensive compilation of legal rules and statutes. Rather, it is mostly based on judicial decisions that have been made in prior similar cases. These precedents are maintained in the records of the courts as well as in historically documented collections of case law known as yearbooks and reports. The presiding judge gets to decide each new case by choosing which precedents he will apply to each individual case. As a result, judges have a massive role in shaping our laws. Common law is basically an adversarial system—meaning a contest between two opposing parties before a judge who moderates. A jury of citizens without legal training or experience on the issue of the case at hand decides a verdict based on the facts of the case. The judge then determines the appropriate sentence based on the jury's verdict and on precedents of similar cases. In my opinion, this system places too much power in judges' hands.

The other most popular form of legal system is called civil law. Its origins are found in the massive compilation of Roman law commissioned by Emperor Justinian, who ruled from AD 527 to 565. This compilation included the codification of old Roman law. Justinian assembled jurists to compile the old law, known as the *jus vetus*, and the new law called the *jus novum*. The digest comprised fifty books including a summary that could also serve as a legal text. Roman law contained the elements of due process and asserted that even emperors derived their powers from the people. Decades after its creation it was lost, but the principles surfaced again in the eleventh century in Italy and Western Europe due to issues regarding the Crusades. The laws of western Europe were heavily influenced by the Codex Justinianus, and legal scholars of Europe modified the principles of these ancient Roman laws to meet the needs of the time. Combinations of legal codes and customs throughout Europe, shaped by the Roman law tradition, are the models of today's civil law systems.

Traces of the civil law tradition may be found within state legal traditions across the United States, but certain practices traditionally allowed under English common law were outlawed by the Constitution. These include bills of attainder, which was a legislative act that singled out one or more persons and imposed punishment on them, without benefit of trial. Also outlawed by our Constitution are general search warrants. The Fourth Amendment of the Bill of Rights states, "The right of the people to be secure in their persons, houses, papers, and effects, against unreasonable searches and seizures, shall not be violated, and no warrants shall issue, but upon probable cause, supported by oath or affirmation, and particularly describing the place to be searched, and the persons or things to be seized." This right has been eroded by our government to a great degree in current times.

From common law, the United States inherited the principle of *stare decisis,* which binds judges to precedents of the rulings of a higher court. American judges not only apply the law, they also make the law, because their decisions become the precedent for decisions in future cases. In essence, the system relies on traditions and judge-made laws. Much is left to the discretion of the judges. The advantage of common law is that because judges are not bound by written rules, they can tailor legal principles to suit the case at hand. Additionally, common law more fluidly adapts to a changing society than civil law, because it is easier and less costly for judges to decide than for legislators to pass laws about every situation. There are disadvantages; sometimes judges make questionable rulings that continue to affect future cases for a long time because of *stare decisis*. Also, if a court has not ruled in a particular area, thereby setting a precedent, there is a fair degree of unpredictability as to the outcome. Federal courts are not given the plenary power possessed by state courts to simply make up law, with a few exceptions such as in maritime law. State courts are able to do this in the absence of constitutional or statutory provisions replacing the common law. Fortunately, common law offers the court of appeals.

CIVIL VS. CRIMINAL LAW

Civil law and criminal law are separate entities with separate sets of laws and punishments. Examples of criminal law include cases of burglary, assault, battery and murder. Civil law applies to cases of negligence or malpractice, for example. One of the main differences between civil law and criminal law is the punishment. In the case of criminal law, a person found guilty is punished by incarceration in a prison, a fine, or in some exceptional occasions the death penalty. In civil court, the losing party must pay the winning party a certain amount of money as well as reimburse them for court costs.

CIVIL LAW

A civil case begins when a person or entity (referred to as the plaintiff), which can be an individual, an organization, a corporation, or the government, files a complaint that another person or entity (called the defendant) has failed to carry out a legal duty owed to the plaintiff. The plaintiff may ask the court to tell the defendant to fulfill the duty, or make compensation for the harm done, or both. In criminal court the burden of proof lies with the government's prosecutor, but in civil law the burden of proof first lies with the plaintiff, and then with the defendant to refute the evidence provided by the plaintiff. In civil litigation, if the judge or jury believes that there is a majority of evidence favoring the plaintiff, the plaintiff wins. This is a very low standard as compared to the standard of "beyond a reasonable doubt" for criminal law. A civil law case does not involve criminal charges or allegations. If someone loses in civil court, that person may be ordered to make restitution to the other party but they do not go to jail. Most civil cases are about contracts, property, family matters, bankruptcy and wills (probate), injuries, traffic violations and civil rights violations.

Civil suits are brought in both state and federal courts. An example of a civil case in state court would be if a citizen (including a corporation) sued another citizen for not living up to a contract. Individuals, corporations and the federal government can also bring civil suits in federal court claiming violations of federal statutes or constitutional rights. An individual could sue a local police department for violation of their constitutional rights—for example, the right to assemble peacefully.

CRIMINAL LAW

In criminal law, the case is filed by the government, usually referred to as the "State" and represented by a prosecutor. The person accused of the crime is called the defendant. The government must prove that the defendant is guilty "beyond a reasonable doubt." An individual can never file criminal charges against another person. An individual may report a crime, but only the government can file criminal charges in court. The concept is that criminal law deals with looking after the public interest. It involves the police and prosecutor who use public funds—taxes—to pay for these services.

A criminal legal procedure typically begins with an arrest by a law enforcement officer. When a person is accused of a crime they are charged in a formal accusation called an indictment. The government prosecutes the case through the US Attorney's Office if it is a federal crime or the state's attorney's office (often called a district attorney) if it is a state crime. A crime does not always involve a victim; one such example is driving while intoxicated, because society regards that as a serious offence which can result in harm to others. If the person is found guilty, they receive a sentence from a judge. Depending on the crime the person must pay a fine and/or restitution to the victim, go to prison, undergo supervision in the community by a probation officer, or a combination of the three.

There are different categories of crimes. Felonies are the most serious and include crimes such as murder, rape, burglary and sale of illegal drugs. Being convicted of these crimes usually means receiving a sentence of a year or more in a state prison (penitentiary). Misdemeanors include shoplifting, drunk driving, assault, and possession of an unregistered firearm. These crimes usually come with a punishment of less than a year in county jail. Often, the second time a person commits the same crime, it is tried as a felony. An infraction is a less serious offense, such as breaking traffic laws. These usually do not go to a jury trial and only involve a fine. Some states consider traffic violations to be civil rather than criminal offenses. Lastly, there are ordinances, which are municipal laws that are enacted by the city or county, such as parking violations or smoking inside a public building. These usually involve a fine as well.

The Grand and Petit (Trial) Jury

A grand jury's main role is to determine whether there is *a prima facie* (Latin meaning at first glance) case; they decide whether or not to indict a potential criminal defendant of crimes alleged by the government. Basically, the grand jury serves as a screening process to protect citizens from false charges. The grand jury dates back to twelfth century England and was mainly to keep the religious courts in check. Over time it was transformed into a safety net for citizens against the monarchy to ensure that the government was not charging people for malicious purposes. This "people's panel" or "voice of the community" was so important that the Founding Fathers wrote it into the Constitution in the Fifth Amendment. It states "that no person shall be held to answer for a capital or otherwise infamous crime, unless on a presentment or indictment of a Grand Jury . . ." Although each state is different, on the federal level under the Fifth Amendment, criminal prosecution of any federal crime that would be punishable by more than one year imprisonment must be initiated by a grand jury's indictment.

The function of the grand jury is not to determine whether someone is guilty or not guilty of a crime, as that is the petit jury's responsibility, better known as the trial jury. The terms refer to the number of jurors serving on each jury rather than the importance of their roles. There are approximately sixteen to twenty-three jurors on a grand jury at the federal level, but no more than twelve on a trial jury.

After the charge is presented, the grand jury hears testimony and reviews the evidence the state provides. The hearing is held in complete secrecy and the jury only hears from the prosecution. The prosecutor has complete influence over the jury since he or she is the only one who selects the evidence to present and does not need to present exculpatory evidence (evidence that would show the defendant innocent). The only other person in the room is a court reporter. The grand jury has the power to compel witnesses to attend its hearing. The accused and any witness on behalf of the accused generally are not asked to testify. The grand jury votes to determine whether sufficient evidence has been presented for each of the proposed charges. While the number of votes required varies by jurisdiction, only a majority or supermajority—not a unanimous vote—is required. If the required number of grand jurors agrees that the evidence establishes probable cause, they vote to "return" the indictment. But even if the grand jury does not vote in favor of an indictment, there remains the possibility of criminal prosecution, as the prosecutor can still pursue charges through a preliminary hearing with a judge.

THE JUDGE'S ROLE

The judge is responsible for making sure that the trial process proceeds in a proper manner. The judge is also responsible for deciding issues of law and procedure that may occur during the trial and for instructing the jury on the law. Judges rule on the admissibility of evidence and the methods of conducting testimony. If an unusual circumstance arises for which standard procedures have not been established, judges interpret the law to determine how the trial will proceed. During the trial, the prosecutor or defense attorney might request a judge to take certain action. This is usually done by making a motion. For example, a lawyer may make a motion to strike certain testimony because it was not properly received. If the judge orders the testimony stricken, the jury must disregard it and may not consider it during deliberations. A lawyer may also make a motion to prevent a witness from testifying. Attorneys may also file pre-trial motions, which are a list of requests to the judge. Some commonly filed pretrial motions are to modify bail, dismiss complaint, reduce charges, change the venue, strike a prior conviction, preserve evidence, disclose identity of an informant, or suppress evidence. A motion for discovery is a formal request for the prosecution to turn over all the evidence they possess regarding a defendant's case. Depending on the decision of the judge, the motion affects the trial, courtroom, defendants, evidence and/or testimony. The judge's rulings can alter the appearance of the facts of the case through the motions he or she allows or declines. If the defendant is declared guilty by the trial jury, the judge then determines the defendant's sentence based on common law precedent.

COURT OF APPEALS

After a criminal or civil case is tried, it may be appealed to a higher court—a federal court of appeals or state appellate court. A litigant who files an appeal, known as an "appellant," must show that the trial court or administrative agency made a legal error that affected the outcome of the case. An appellate court makes its decision based on the record of the case established by the trial court or agency—it does not receive additional evidence or hear witnesses. It may also review the factual findings of the trial court or agency, but typically may only overturn a trial outcome on factual grounds if the findings were "clearly erroneous." If a defendant is found not guilty in a criminal proceeding, he or she cannot be retried on the same set of facts.

TRIAL BY JURY

Article III of the Constitution of the United States guarantees every person accused of wrongdoing the right to a fair trial before a competent judge and a jury of one's peers. The second President of the United States, John Adams, wrote, "Representative government and trial by jury are the heart and lungs of liberty. Without them we have no other fortification against being ridden like horses, fleeced like sheep, worked like cattle, and fed and clothed like swine and hounds." He meant that the two areas that allow for a level playing ground for our freedom are honest and legal elections and trial by jury. Thomas Jefferson wrote, "I consider [trial by jury] as the only anchor yet imagined by man, by which a government can be held to the principles of its constitution." US Supreme Court Chief Justice William Rehnquist later stated, "The right to trial by jury in civil cases and common law is fundamental to our history and jurisprudence. A right so fundamental and sacred to the citizens should be jealously guarded."

The Sixth Amendment guarantees the right of criminal defendants to a public trial without unnecessary delay, the right to a lawyer, the right to an impartial jury, and the right to know who your accusers are and the nature of the charges and evidence against you. The defendant is also constitutionally entitled to be presumed innocent until the jury finds otherwise. More proof is required to find a person guilty of a crime than to return a verdict for a plaintiff in a civil case. In order to return a verdict of guilty in a criminal trial, the charges must be proven beyond a reasonable doubt. In criminal trials, the twelve jurors must be unanimous in their verdict. Jurors do not determine a defendant's sentence, except in a murder trial in which the prosecuting attorney is seeking the death penalty. In that case, the judge gives special instructions to the jury. In every other criminal trial, it is the judge who imposes the sentence if a jury determines that a defendant is guilty. If the defendant is found not guilty, the charges are dismissed.

The Seventh Amendment requires civil jury trials only in federal courts. It only governs federal civil courts and has no application to civil courts set up by the states when those courts are hearing only disputes of state law. At the time of the Constitutional Convention in Philadelphia in 1787, there were mixed opinions regarding a civil jury, and there has been dispute over not having a jury in state civil cases since the Supreme Court decided this ruling. James Madison drafted the Seventh Amendment, which has two clauses. The first is known as the Preservation Clause. It states, "In suits at common law, where the value in controversy shall exceed twenty dollars, the right of trial by jury shall be preserved." The second clause, known as the Reexamination Clause, states, "No fact tried by a jury, shall be otherwise re-examined in any Court of the United States, than according to the rules of the common law." This clause prevents federal judges from overturning jury verdicts. In a civil matter, in order for a plaintiff to win a case, it is only necessary for the plaintiff to prove his or her case by a majority of the evidence, or in some cases by clear and convincing evidence. In most civil cases, six jurors sit to hear a matter, although there may be as many as twelve jurors. Five out of six jurors are needed to return a verdict in favor of one party or the other; when there are twelve jurors, ten jurors are needed to return a verdict.

THE HISTORY OF TRIAL BY JURY

Around two thousand years ago, in ancient Egypt, there was a form of trial by jury that consisted of eight jurors composed of four from each side of the Nile. Trial by jury became the norm in Greece in the sixth century B.C. This was carried over into Rome and arrived in Britain via the Roman Conquest. By the late 800s, under the leadership of Alfred the Great, trial by a jury of one's peers became the norm throughout England. In 1215, the Magna Carta ("Great Charter") was signed by English King John I. The Magna

Carta protected the civil liberties of English subjects and guaranteed the two great pillars of democratic society—representative government and trial by jury. Chapter 39 of the document reads, "No man shall be taken, outlawed, banished, or in any way destroyed, nor will we proceed against or prosecute him, except by the lawful judgment of his peers and by the law of the land."

But trial by jury began to break down in the sixteenth century when King Henry VIII declared himself supreme ruler of Great Britain. He suppressed and intimidated the court system and reinstituted the Star Chamber his father had developed, which was a political weapon to take down those who challenged his authority. Star Chamber sessions were held in secret, with no indictments, no juries, no witnesses and no appeals. The Star Chamber continued for around another hundred years under the Stuart kings and Oliver Cromwell, who overthrew the Stuarts. The Star Chamber showed rulers' complete disregard of basic individual rights. Charles II was no help as he even went so far as to dissolve Parliament whenever it convened. Finally, after nearly two hundred years of abuse, the British people asked William and Mary to guarantee that the liberties and rights in the Magna Carta, especially the trial by jury, would never be taken from them again. William and Mary had to sign the British Bill of Rights before they could be crowned; they signed it in 1689. But many British subjects had already sailed for America in search of the rights that had been promised them, and to escape the threat of more loss of freedom.

In 1734, the publisher of the *New York Weekly Journal*, Peter Zenger, wrote a column that criticized the Royal Governor William Crosby. Crosby had Zenger imprisoned for seditious libel. Zenger was tried before a jury of his peers the following year and was found not guilty, as he had printed the truth. This case established freedom of the press, guaranteeing that editors and publishers could not be found guilty of libel if they printed the truth. Gouverneur Morris, who helped write the US Constitution, stated, "The trial of Zenger in 1735 was the germ of American Freedom, the morning star of liberty that subsequently revolutionized America." Unhappy with the outcome of the Zenger trial, the British authorities suppressed the right of trial by jury with the goal of subduing those pushing for American independence. Needless to say, this just added fuel to the fire.

The right of trial by jury was instrumental in the quest for independence and shows up in The Stamp Act in Congress of 1765, where it is written that "trial by jury is the inherent and invaluable right of every British subject in these colonies." John Jay, who would later become the first chief justice of the United States Supreme Court, wrote, "Know then that we claim all the benefits secured to the subject by the English Constitution, and particularly the inestimable right of trial by jury."

However, British rulers continued to deprive the colonials of their right to trial by jury. In the Declaration of Causes and Necessity of Taking Up Arms, the Continental Congress cited the denial of "the accustomed and inestimable privilege of trial by jury, in cases of both life and property." Our Declaration of Independence states that the charges against Britain's King George III included "Depriving us in many cases, the benefits of trial by jury." Following the Declaration of Independence, each colony had to write a new state constitution. These constitutions were based on the principles and rights found in the Magna Carta and the British Bill of Rights, as well as interpretation of British common law.

The years following The Revolutionary War presented the new nation with difficulties such as financial trouble, interstate conflicts and domestic insurrection. The Articles of Confederation were insufficient for this new era. The Philadelphia Convention of 1787 brought together fifty-five delegates from the thirteen colonies. They would end up completely rejecting the Articles of Confederation and writing the first constitution for any nation in world history. For four months the group debated heatedly about what to include in the Bill of Rights. There were two camps: the Federalists, who wanted a strong centralized government, and the Anti-Federalists, who wanted to protect the rights of the states and citizens from an overpowering central government. The Anti-Federalists refused to ratify the Constitution unless it included a Bill of Rights. Chief among their concerns was making sure that the Constitution included the right of trial by a jury of peers as well as freedom of the press. The first draft allowed a jury trial for criminal cases but not for civil cases. Elbridge Gerry of Massachusetts stated, "A tribunal without juries would be a Star Chamber in civil cases." One thing that the Federalists and Anti-Federalists agreed on was trial by jury for criminal cases. Eventually, John Adams and John Hancock brokered the Massachusetts Compromise, which allowed ratification of the document as long as they could get enough states to support it. Many states debating the issue followed the Massachusetts Compromise, and the Constitution went into effect on March 4, 1789. When the First Congress convened, they agreed that a Bill of Rights was needed. James Madison drafted the legislation outlining the first ten amendments; it was passed by Congress on September 25, 1789. Madison wrote, "Trial by jury is essential to secure the liberty of the people as any one of the pre-existent rights of nature."

PLEA BARGAINS

How did we get from a new country based on individual freedoms and rights to the country that has more men and women imprisoned than any other in history? Is this really the "Land of the Free"? One of the two pillars of a free society—our right of trial by jury—has been decimated by the plea bargain. Our Constitution guarantees our freedom, but those who lack the virtues espoused by our ancestors have found this way to dismantle our almost perfect system. A plea bargain is a negotiated agreement for a criminal defendant whereby he or she agrees to plead guilty in exchange for a more favorable outcome. This outcome may be the dropping of additional charges, a reduction in the sentence, or being charged with a lesser crime. The late Harvard law professor William J. Stuntz wrote about the history of the plea bargain in his book, *The Collapse of American Criminal Justice*, saying that as a result our system has become "the harshest in the history of democratic government."

Plea bargains did not exist in colonial America. There were few law books, lawyers, or prosecutors. Most judges had little to no legal training, and victims ran their own cases (with the exception of homicides). Trials were short, and since the people generally knew each other, the defendants spoke directly to the witnesses and answered their questions. In fact, there is not much history on plea bargaining because in most jurisdictions it was considered inappropriate until the late 1960s. However, some of the earliest accounts come from the 1692 Salem Witch Trials. The accused were told that they would not be put to death if they confessed to being a witch, but would be executed if they did not. The magistrates encouraged "witches" to confess in order to uncover more witches. The Salem Witch Trials are used to illustrate one of the strongest arguments against plea bargaining—that the practice encourages innocent defendants to plead guilty and accuse others to save themselves.

Plea bargains were still practically unheard of prior to the Civil War. Following the war, due to many displaced Americans and immigrants moving into cities, the crime rate increased. A system similar to the current plea bargaining helped to lighten the case load. But Albert Alschuler, a retired law professor who has studied plea bargains for fifty years, said the appellate courts at the time "all condemned it as shocking and terrible." The Wisconsin Supreme Court in 1877 wrote that pleas were "hardly, if at all, distinguishable in principle from a direct sale of justice." The practice took on the appearance of shady, behind-closed-door deals, as someone could hire a "fixer" to arrange for alternatives to a prison sentence. Police toured jails to "negotiate" with the inmates.

By the twentieth century, our modern criminal justice system was morphing into the current disaster that we have today. Career prosecutors emerged, more defendants hired lawyers to represent them, and the courts developed more formal rules for evidence. Instead of trials taking minutes or hours, they started to last for days. This caused a backlog of cases, inducing more judges to start accepting pleas. Many judges today actively encourage prosecutors and defense lawyers to work out plea agreements so that the docket is not as full.

During the 1960s, the landmark case of Gideon v. Wainwright significantly changed the way that criminal cases are handled. The court ruled that indigent defendants (those who couldn't afford to pay for a lawyer) had the right to legal counsel. Criminal cases now had a defense lawyer representing the criminal defendant and another lawyer—the prosecutor—representing the interests of the state. In 1969, the Supreme Court changed its stance from fewer than one hundred years earlier when it ruled unanimously that pleas are constitutionally acceptable in that they are "inherent in the criminal law and its administration." In 1971, Chief Justice Warren Burger wrote regarding the morals of this reasoning, "An affluent society ought not be miserly in support of justice, for economy is not an objective of the system."

Despite the warning from Chief Justice Burger, plea bargaining has continued to be sold to us under the banner of enhanced efficiency, and we have accepted it. The cost of this sale has been the erosion of our freedoms. This so-called economic and efficient system comes at too high a cost: many innocent people, mistrustful of the system and afraid to take a chance of being convicted at trial, are induced to plead guilty in order to receive a lesser charge. More innocent defendants are convicted by plea bargains than would be by trials alone. Pleas are based upon coercion even though they claim not to be. They make people feel they have no option but to plead guilty, even though they are innocent. Imagine someone being told by the prosecutor that if their case goes to trial and they are found guilty, they would get thirty years in prison (due to the discretion of the prosecutor's charge), but if they take a plea, they would only get four years and a chance for probation after one year. Out of complete fear, they often choose the plea. Very few are willing to take the chance. Trials have court reporters to take complete and accurate notes of what is said at trial, yet plea bargains are done on the side with little or no written trace of what has transpired.

Prosecutors are overwhelmed and do not have the time to thoroughly review every case. Often, they intentionally set higher charges to scare the accused into pleading to the lesser charge, thereby avoiding trial and decreasing their workload. And if the prosecutor thinks that they have a losing case, this is a way to keep the loss off their record. Some critics argue that the practice should be abolished, as it is unconstitutional. I certainly agree. As I see it, and as I experienced in Tristan's case, the criminal justice system is no less criminal than who they are prosecuting. Jed S. Rakoff, a United States district judge in New York, wrote about the abuses of plea bargains in 2014 in *The New York Review of Books*: "A criminal justice system that is secret and government-dictated, ultimately invites abuse and even tyranny."

Most people adjudicated in the criminal justice system today waive the right to a trial and the host of protections that go along with one, including the right to appeal, by pleading guilty to lesser charges. The majority of felony convictions are now the result of plea bargains. It shocks me that plea bargaining has very little to do with actual guilt or innocence, yet it is the method by which almost all criminal convictions are obtained. In fact, approximately 94 percent of defendants take a plea at the state level, and approximately 97 percent do so at the federal level. Misdemeanor convictions run even higher. Only three to six percent of all people charged with a crime actually go to trial to use their constitutional right to be heard by a jury of their peers!

These are frightening statistics. We have a system here that undermines its own legitimacy. Pleading guilty to a felony makes someone a convicted felon forever—it matters not whether they were innocent but took the plea bargain due to fear or were found guilty in a trial. Unfortunately, conviction by plea and conviction by trial carry identical, high consequences, including temporary or permanent ineligibility for federal welfare benefits, educational grants, public housing, voting rights, handgun licenses, and military service as well as prohibitions from many types of employment—not to mention the moral stigma. Also, if that person is ever charged again in the system, the next sentence will be much more severe. Society treats all convicted felons alike. No one thinks to ask a "convicted felon" if their case was pled out or went to trial. We hear the words "statistics" and "cases," but we must acknowledge that every "statistic" and every "case" is a person's life, and his or her loved ones are affected as well. Supreme Court Justice Anthony Kennedy acknowledged this reality in 2012, writing for the majority in *Missouri v. Frye*, a case that helped establish the right to competent counsel for defendants who are offered a plea bargain. Quoting from a law review article, Kennedy wrote, "Horse trading [between prosecutor and defense counsel] determines who goes to jail and for how long. That is what plea bargaining is. It is not some adjunct to the criminal justice system; it is the criminal justice system." Plea bargains are, at best, coercions. At the worst, they are thievery of one's rights, liberties and sovereignty. Even though the courts say that the defendant affirms the plea freely and voluntarily, it most likely is due to the threat of a greater loss of freedom.

Due to the explosion of new laws on the books in the last several decades, brought to us in part by our elected legislators having criminalized so many behaviors, police are arresting millions of people annually—almost eleven million! If most of those charged ended up going to trial, there would be such a backlog that the court system would come to a complete standstill. In my research, it appears that plea bargains are the path of least resistance for prosecutors to secure convictions. It is how they win the game. Instead of throwing out weak cases, which would make the prosecutors actually have to screen them vigorously, they "up" the charges and the defendant is coerced—some might even say threatened—into accepting a plea, even if they're innocent. According to Stephanos Bibas, a professor of law and criminology at the University of Pennsylvania Law School, the criminal justice system has become a "capacious, onerous machinery that sweeps everyone in," and plea bargains, with their swift finality, are what keep that machinery running smoothly.

Because of plea bargains, prosecutors are able to handle the cases of millions of Americans each year, everything from petty violations to violent crimes. However, those people who do not present a danger to society, such as people suffering from poverty, mental illness, or addiction, still get caught up in the legal dragnet and punished instead of helped. Our justice system has turned into not much more than a conviction mill. Plea bargaining increases the number of innocent persons found guilty because every person who pleads guilty is convicted, whereas only a portion of those who go to trial are convicted. Even though innocent defendants can still be convicted at trial, they at least have a chance of being acquitted. Therefore, increasing the number of persons who plead guilty through plea bargaining increases the number of wrongful convictions. Plea bargains undermine the accuracy of the justice process. The legitimacy of the legal system is compromised and confidence in the system is destroyed. Sir William Blackstone, in commenting on English laws, wrote in 1783, "For the law holds, that it is better that ten guilty persons escape, than that one innocent suffer." In 1785, Benjamin Franklin expounded on this, writing, "It is better 100 guilty persons should escape than that one innocent person should suffer." It is why the framers of the Constitution imposed such a high burden of "beyond a reasonable doubt" on the government—which can only happen with evidence in a trial—before we convict people of crimes, revoke their liberties and put them behind bars.

THE ROLE OF THE PROSECUTOR

Prosecutors have become the most powerful officials in the American criminal justice system. We have an ideal concept of our legal system in which prosecutors and defense lawyers are equal, with dispassionate judges presiding over everything. In truth, this has not been the case over the past several decades. Prosecutors have accumulated power while judges and public defenders have lost it. Now prosecutors wield unlimited power, deciding whom to charge, who gets a second chance, and, in some cases, who lives and who dies. Their power starts with the charge, then it moves to the bail. Judges set bail, but the demands that prosecutors make influence the judge's decision. It seems to me that many judges don't want to take the political risk of letting someone go. This is the underreported piece of our mass incarceration problem.

Prosecutors control the direction and outcome of all criminal cases mostly through their charging and plea-bargaining decisions. Their decisions have greater impact and more serious consequences than those of any other criminal justice official. The prosecutor's decisions are totally discretionary and virtually unreviewable. These negotiations vary from individual to individual, from office to office, and from jurisdiction to jurisdiction, so that cases involving similar charges and even similar defendants may have decidedly different results. There has been a shift from the judge as a neutral referee to someone who is no longer making the key decisions. The prosecutor gets all the evidence from the police. They have a constitutional obligation before a trial to turn over anything that could help the accused prove their innocence, but if they don't, it's likely that no one will ever find out. Incredibly, there is no actual check in the system that effectively oversees their power. We more or less just rely on them to do the right thing.

Adding to their overarching power is the fact that over the last thirty years, lengthy mandatory sentences have increased greatly. Prosecutors have contributed to mass incarceration in America due in part to this increase in sentencing stemming from mandatory sentencing laws passed in the 1980s. Once the prosecutor knows what the mandatory sentence is, then they are able to make the charge fit the punishment. One of the main reasons for passing the mandatory minimums was to require a minimum amount of jail time for designated crimes regardless of context. The idea was that this would take discretion out of the system, weed out soft judges, and make the whole system more consistent and fairer because everyone was supposed to be getting the same punishment. Yet in reality, the discretion shifted to the prosecutors, and the actual result was that mandatory minimum sentences gave prosecutors a new role and a new kind of leverage. They use that leverage to induce more and more plea bargains, which is why plea bargaining went way up and felony charges doubled around this same time. Prosecutors want to have the maximum punishment as a weapon to coerce the accused to take a plea bargain, so they pick the charge that has the most severe potential punishment.

Another tool that prosecutors use to increase their conviction rate is setting high bail amounts. Higher bail amounts mean that more people must wait in jail until trial because they can't afford the bail. Research shows that people who are held in jail before their trials are more likely to accept plea bargains and less likely to have their charges dropped by prosecutors. Many defendants, including those who pose little to no threat to public safety, see the guilty plea as the fastest way to get out of jail, even though a guilty plea and its consequences will follow them for life. Prosecutors use detention and high bail as powerful leverage and place poor people at the greatest disadvantage. Remember, prosecutors are judged by their conviction rates and their "tough-on-crime" platforms. They are incentivized to think less about what is actually fair and more about winning trials and getting massive sentences.

In the 1970s, the Supreme Court made prosecutors absolutely immune from lawsuits. This means that there's no check from the legal system on prosecutorial abuses. Even if a prosecutor withholds exculpatory (key) information that would help or exonerate a defendant, there's no consequence. With this unrestrained power, and since most prosecutorial decisions are made behind closed doors, there is not much to hold them accountable. Alschuler explains that the only restriction the prosecutor has is that they cannot use illegal threats. "So if a prosecutor says, 'I'll shoot you if you don't plead guilty' then the plea is invalid. But if he threatens to charge someone with a crime punishable by death at trial and the defendant pleads guilty, the plea is lawful."

The Criminalization of Everything

The United States has only 5 percent of the world's population, yet it has nearly 25 percent of its prisoners—about 2.3 million people. Incarceration here has skyrocketed during the last half century. For most of the twentieth century, the US incarcerated about one hundred people per one hundred thousand residents, which was below the current world average. Our incarceration rate began to increase starting in 1972. By 2008, we reached a peak rate of 760 incarcerated persons per one hundred thousand residents. Interestingly, incarceration was increasing while crime rates were going down. In the early 1990s, US crime rates had been on a steep upward climb since the Lyndon B. Johnson presidency. The crack cocaine epidemic in the mid-1980s added fuel to the fire, and handgun-related homicides more than doubled between 1985 and 1990. Politicians ran on tough-on-crime platforms and enacted harshly punitive policies. Experts warned the worst could be yet to come.

But then crime rates went down. And then they kept going down. By the end of the 1990s the homicide rate had declined a whopping 42 percent nationwide and violent crime had decreased by one-third. This is a national statistic—it happened in each region of the country, in large and small cities as well as in rural and urban areas.

The increase in incarceration, therefore, cannot be explained by a rise in crime. Research also shows that the severity of the punishment does not deter a person's decision to commit a crime. What does influence them is whether they think they can get away with it and not get caught. Incarceration rates soared mostly due to laws making a wider variety of crimes punishable by incarceration and lengthening sentences. This harsh increase was driven in part by the implementation of mandatory minimums for drug offenses starting in the 1980s. These laws demand strict penalties for all offenders in federal courts, no matter the circumstances.

As I have witnessed, every time the government claims to help us with a program, we can be sure that it will result in a loss of rights and freedoms, an expansion of federal powers and an increase in incarceration.

Let's take a look over the last eighty years of government programs:

- President Lyndon Johnson declared a national "War on Crime" on March 8, 1965, shortly after his declaration on a "War on Poverty." Johnson called crime a crippling epidemic hindering the progress of our nation. Really, the target of the War on Crime was not merely criminal behavior, but rather the sociological and economic factors that the national government believed led to criminality. It made police and other law enforcement officials responsible for monitoring "poverty, racial antagonism, family breakdown, [and] the restlessness of young people," according to President Johnson's Commission on Law Enforcement and the Administration of Justice. It filled the streets with uniformed and plainclothes police. This policy led to police targeting black youth on the street, often arresting them for minor offenses or for nothing at all. This was not effective in combating actual criminal behavior. The War on Crime did not correspond with any increase in the crime rate—it just expanded federal powers. It put federal money into local jurisdictions, and the states and cities had to accept federal task forces taking control away from local law enforcement.

- Nixon declared a "War on Drugs" in the 1970s, which has cost the federal government (your tax dollars out of your paycheck) more than fifty billion dollars annually. It overwhelmingly targets the poor and minorities, contributing to the highest incarceration rate in world history. This has made the government more powerful and citizens less free, but it hasn't helped drug users or addicts. (It appears it wasn't meant to anyway.)

- The 1984 Comprehensive Crime Control Act, during the Regan presidency, established mandatory minimum sentences and eliminated federal parole, which had been given to increasing numbers of people since the 1970s.

- During the heyday of the "War on Drugs," from 1985 to 1992, legislators began to lengthen drug sentences. The Anti-Drug Abuse Act of 1986 was established, which imposed even more mandatory minimum sentences. As if that wasn't punishment enough, two years later a five-year mandatory minimum sentence for simple possession of crack cocaine, with no evidence of intent to sell, was passed.

- In 1994, during the Clinton presidency, "Three Strikes Laws" were introduced in many states, which sentenced any person with two prior convictions to life without parole upon a third conviction.

- "Truth in sentencing" policies also demanded that people serve their full sentences. This culminated in The Violent Crime Control and Law Enforcement Act of 1994, which included a three strikes provision at the federal level. The mandatory minimum drug laws and sentencing guidelines contributed to a dramatic growth of the federal prison system; it has become the largest prison system in the United States.

- In 2001, during the George W. Bush's administration, the USA PATRIOT Act was passed in reaction to the attacks on the World Trade Center on 9/11. No member of Congress was able to read the first USA PATRIOT Act, as its three hundred pages were printed at 3:00 a.m. for a vote that took place at 11:00 a.m. that same morning. This act gave the federal government the ability to wiretap, conduct electronic surveillance, pry into private medical records and access financial records such as bank and credit card statements.

- On November 25, 2001, President Bush created the Department of Homeland Security, which has become the third largest cabinet department after the Department of Defense and the Department of Veterans Affairs, with more than two hundred thousand employees.

- On January 14, 2005, the Department of the Army published Army Regulation 210–35: Civilian Inmate Labor Program, which provided the army policy and guidance for establishing civilian inmate labor programs and civilian prison camps on army installations.

- On October 17, 2006, President Bush signed into law the John Warner Defense Authorization Act expanding the president's power to declare martial law and take charge of the US National Guard troops without state governor authorization.

- That same day, October 17, 2006, President Bush also signed into law The United States Military Commissions Act of 2006 "to authorize trial by military commission for violations of the law of war and for other purposes."

- On May 9, 2007, President Bush signed National Security Presidential Directive 51 and the Homeland Security Presidential Directive. These essentially say that when the president determines a national catastrophic emergency has occurred, he can assume dictatorial powers.

- On May 26, 2011, President Obama signed a four-year extension of three key provisions in the USA PATRIOT Act allowing for roving wiretaps, searches of business records and conducting surveillance of "lone wolves," which are individuals suspected of terrorist-related activities not linked to terrorist groups. (You would be astonished to see what's on the long list of terrorist activities.)

- On New Year's Eve 2011 (Christmas Eve and New Years Eve seem to be very popular dates to sign unpopular bills and laws), Obama signed the National Defense Authorization Act, which gives the office of the president dictatorial, unconstitutional and treasonous powers: the authority to arrest any American citizen, or anyone for that matter, without warrant, detain them indefinitely in offshore prisons without charge, and keep them there until the end of hostilities. (Oh and by the way, no one, not even your family, will know.)

- On March 10, 2012, Obama signed The Federal Restricted Buildings and Grounds Improvement Act of 2011, commonly known as the anti-protest "Trespass Bill." This bill makes any trespass in an area that is under Secret Service protection, such as a campaign event, a federal offense punishable for up to ten years.

- On September 20, 2011, Anwar al-Awlaki—who was an American citizen—and his teenage son were assassinated under Obama's orders, without regard for a previous executive order that forbids assassinations. A US federal judge asked, "Can the executive order the assassination of a US citizen without first affording him any form of judicial process whatsoever, based on the mere assertion that he is a dangerous member of a terrorist organization?"

Wouldn't it be more constitutional and transparent to the citizens of the United States if the government was made to name a bill or law by its intention? "Bill to ransack your home and confiscate anything the feds want without a warrant." "Law allowing the feds to arrest you if you speak up at a county school board or city commission meeting." Or how about "Bill allowing prosecutors who hold back exculpatory evidence proving your innocence to be immune from being sued"? If this was the case, I am certain there would be far fewer of these bills and laws passed—especially those passed in the middle of the night.

The number of inmates across all federal facilities continued to surge under Obama's presidency, peaking in 2013. In 2010, the Fair Sentencing Act was passed, which included sentence reductions for crack cocaine offenders. The prison population began to drop as penalties changed and people were released. In the summer of 2015, Criminal Justice Policy Foundation Executive Director Eric E. Sterling called on President Obama to address mandatory minimums during his remaining months in office. Hopes were high for reform to pass in the 114th Congress, but President Obama's advocacy was inadequate, and no legislation was enacted before Congress adjourned in 2016.

On December 21, 2018, President Trump signed into law the First Step Act (FSA) of 2018 (P.L. 115–391). The act was the culmination of a bipartisan effort to improve criminal justice outcomes, as well as to reduce the size of the federal prison population while also creating mechanisms to maintain public safety. The FSA modifies mandatory minimum sentences for some drug traffickers with prior drug convictions by increasing the threshold for prior convictions that count toward triggering higher mandatory minimums for repeat offenders. It reduced the twenty-year mandatory minimum (applicable where the offender has one prior qualifying conviction) to a fifteen-year mandatory minimum, and reduced a life-in-prison mandatory minimum (applicable where the offender has two or more prior qualifying convictions) to a twenty-five-year mandatory minimum. It also expanded judges' discretion to ignore mandatory minimum sentences in some cases. The law also shortened some mandatory minimum sentences, such as from life to twenty-five years, or from twenty years to fifteen years, for various offenses. After the passage of the First Step Act, the Bureau of Prisons increased its use of compassionate release sentence reductions and home confinement. So far, thousands of people have been released from prison due to the First Step Act. Finally, there was some relief from the damaging effects of mandatory minimums.

John McAfee, the creator of the anti-spyware software company, put this message out on social media the day of his death from a prison cell in Spain: "The Deep State is a conspiracy theory of—it's defined as the people within the US government and military who are in secret control of government policy. Secret? Please people. The Deep State is those people within the US government that are career employees that cannot be fired by people that we elect by the congress or the president. There are the SEC, CIA, Securities and Exchange Commission, IRS—are these people in control? Can they enact laws? F—yes! They're called regulations. For every law that congress passes—and we elect congress to pass our laws—there are 20 regulations enacted by federal agencies that have far more impact on our lives than anything congress can possibly pass. Is there a Deep State? Yes! Can we fire these people? No! Can presidents fire them? No! It's designed that way so that political parties and political interests cannot affect the Deep State. Do you understand the nightmare of our situation people? I'm sorry, it's not secret. It's as open as anything could be. In the past, since 1975, 200,000 regulations have been passed by federal agencies encompassing 800,000 pages of fine print. People, it is no secret. It is as open as it can be. The Deep State does control America. Wake up people, please. God, use some common f---ing sense. Thank you."

Where am I going with all of this? You may not have been personally affected—yet—but when something happens to you, a friend or a loved one, you will see first-hand the atrocities that we've allowed to go on for a very long time. People may feel that they have achieved a certain level of success or comfort, but that ship can sink in a blink of an eye. Is it OK to stay in your comfort zone while many people suffer from poverty, unfair imprisonment, violent crime and unconstitutional, corrupt government policies? After World War II ended, German citizens were actually forced to go into the prison camps to witness the abomination and genocide that had occurred. They didn't want to see—it was too uncomfortable. But the Allied military wanted people to see that horror to make sure it would never happen again. Horrors are happening in our country every day, and most of us don't see it. The malevolent, greedy, evil and corrupt people behind the horrors are geniuses. They know how to hide "like a thief in the night," leaving many unaware. As my teacher and mentor John Barnes of the Barnes Myofascial Release Approach has said, "Without awareness there is no choice."

That is the purpose of our book. To increase the awareness that we the people have had our hands off the wheel for far too long. How do we stop this insidious corruption that has been torturing the good souls on this planet? I go back to awareness. As we come together in like-minded intention, I believe the answers will come. As we have been told, "love conquers all." We have allowed artificial separation and divisiveness to pull us apart until we fear and hate each other. Nothing good ever gets accomplished when we are divided. Is this the world we want to pass on to our children and future generations? I say, turn off your television and tune in to your Divine Source. Work with your community and make changes where you live. Expect and envision a peaceful planet based on truth and, yes, as our "Master of Love" has said, "peace on Earth and goodwill to all." We have work to do.

Tristan on the Criminal Justice System (3/21/21)

(On this day, I had just finished a lovely meditation which ended by me picturing myself sitting in a rose garden.)

Tristan: This is beautiful, why don't we start here? I am not by myself as I impart this message to you. There are many others who were victims of the corrupt criminal injustice system, as well as many others who had direct experience in the system, such as judges and others who were employed or played some sort of role in the judicial system on Earth. Also joining me today are great souls who understand true justice and would like to share with you how true justice could be served and brought about on the Earth plane.

Many of us came home (Heaven) after being mistreated and abused or were falsely accused on Earth. There are those who were the perpetrators of injustice who have seen the damage done by their choices and bad behavior. At the time they were in their role, they were more concerned with how they appeared, what promotion they would earn or how they would be treated by their fellow comrades. As you know, they were more concerned with winning their case and truly not the humane treatment of another person and the truth. It is a game to many. Certainly, this depends on what part they played such as police, detective, attorney, judge, etc. These people come home and they have to feel everything they did to another person—like in first person. They must reap what they have sown—on this side. They see the damage they have done and are charged with reversing the energy of the damage they have inflicted on others. Those are mostly the ones with us today, as they are charged with fixing the errors and injustices that they enforced on others. Many don't do the work on this side and must reembody and either be on the receiving end of a similar energy or situation or they are placed in a role where they have the opportunity to set things right and to undo some of their past errors. They have all of eternity to get it right. Once they are on this side, they see what they have done, but can still remain belligerent and go back to Earth to repair past mistakes yet get caught up in the same system and get heavier karma each time. Woe to them, as it is said. But let us not place too much thought on those souls. Earth will not be supporting that kind of low energy for much longer. It will not only not be tolerated, but the frequency of Earth will not support it.

Let us instead talk about and with those who wish to initiate a higher system of justice on the planet.

[New communicator:] By way of rules and regulations we have been controlled as well as manipulated. Controlled by the laws and manipulated by the courts. Most people are blind to all the rules and regulations that they exist under—it is a heavy burden.

Yes, of course there needs to be accountability for one's actions to others and their communities, but it has gotten beyond out of control. Know that for every crime committed, someone in the system—usually many people—make money. Crime is big business. The more crime committed, the wealthier people in the system get. Yes, that is the truth. We know you have never thought of it in this way but as you think about it, it becomes apparent that it is truth. So then why wouldn't it become advantageous to support crimes, to make crimes look enticing, to create more laws that people will "break?" How about the worst of it? Yes, my dear, the same group—not the ones at the ground level but the higher ups, we shall say, create the environment so people get caught up in criminal activity. They get swept up in a way likened to a dragnet. You have memories of an old TV show now called Dragnet. See how they—the true criminals—create the situation and even prime the citizens of what they are deceptively planning? [By this, they mean the use of movies and television shows to prepare us subconsciously.]

Think of the horrible mess there is with horrible intoxicants— drugs—put out in the population. My dear, this has been going on for centuries. It is an old trick, you know—used in Asia hundreds of years ago. People get addicted to it, then it becomes illegal. So now the same government (they like to call themselves leaders) say there is a problem. Instead of helping the poor people who now have trouble functioning because of these intoxicants, they now claim it is illegal, and they are punished. As well, there is now a black market of people who will take advantage and sell the drugs to those who are desperate. Look what fun these leaders have now—it is a cash crop. Their plans pay off as there is a new industry from the law enforcement, courts, prisons, and social workers, etc. Of course, the prisoners must be fed and taken care of and that is another industry. Then the prisoners must pay fines without the means to do so. More crimes are committed by the desperate ones who will steal and do horrible things just to get more intoxicants—even sell their bodies, and many, their souls. This is one industry. There are many more—even the sexual exploitation industry. It is an abomination and true justice happens in spirit on this side for those who will exploit anyone else—and children—well . . . it is not anything that needs to be discussed here but Creator will not stand for this abuse. But allow us to say that this was a purposefully created industry—the way it is today with trafficking of souls . . . trafficking of souls! Do not think this just started, but it is alarming and the sirens have been sounding for many many years, but as you say, until it happens to you or someone you know and love, you have no idea. It is now front and center for all to see.

Every culture has its unique ideas as to what is acceptable behavior, simply bad behavior and what is criminal behavior. It is usually based on their religious beliefs, in part, at least that was once the foundation. However, as we have pointed out, it has become big business as the governments have created big business out of crime. Like the expression—"follow the money." What once a community would handle on an individual basis has grown into many staggered layers of government. The authorities are the criminals. They receive kickbacks, receive and give favors, make high salaries with great benefits, get to exist in a limelight and receive accolades from their fellows—all while standing on the backs of those who they helped put asunder including the families that are torn apart.

[There was a pause while they told me they were changing authors. It was apparently someone who suffered in the criminal justice system and is speaking for others in the group.] . . . *We watch from this side the terrible mess in the wake of our actions that we committed. How the courts had to come into play, the losing of our freedom and how our families were terribly hurt. We made mistakes yet some of us who committed crimes and were given harsh sentences watched as those who did much worse got off easy due to who they knew or some other situation that allowed them to go free. There is no consistency or fairness to the system. There is too much power in the hands of those in the system. You lose your identity and become a number—another cog in the wheel that keeps the system going and growing.*

[I asked, "Well, what did you learn and what are you going to do about it?"] *We know that it is more about treating your fellow man with compassion and kindness and to take a higher road. We see what we have done to others from this side, and it doesn't feel good. It is even more than this. It is about soul growth. Sometimes we have good intentions, but we go astray—enticed by the "rewards" of taking what is not ours to take. While there may not be true justice and fairness on Earth, there is here at home.*

[Tristan returns:] *Mom, as you know, I knew I was set up. This is how it works. The prosecutor needs a win or is told by his higher ups how they want the case to end up. The jury pick and the motions allowed by the judge will set the stage. I was a sitting duck and it became apparent to me as it was getting close to the trial. Know the truth, and the truth is well-known on this side. Justice supports truth. All is known and accounted for on this side, so have no despair. No one "gets away" with anything. They have a choice in their free will how they will play their part and how they will evolve their souls by their moment-to-moment decisions.*

[Tristan pulls back and a new speaker appears—this seems to be a guide. I ask, "How is this repaired?"] *As Tristan has showed you before, the fire has been blazing for a very long time. The fire is out but now you have the ashes, smoke and total destruction. You have to analyze the damage, consider how to rebuild, then create anew. Yes, this change will take several more years as all must become aware of the truth of what has been occurring. Those responsible must be held accountable—not such a small endeavor as there are many layers. The population on Earth will become acquainted with the fact that they have been bought and sold by the system and they have not had freedom. It will be overwhelming and many will have difficulty understanding that on one hand they have been manipulated and on the other, what does one do with themselves when they are not being told what to do, when and how to live, what to believe, how to exist. There is the repair of the human psyche—a cooling-off period of sorts. Then there are the people who have come in to rebuild a more beautiful system—but realize, there will be less crime as people won't be enticed and rewarded to create it. There will be no need for the massive bureaucracy as there is now. The people will be in charge. There will be transparency— no "behind closed door" deals. Knowledge of the spiritual laws will be understood. Therefore, we know that what we do to another is what we will reap and how it will affect the collective mind as well. This will take time. You just now are realizing the fire has been blazing for centuries and now you all on a mass scale are analyzing and observing the mess in its wake. Know that we are all responsible, so we all must participate in some way. No longer can anyone not participate in one way or another. All must be a part of the clean-up crew. It has to be dismantled. Some people come in and expose the corruption. It is like a life of sacrifice. We honor all those who come to Earth and play these roles. Not being aware is not part of the solution. It is Earth's time to rise and shine. Many of us are now standing in the wings helping to direct circumstances from this side and waiting our turn to be reborn in the right place and time to continue our missions. Take care, all is in place, just know that how long it takes is up to you. We laugh here when you tell us to just rip off the band-aid because it is worse to pull it off excruciatingly slow. We wait for your next thought, request, and action. It truly is all up to everyone. It really does take a village, and that is all of us. We welcome your requests and appreciate you giving us an ear, so to speak.*

[Tristan:] *There are many over here, Mom, that are working on this, as this is the biggest situation that is happening on Earth now—cleaning up of all the corruption and those responsible for it.*

As always, my love to you. Tristan

CHAPTER 8

Guns

"Guns are bad news in the wrong hands, and never should they be in the hands of children."

-TRISTAN

Barbara's Research and Experience:

Let's face it, to keep guns in a household with children is very dangerous. How many times have I heard, "I was raised around guns and we knew how to handle them and respect them . . . I have taught my children how to use a gun since they were little . . . Only careless people have gun accidents . . . My children know where my guns are stored and they know not to touch them . . ." To those people I say, how fortunate you were to never have had a terrible accident. Even the most careful gun handlers can have accidents. During the interviews that our defense attorney had with ATF (Alcohol, Tobacco and Firearms) officers while working on Tristan's case, the officers said that there have been times when someone had been cleaning their gun in the ATF office and it accidentally went off and the bullet went through the cubicles. If an accident can happen to the most highly trained experts, it can happen to anyone.

We knew the Lugners were gun owners. We knew that Mr. Lugner would take his sons and Tristan to their private property to shoot, and we allowed it. We knew that Tristan wanted to be a police officer and felt that it was a good way for him to see if he really wanted to pursue that career path. We did not know how many guns Mr. Lugner had. We did not know that the boys were allowed to play with the guns unsupervised, and we did not know how irresponsible Mr. Lugner was. I will forever feel guilty that I did not insist on going over to their house to inspect the situation. I will be forever sorry.

Eight children are accidentally injured or killed every day by unsecured firearms in the home. This is referred to as "family fire." Thirteen million households owning guns in the US have children present, according to a 2018 study. In approximately 2.7 million of those households, gun owners store their firearms loaded and unlocked, which means that there are an estimated 4.6 million kids living with guns they can easily access. Surveys have shown that many children know the location of their parents' gun even when their parents think they don't. Some children have even handled the gun in their home without their parents' knowledge. In 2016 alone, 3,000 children were unintentionally shot and 127 were killed in family fire incidents due to improperly stored guns. Another 1,100 children shot themselves to death in suicides, in many cases with unsecured firearms owned by their parents. Studies have shown that having a gun in the household significantly increases the risk of adolescent suicide.

There is an organization called the Brady Campaign to Prevent Gun Violence. They say the first step toward ending family fire is to reach gun owners and encourage more responsible gun ownership. A slide on their website says gun owners can "start by storing your gun in a secure and inaccessible location away from children and guests." (Do people really need to be told that?) Another message urges people to store their firearms with a gun lock or in a safe, and to keep the guns separate from ammunition. There was discussion about Brady partnering with a manufacturer of biometric gun safes, which allows people to get to their firearms in just seconds. I would guess that parents who have a "that will never happen to me" attitude will not take these recommendations seriously.

Also of note is the fact that firearms are a popular target for burglars and thieves, and that locking them up can help keep guns off the street.

According to one man who lost his nephew to family fire while at a friend's house, "The truth of the matter is, if you have an irresponsible gun owner in your neighborhood, your community's not safe." I often thought about this after the accident. Here was a home in a neighborhood with minimal lot lines, and a man with two teenage sons who allowed friends over, with more than fifty loaded guns scattered around the house. Any type of accidental discharge could have affected a neighbor. I am sure the neighbors had no idea.

A 2019 study in the *American Journal of Preventive Medicine* found that the best predictor of a state's youth suicide rate is the proportion of homes that contain a firearm. Remarkably, one of the study's authors said that single piece of data is a "far more accurate" indicator than the percentage of children in the state who have previously attempted suicide. According to Denise Dowd, a physician and researcher who has treated more than five hundred pediatric gunshot victims, "There's this mythical idea that you can teach kids not to want to handle a gun. You can't train or educate curiosity out of a little kid, and teenagers are impulsive, and they act without any thought to the future. You have to separate the guns from the kids; the thing that does harm from the thing that's harmed."

Let's put some perspective on how big an issue accidental shooting deaths really is in the United States.

- In 2018, accidental gun deaths accounted for 1 percent (458) of total gun-related deaths (39,740) in the United States.

- Shelter-in-place orders during the coronavirus pandemic led to major spikes in accidental shootings at home by children. Deadly unintentional shootings were up 43 percent in March and April 2020, compared to the same months in the previous two years.

- Around 77 percent of accidental gun deaths happen in the home.

- From 2006–2016, almost 6,885 people in the US died from unintentional shootings. In 2016 alone, there were 495 accidental firearm deaths.

- Accidental gun deaths occur mainly to those under twenty-five years old. In 2014, 2,549 children (age 0–19) died by gunshot, and an additional 13,576 were injured.

- Adolescents are particularly susceptible to accidental shootings due to specific behavioral characteristics associated with adolescence, such as impulsivity, feelings of invincibility, and curiosity about firearms.

- The majority of people killed in firearm accidents are under age twenty-four, and most of these young people are being shot by someone else, usually someone their own age. The shooter is typically a friend or family member, often an older brother. By contrast, older adults are at a far lower risk of accidental firearm death, and are most often shooting themselves.

- A statistically significant association exists between gun availability and the rates of unintentional firearm deaths, homicides and suicides. Around 31 percent of accidental deaths caused by firearms might be prevented with child-proof safety locks and loaded chamber indicators.

- A study from 2014 showed that people that who died from an accidental shooting were more than three times as likely to have had a firearm in their home.

Many people don't want to have this discussion. They feel restricting guns in any way would infringe on their Second Amendment right to own a firearm. But this is not the case. It is simply the most obvious way to protect kids from injury and death. As you can see, Van and Tristan's gun accident fits into the above statistics with the probability of an accident being extremely high. They would be alive today, and Tristan would not have had to go through seventeen months of trauma, multiple horrific surgeries and severe pain. Demanding, by law, that people with guns must prevent them from falling into the hands of a child does not mean they can't own them. It simply means they must behave responsibly with the ones they own. If everyone in the United States locked up all their firearms, researchers estimate, the number of gun-related accidental deaths and suicides among children and teenagers would drop by as much as a third. And yet a huge number of Americans do not take that simple step because of ignorance or negligence. I will add to that arrogance. Researchers who surveyed gun-owning families in the rural South found that a significant proportion of parents had no idea what their children knew about or had done with their firearms, according to a study in *JAMA Pediatrics*. Nearly 40 percent of parents who claimed that their kids did not know where they stored their guns were wrong; the kids said they knew. More than 20 percent of parents who claimed that their kids had never handled one of those guns were also wrong; the kids said they had. Notably, children who had been educated on gun safety were just as likely to say they had played with the weapons.

How do we save children from having to take on the responsibility for their parents' negligence? By responsibility, I mean injury, or post-traumatic stress disorder when they have to relive the moment of injuring themselves or a friend—or even killing a friend. They relive that horror every time they close their eyes. I ask, if a minor gets his or her hands on your gun in your home and shoots another child, should we charge you or the child? (And I answer: you.) Accidents happen even to those who are educated and trained—are you willing to take that chance? Gun owners must take responsibility. We can equate it to driving a car. First you must be trained. You must learn the rules of the road, how to physically handle a vehicle, and how to have responsible behavior while on the road. Why is this training required before you can get a driver's license? Because you are handling something that can injure or kill other people. This is required of everyone before they receive a driver's license. We must have some sort of criteria and education required for having a gun in your home as well. Should there be a training certificate? I remember watching movies in Driver's Education class in high school about horrible auto accidents that were intended to impress on us new drivers the importance of being responsible. Should there be something similar when one goes to buy a gun? Should there be a responsibility and safety course required along with the standard background check? What actions can we take to lessen the chances of childhood injuries and deaths while securing our Second Amendment rights? These are questions we need to ask ourselves. In my opinion, negligent behavior and irresponsible handling and storage will erode those Second Amendment rights. Gun ownership is a right, but it is also a responsibility.

As we get older, we have more experiences under our belts, so we have a greater ability to respond when life throws us sudden curveballs. Children have not acquired that skill yet. Tristan, because of his young age of seventeen, knew no other thing to do in the moment the gun accidentally went off and killed his friend but to try to take his own life. Think back to your teen years. What would you have done? He had no law enforcement or military training that could have prepared him for a moment like this.

This was a terribly unfair accident; these two beautiful boys were just getting started in life. Mr. Lugner has taken zero responsibility for the deaths of these two young men who had such great potential. There have been no consequences of any type for his negligence. Here is a man who not only is an alleged alcoholic with multiple DUIs but also kept loaded guns unsecured around the house—and yet no one ever questioned his role in what happened.

After Tristan died, there was an incident involving Mr. Lugner's younger son and his guns. This incident triggered a "red flag" law, which is a gun control law that permits authorities to remove guns from a person who may present a danger to themselves or others. (This is the incident referred to in the newspaper article quoted at the end of Chapter 1.) The guns were removed from Mr. Lugner, but he won them back in court. (We have discussed the corruption of the court system, so this is no surprise. I wonder who he knows?) A state representative in Jacksonville, Florida, was supportive of Lugner's case because he was against the red flag law, but he soon pulled it from his website. Maybe he found out there was a lot more to Mr. Lugner's story. The younger son was committed to a mental health treatment center under the Baker Act. When the mother picked him up from rehabilitation, she said in a newspaper interview that her son would be able to get his guns back as soon as the courts said he could. I guess some people never learn.

Most states have laws on child access prevention; negligent storage; imposing criminal liability for allowing a child to gain access to the firearm regardless of whether the child uses the firearm or causes injury; prohibiting intentional, knowing or reckless provision of firearms to minors; and other similar topics. Florida Statute 790.174, on the "Safe storage of firearms required," states the following:

> (1) Person who stores or leaves, on a premise under his or her control, a loaded firearm, as defined in s. 790.001 and who knows or reasonably should know that a minor is likely to gain access to the firearm without the lawful permission of the minor's parent or the person having charge of the minor, or without the supervision required by law, shall keep the firearm in a securely locked box or container or in a location which a reasonable person would believe to be secure or shall secure it with a trigger lock, except when the person is carrying the firearm on his or her body or within such close proximity thereto that he or she can retrieve and use it as easily and quickly as if he or she carried it on his or her body.

> (2) It is a misdemeanor of the second degree, punishable as provided in s. 775.082 or s. 775.083, if a person violates subsection (1) by failing to store or leave a firearm in the

required manner and as a result thereof a minor gains access to the firearm, without the lawful permission of the minor's parent or the person having charge of the minor, and possesses or exhibits it, without the supervision required by law:

(a) In a public place; or

(b) In a rude, careless, angry, or threatening manner in violation of s. 790.10.

This subsection does not apply if the minor obtains the firearm as a result of an unlawful entry by any person.

(3) As used in this act, the term "minor" means any person under the age of 16.

Florida Statue 784.05, "Culpable negligence," states:

(1) Whoever, through culpable negligence, exposes another person to personal injury commits a misdemeanor of the second degree, punishable as provided in s. 775.082 or s.775.083.

(2) Whoever, through culpable negligence, inflicts actual personal injury on another commits a misdemeanor of the first degree, punishable as provided in s. 775.082 or s. 775.083.

(3) Whoever violates subsection (1) by storing or leaving a loaded firearm within the reach or easy access of a minor commits, if the minor obtains the firearm and uses it to inflict injury or death upon himself or herself or any other person, a felony of the third degree, punishable as provided in s. 775.082, s. 775.083, or s. 775.084. However, this subsection does not apply:

(a) If the firearm was stored or left in a securely locked box or container or in a location which a reasonable person would have believed to be secure, or was securely locked with a trigger lock;

(b) If the minor obtains the firearm as a result of an unlawful entry by any person;

(c) To injuries resulting from target or sport shooting accidents or hunting accidents; or

(d) To members of the Armed Forces, National Guard, or State Militia, or to police or other law enforcement officers, with respect to firearm possession by a minor which occurs during or incidental to the performance of their official duties.

When any minor child is accidentally shot by another family member, no arrest shall be made pursuant to this subsection prior to 7 days after the date of the shooting. With respect to any parent or guardian of any deceased minor, the investigating officers shall file all findings and evidence with the state attorney's office with respect to violations of this subsection. The state attorney shall evaluate such evidence and shall take such action as he or she deems appropriate under the circumstances and may file an information against the appropriate parties.

(4) As used in this act, the term "minor" means any person under the age of 16.

As you can see in the above Florida statutes, Mr. Lugner would have been guilty of both. However, since Tristan was seventeen at the time, he escaped being charged. I question these statutes defining a minor as being a person under the age of sixteen. In most ways, one is still considered a minor until age eighteen. Are sixteen- and seventeen-year-olds considered fully mature and responsible? Why isn't a firearm owner responsible if an accident happens to a sixteen- or seventeen-year-old versus a fifteen-year-old? I claim that this law needs to be changed. In this statute, a minor should be anyone under eighteen. These are areas in urgent need of change.

I will finish with this statement from Jesus, found in Luke 17:2: "It would be better for him if a millstone were hung around his neck and he were cast into the sea than that he should cause one of these little ones to stumble."

TRISTAN ON GUNS (11/5/18, JUST SIX MONTHS AND ONE WEEK AFTER HIS PASSING)

W*elcome back, it's been a while, Mom. You so want to talk to me, but it also feels like an overwhelming sadness that it has to be like this—communicating in spirit rather than face-to-face. But it seems like that to you, but I am right here—so near to you—feel me here in your heart. I love you and am here for you. The crying is so sad and yet a beautiful cleansing as souls come in and go out of each other's lives while in the physical on Earth. I wish I could be there in physical with you too sometimes, but that is not the case, and all is truly well over here. There is no time, no change really—just moving on in love. There is also no sadness. It is just like a disappointment that it had to play out the way it did. My soul's evolution is processing what happened and healing from it. You must heal from this too. I have grown up a lot over here. My work continues—it is what we do—it doesn't end in so-called death. We are just aware now of our mission or soul's work. It is not blocked out like when we are in a body. It is really hard, yet you are creating a new planet—one that will be based in love and not fear and that has to start at the densest layer and move up through the finer layers of consciousness.*

We ask why, why, why? Meditate and you will be surprised at some of the answers to your questions. It is how Creator planned it—like all other planets that have evolved. It starts at the physical—so you work your way through the illusions to the truth. The vibrations are low because of low vibration people who have greed in their hearts. If they knew how to work the ethers completely the Earth would cease to exist because they would blow it up! So only so much awareness of truth can be let out—like inventions—because those higher ups would hijack it. They already have to an extent— they know what they are doing but love will win the day. Those of us who left early are learning much over here to bring it—the knowledge—the higher knowledge—back in with us. It will be a battle but the children of the Light are coming in and God's power will win—the tide will turn. They can't kill God's children— they can't destroy them. Oh, it looks like they are winning but we reincarnate and bring the greatness in with us. We can't be stopped. The dark has lost the fight. It is their last gasp for control of this planet. Do not fear—it looks bad but we know our mission.

Feel my hand on your shoulder—it is always there now from this side. Just ask us—through God—and we will do our best from this side to help you. If you could only see what it is like over here. So beautiful—so many of us—another world! We work hard over here helping souls on Earth. Yes, I was disfigured, and I was very self-conscious of it, and now I am helping those on your side and this side to heal from that. It is not something that lasts—you get your beauty back on this side. I look pretty good—told you that before—just want to tell you again to make you feel better. I love myself over here again. Love and acceptance are all we have over here. Even for those who hurt us—really—I know that is hard to accept—all the people you feel were responsible for my departure— you call death—still here you know. We ask, "How did this evolve my soul?" "Did I understand this?" "What did I leave unfinished?" "What am I going to have to re-experience in another way again?" It is peaceful on this side while analyzing your past lives and your last life. It's when the veil of illusion comes down at birth—well, a few years after birth—that things become fearful, because you don't know why you're experiencing it.

Guns—they really are a big deal. I was enthralled with them on Earth as Tristan because they were like the "forbidden fruit" and I got to play with them at the Lugners' and that made me feel so grown up and powerful. It was Van's time to go, and so Spirit set it up that this was how it would play out due to what we were doing. Shit—that is nothing I would have ever thought could or would happen. I loved him so—a real friend—we would do anything for each other. Van came in for a short life. Something about lessons his parents had to learn and feel responsibility for their actions. I too came in for a short life. I used to tell you that too—you remember— but I couldn't explain how I knew it. Yes, we have free will and can always change our minds (on a spiritual level), but my path went far off the path. Yes, things were going to happen, but this was harsh. I was a systems buster as we talked about, and I was to show people about the Earth's old energy systems, but the path was too difficult. Like I said, it looks good when you're planning it on this side but when you're in it, however, it really sucks! We never should have been allowed to play with guns. You will know eventually that guns are for one thing and that is death and killing. Too many deaths of young people occur because of the misuse. I am not saying that there should be no guns at this time as there is still so much low energy, but over time people will not feel the need to stock up on guns and weapons. There will be less fear and governments will be benevolent and for the people. But guns in the wrong hands are the problem—even police—so much misuse of their weapons. Everyone feels that they have to protect themselves from everyone else—even protect from the police. They can be fearful themselves or get into an ego power trip and misuse them and hurt people.

Guns will eventually, over time, phase out because people won't be fearful as they are now. There has to be accountability from those who choose to own them. They must bear responsibility if someone gets hurt with their gun. Your gun—your responsibility. People must own up to their responsibility. If you choose to own a gun, then there are severe rules and penalties if someone gets hurt from it. If it gets stolen, you are still at fault because of how you handled it. It can be no other way. We should never ever have been allowed to just carelessly play with the guns. My life was ruined—over— when I saw Van, my best friend, go down. I couldn't recover from that trauma. I just freaked out and I couldn't live it over and over again. Guns are bad news in the wrong hands and never should they be in the hands of children. You say what about hunting? You have to know that difference between properly handling a gun and misuse of one. We were allowed to misuse them—you didn't know it. But even if a child gets hurt hunting or hurts someone else, can you, as an adult who gave them the gun, live with that? Why? Is it your ego that your child can shoot a gun? You must ask yourself these questions. Does your child need to kill food at such a young age to eat? Where do you live—what are your circumstances? Circumstances—one size or answer does not fit all. Make up your mind—guns or no guns? Will you be able to bear the responsibility if a child gets hurt with your gun? It must be so.

Children on medication get their parents' guns and kill themselves or others. If they can get to your gun, then you are responsible. That is how things will change. In my case—yes, it should have been Mr. Lugner's fault, but he got his attorney, Patrick Batemans, and the law makes things so confusing. People win a case because they have money or clout and political pull or the right friendships, etc., and they don't have to bear the responsibility for their actions. This is where the change needs to come about.

Your gun—your responsibility. Guard and store it appropriately. It will make people think twice if they should want to own one. Unregistered guns should not be allowed. When people give up their responsibility, they give up their rights as well. Van and I shouldn't have been playing with them, and yet in the long run the truth of the matter is Mr. Lugner should never have made them available. Period.

Mom, it is with great love that I speak with you today. I know it is a difficult time for you and difficult subjects, but the truth must be heard. Stay brave. I am always here when you want to talk. And yes, the little white feather was from me.

I love you, Tristan.

SECTION III

Awakening to a New Era: The Golden Age

"Our birth is but a sleep and a forgetting
The Soul that rises with us, our life's star
Hath had elsewhere its setting,
And cometh from afar,
Not in entire forgetfulness
And not in utter nakedness,
But trailing clouds of glory do we come
From God who is our home.
Heaven lies about us in our infancy."

WILLIAM WORDSWORTH

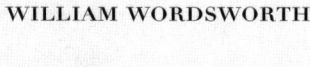

CHAPTER 9

The Universal Spiritual Laws

"The time will come where people will no longer need to read and study these Laws as they will become the Laws unto themselves. This is the Decree from God: All is One."

-A SPECIAL MESSENGER

BARBARA'S RESEARCH

The timeless and truest laws for all of humanity can be found in the Universal Spiritual Laws. These are our Creator's statutes, which are based in pure love. They are uncompromising, but they allow us to have free will. We can choose to be aware or unaware that all that is happening in our lives is a result of these concepts. This can be difficult to understand when we witness atrocities such as what happened to Tristan, and how mankind has historically treated others. We ask, how can a loving God allow such horrors to happen? But when we seek to truly understand these universal concepts, we realize that God is one constant loving force, and we are playing our own hand in this time/space continuum. Those who commit these crimes against humanity also live under the same laws. They therefore will reap the consequences of their actions and behavior. That gives me solace and comfort, as I trust that "God's got this"—God's justice is always at work, even if we can't see it.

There are Universal Laws. Some people have condensed them down to just a few and others have expanded on them. There are also subsets of these laws. However, I am going to list the main twelve, as they are what I am most acquainted with. To fully grasp the concept of the laws, it is important to understand that everything is energy and has its own unique frequency. One of the principles of physics is that energy cannot be destroyed—it can only be transformed into another form of energy. It also helps to know that even thoughts have energy—especially repetitive thoughts with a lot of emotion behind them (e-motion is energy in motion). Thoughts are expressed in other forms of energy, such as feelings, words and actions. Once we understand this, it can lead to freedom, happiness, peace and true equality, as we realize that we are in control of our own thoughts and responses—and therefore of the reality they create.

These spiritual laws that govern our Universe are believed to have been in existence from the beginning of time. They were known to ancient cultures, who lived by them. Some of these laws may have originated from ancient Hawaiian culture in a spiritual technique called Ho'oponopono, used for reconciliation and forgiveness. Many come from the Hermetic philosophy derived from Egyptian culture, as described in *the Kybalion*, which was the first book to chronicle this philosophy of seven laws of the Universe. The *Kybalion* was published in 1908. Since then, many authors have published their versions of Universal laws.

Hermetic philosophy is named after Hermes Trismegistus. He is believed to have been an actual living king, philosopher, priest, sage, scientist and sorcerer. In these various "incarnations," his main purpose was to transcribe the word of God, which included the spiritual laws of the Universe.

Hermetic philosophy, or Hermeticism, is one of the oldest religious and philosophical traditions. Hermeticism is not a religious order, but rather a belief system that is at the root of many of today's religions. It is said to hold "prisca theologia," a doctrine that claims one true theology exists and threads through all religions, and is a combination of ancient Egyptian religion, philosophy and science; Greek Paganism; Alexandrian Judaism; ancient Sumerian religion; Chaldean astronomy; and Zoroastrianism. The Hermeticists believe in a monotheistic God and that "All is One" in the Universe. Hermeticism influenced Judaism, Islam and Christianity, especially the early Christian Gnostics (who, as we read in the chapter on religion, were considered heretics). However, the Christians, starting with Emperor Constantine, erased almost every trace of Hermeticism from AD 312 until the sixth century. They put to death thousands of pagans, many of whom were Hermetic, and destroyed temples and sacred texts. Much of the Hermetic and alchemical literature was destroyed; the remainder ended up in the Islamic world between AD 400–600. Hermeticism emerged again in medieval Europe during the Renaissance era.

Religions and schools have not specifically taught this curriculum. (This should be no surprise to you by now, after reviewing the history of education and religion.) It may also be because up until recently, the concept of quantum reality was not widely known or understood. But we now have the science to back up what Jesus and the prophets meant when they said "love your neighbor as yourself," "you reap what you sow," and "what you do unto the least of those, you do unto me." These are the universal laws, just condensed into what humanity could understand at that time in history. Can you imagine what the world would be like without those simple yet profound truths? When you strive to live within these universal concepts, you are set free and realize that you have the power to serve your fellow man and create Heaven on Earth. It becomes clear that we are our brothers' keepers.

LAW OF DIVINE ONENESS

Tristan mentions many times in his messages that we are all One. It must be such a wonderful existence that we go to when we cross back to Heaven and truly realize and experience this essential truth. The concept of Oneness is the realization that everything is part of the same life force. Different schools of spiritual thought call it prana, life force, chi, etc., but it is all the same quantum or subatomic substance, which we can call the Mind of God or Universal Mind. We are part of this mind. In other words, we are one with this Universal Mind. We co-create with our minds and with our thoughts, which become words, actions, and objects. These energies affect others as well as the world. Our mind, emotions, spirit and body are one and each affects the other. Thoughts create your reality whether they are of a lower, negative vibration or a higher, healthier and more loving vibration. When you send a negative thought toward another person, it's like putting a hurdle in their way energetically. It puts out a negative frequency that affects the delicate, subtle Universal field. But when you send thoughts of compassion, understanding and acceptance toward others, it puts a positive frequency into the field, fostering harmony and peace.

Law of Vibration

Physical properties and physical changes are the result of how particles of matter behave. All of the particles that make up matter are constantly in motion. As a result, all particles in matter have kinetic energy. The kinetic theory of matter helps explain the different states of matter—solid, liquid and gas. We can also include the movement of photons (light particles). This can be described as a discrete bundle (or quantum) of electromagnetic (or light) energy. Photons are always in motion at the speed of light. Science can validate now that everything in the Universe is in motion and therefore has a vibration.

Everything has its own unique vibrational frequency, and these frequencies lie on a continuum from the lowest dimension of the densest matter, such as rocks, to the highest dimension of spirit. Emotions such as hate and greed are the lowest level of vibrations while love, peace and awareness of God have higher vibrations. The differences between the planes is that the particles vibrate at different levels. Even though all the vibrations are unique, they all reside in the Oneness of Universal Mind. Our mission is to become aware of the thoughts, feelings and experiences that cause us pain and replace them with thoughts of a higher vibration such as forgiveness, understanding, love and peace. This is authentic healing. It is a simple concept, yet not always easy to put into practice. The higher vibrations will overcome the lower ones and influence the environment around us as higher vibrations raise and transform lower vibrations. This can explain, in one way, how prayer works.

LAW OF ACTION

Our actions mirror our emotional and mental states. For instance, when you are frustrated you may scream or throw something and your blood pressure may increase. When you are angry you may stop communicating or slam a door. When people are unaware of their emotions—and the vibrations they cause—they are also unaware that they are creating exactly what they are consciously (and, mostly, unconsciously) thinking and feeling. Like attracts like. Actions on the physical plane create changes in what is manifested physically as well as energetically. We must raise our vibrations to create a better life.

To do this, first, we must become aware of what we want to have, be or accomplish. Then we must apply action steps. But many times we aren't aware of what we want. To get clarity, we can notice what makes us happy, brings us joy, gives us energy, motivates us to get out of bed in the morning, and what we are good at. What natural talents were you born with? Yes, everyone has them! Most of the time, our gifts are right in front of us and we don't see them. Be aware of what situations or people keep coming up. Spirit will give us nudges and clues. How do we respond to situations? Where do we feel compelled to help others and be of service? Once we become aware, then we can create an action plan with step-by-step goals.

Make a commitment to yourself and your goals, but be flexible to allow them to change as new thoughts and experiences arise. Persistence and discipline are key. It is easy to stay in your comfort zone and not step out and do or say things that feel difficult or intimidating. Remember, the definition of insanity is doing the same things and expecting different results. You have to change your actions to get new results, and thoughts power actions. If you can think about it, you have the power to create it. When you know what you want and ask Spirit to help, the Universe will maneuver things around to help—but the bottom line is that you are God's boots on the ground. Nothing happens until you take action.

Law of Correspondence

"As above so below, and as below so above" is the basis of this Law. Correspondence is defined as "a strong connection between two things; conformity, similarity, communication." We understand the Law of Correspondence first by acknowledging that there are three planes of existence: the physical, mental and spiritual planes. Each of these planes have may subcategories and dimensions. Since everything has its unique vibration and all exists on a continuum, divisions of the planes are simply arbitrary within the Oneness or Mind of God. The physical plane vibrates at the lowest rate and the spiritual vibrates at the highest. The Law of Correspondence is the glue that holds it all together by connecting the physical, mental, and spiritual planes.

The significance of the Law of Correspondence is that all planes of existence affect all others simultaneously. This includes thoughts, words, and actions. The quality of our thoughts is what is manifested in the material world. Our decisions influence and affect others. We create from our minds consciously, but also unconsciously. This is where our shadows come into play. This law encourages us to work on our own issues. What keeps coming up in our life? It is most likely an aspect in need of healing—an old trauma, unforgiveness, anger or grief. What we are experiencing in our outer world stems from our inner world. It is the great mirror, our external reflection of our innermost beliefs. We are more in control of creating our reality when we understand that we can choose to transform our beliefs, emotions, thoughts and actions, thereby transforming our lives.

The Law of Cause and Effect

The *Kybalion* is a teaching manual that compiles traditional ideas and verbal lessons passed down over thousands of years. A famous quote from it regarding the Law of Cause and Effect is, "Every Cause has its Effect; every Effect has its Cause; everything happens according to Law; Chance is a name for a Law not recognized; There are many planes of causation, but nothing escapes The Law." The basic understanding of this law is that nothing happens by chance or independent of the spiritual laws of Divine Order.

This law refers more to events and experiences. Every event has its cause. Karma is an aspect of this law; what you sow is what you reap. This could be from past lives or your current incarnation; the cause is not usually obvious, because there are most often many chains of events from past lifetimes or ancestors. To believe in coincidences is to believe that some things lie outside of Universal Law. Knowing we are all of One Universal Mind, we understand now that nothing can escape the Laws and all is in Divine Order.

When we understand that we all participate in the creation of our reality through our own actions, it's empowering. Even though it may look like we are victims of circumstances or of others, we can learn to become aware that we are more in control of our lives than we may think. By choosing higher vibrations of thoughts, feelings, words and actions, we can change our perceptions of our life's events and change its course. If not, we are tossed around like the proverbial ship without a rudder, as we give up our power to the stronger will and power of others. Fear, lack of self-worth and low self-confidence cause us to be people pleasers and seek external approval.

This keeps us from acknowledging our own uniqueness and prevents us from learning our soul lessons. Our soul stays on the hamster wheel of karma until it can release itself from what has been hampering its soul growth.

We experience unpleasant events either because there is unfinished business that must be resolved before the soul is allowed to move to a higher plane of existence, or there are lessons that must be learned to achieve a higher state of enlightenment. Becoming aware of our responsibility for our life's events and understanding the lessons is key in learning how to move on to higher planes of life.

The Law of Compensation

The Law of Compensation is connected to the Law of Cause and Effect. It is about giving and receiving and service to others. The Law of Cause and Effect applies to events and experiences in our lives, whereas the Law of Compensation applies to the gains we receive in life, materially, mentally and spiritually. They are both about reaping what you sow. In the *Kybalion* we find the statement, "The measure of the swing to the right is the measure of the swing to the left; rhythm compensates." Visualize the swing of a pendulum. If it has a short sweep in one direction, there will be a compensatory short sweep in the other direction. The same happens with long swings, and anywhere along that continuum. How does this Law express itself on the mental plane? If someone has gone through terrible suffering, then they also have the potential for great joy. This does not necessarily mean that if someone has experienced immense joy and happiness then they should expect the same measure of pain. It does indicate that if there has been an experience of great pain, then there is a balanced capacity for great joy and happiness. This capacity for joy and pain has a balance with each person. Be careful not to judge when something looks like a punishment in life, as it could be a "Test of Initiation," and if passed, there will be a wonderful reward. Keep the faith, knowing that the gifts of the experience will be revealed.

This Law also applies to the material plane. What one gives freely from the heart is returned or compensated equally. Actually, there is also the Law of Tenfold Return, which says that when a person completely releases the fear of lack, they are gifted with a tenfold return. Fear of lack stems from programming and conditioning from past events, family and other authority figures in this lifetime and past lifetimes.

We also receive gifts and blessings in accordance with the degree to which we have given freely to others—not based in fear, with strings attached, for the wrong motives, due to arrogance, or out of lack of self-love (such as when someone wants to buy another's love). Self-love must come first, as this allows the flow of love that you are then able to give to others. Without self-love, a cycle of lack is created which blocks the flow of giving. One must give equally to themselves as well as to others to maintain the balanced energy. Jesus explained this law beautifully when he said, "Give, and it will be given to you. A good measure, pressed down, shaken together and running over will be poured into your lap. For with the measure you use, it will be measured to you." (Luke 6:38)

THE LAW OF ATTRACTION

This law is probably the most well-known of all the laws. Most simply stated, like attracts like. We live in a belief-driven world. It is not so much that what we think about is what we attract; rather, it's more that what we believe to be true is what we attract to us. Most of our beliefs are unconscious! I think of the old Murphy's Laws. They certainly seem to be the antithesis of what one would want to attract, yet they are often accepted without realizing that we are actually creating manifestations of these beliefs. I'm sure you've heard some of these statements, such as, "Anything that can go wrong will go wrong," "If anything simply cannot go wrong, it will anyway," "The light at the end of the tunnel is only the light of an oncoming train," "A day late and a dollar short," or "Of course things like this always happen to me." With beliefs such as these driving our conscious and subconscious minds, it is no wonder that we actually manifest them.

One of my teachers would illustrate this when a student would ask, "What do you see my life becoming?" She would say, "Well, tell me what you don't want." When the student would tell her what they didn't want, she would reply, "That is exactly what you will be like!" In this way she brought up from their subconscious their fears, anxieties, and hidden beliefs so that they could become aware of them and begin the healing process. We don't always realize how strong the "I don't want" is over the "I want." How many times have you heard people (maybe even yourself) say that they never want to be like their parents, etc., and yet that is exactly what they become! This is because it is in our subconscious patterns. We must be aware of our thoughts and feelings at all times—especially the ones that float around in the very back of our minds—and question their origins. We must be the master of our own thoughts and feelings, or we will unconsciously accept the erroneous beliefs of others and manifest those instead.

"Know oneself" is a maxim that great philosophers have said over thousands of years. Know what energy is yours and what energy is not. We are in a constant state of information overload from our computers, social media, television, so-called news media, radios, movies and commercials. Subliminal messages are rampant and register in our subconscious minds. Discernment is key in mastering the Law of Attraction. If you are not aware of your own thoughts and feelings—and the resulting words and actions—you will keep repeating the old patterns. Old patterns are like a well-trodden path that you repeatedly take. To create a new path you must be very conscious of avoiding the old ones—the old thoughts and actions—and create new ones. Over time, the old path gets covered up with grass and flowers, and the new path becomes clearer and easier to follow. This goes for all things. With free will we get to choose our vibrations. Our frequencies attract like frequencies in people and experiences. Our vibrations determine our Tests of Initiation as well, as mentioned in the Law of Compensation and explained further under the Law of Relativity.

THE LAWS OF PERPETUAL TRANSMUTATION OF ENERGY

This law tells us that nothing is stagnant, and everything is always changing. As we have seen in the Law of Vibration, everything is energy, and energy is always in motion. If everything is always changing, then we can change our lives by knowing we are the creators of our own circumstances. Look at the wording of this law: "perpetual" means constant, ceaseless; "transmutation" means the state of being changed into another form or state; "energy" means the All, momentum. We cannot create energy, as this is the substance of Universal Mind, or God, but we can change or transmute it, and do so continually whether we realize it or not. We do not die, we change form—we take off the body suit and transmute our energy into a spiritual state. Lower energy can be transmuted into higher energy and vibrations. A quote from Mahatma Gandhi that exemplifies this law is, "I have learnt through bitter experience the one supreme lesson to conserve my anger, and as heat conserved is transmuted into energy, even so our anger controlled can be transmuted into a power which can move the world."

All people have the power to change their lives simply by understanding and applying the Universal Laws. When we see that horrible things happen to good people, we question why a loving God would allow this to happen. We get angry and yell at God, and many times come to the erroneous conclusion that there cannot be a God. It helps to understand that God is forever a force of love and light: we simply have unconscious blocks to receiving and comprehending this love. The benevolent gift that we do have is free will, and we can use it to raise our vibrations and transform the darkness into light. We can visualize God's light surrounding, consuming and transmuting all negative situations and lower energies.

Of course, in some instances it is much easier said than done. Yet perhaps we are being called to a higher order—a greater mission. Perhaps we have been called to forgive the seemingly unforgiveable. We do not know God's plan or our soul contract. We do not know our karma or past lives. Because of this, I feel that we can forgive a person as a soul who has made a terrible error even though we may not forgive the act or even the personality. We can forgive on a spiritual level but maybe not an emotional or mental level. At the very least, we can choose not to hate. Remember, most of our behavior is from our unconscious mind, which was programmed when we were children (mainly birth to seven years old). We can forgive the person if we realize that they were acting from a distorted belief in their subconscious. We are responsible for transmuting our lower thoughts and vibrations to a higher level. As beloved Buddha has proclaimed, "Good thoughts will produce good actions and bad thoughts will produce bad actions. Hatred does not cease by hatred at any time; hatred ceases by love."

LAW OF RELATIVITY

The Law of Relativity is considered a more advanced law. It is the answer to the question, "Why me?" It is not about comparing your problems and life situations with others to see where yours lie along a continuum of pain and difficulties. That would be looking at your life from the lower ego vantage point. From this perspective you could have the potential to either feel more blessed than other people, resulting in a feeling of arrogant superiority, or feel like you have it worse than others, leading to a victim mentality.

Each event is individual and stands alone without comparison to anyone or anything else. It has its own frequency and own lesson to learn—a lesson that is that soul's alone, based on whatever the soul came in to learn. The way to look at each situation is with the intention of understanding what the lesson is and somehow finding a way to be grateful for it. We need to both mentally understand it and emotionally feel it in our hearts. We need to own it and dig deep to uncover the gift within it. Instead of problems, we can understand them as Tests of Initiation.

Tests of Initiation are set up when our soul is ready to advance. By using our free will, we can respond negatively with anger, fear or self-pity, or positively by learning the lesson and seeing the opportunity in and meaning behind the experience. We've all heard the success stories of people who created amazing lives that they claim would never have happened if it wasn't for the fact that they had first lost everything. When the loss is a child, a parent cannot see anything good about that. The heartache is unbearable; you would give anything to be the one to die and let the beautiful younger soul live. Yet, we have to look beyond the death and see what gifts that soul left, how the world is a better place because they were here, and who was touched by their acts of kindness, love or lessons taught. In my case, my heart cracked open and my spiritual gifts exploded. I always knew I had them; I just felt they were my personal connection to God and my guides. After Tristan's passing, I knew that I had to use them not only to comfort myself to be able to get through the rest of this life, but also to help other people who had lost loved ones, especially children. As you know, Tristan helps me with this from Heaven.

When a Test of Initiation is passed, there is an advancement of the soul along their unique journey. As was explained in the Law of Compensation, when there has been great perceived sadness or negativity, there is an equal compensation of joy, peace and love. There is a greater capacity for love because higher frequencies dissolve lower frequencies and the pendulum now can swing to the opposite polarity. If the lesson is missed, or only learned by the mind and not the heart, there is no judgment—but the lesson will come around again, in this life or another one, a bit more strongly. It will keep repeating until the soul gets it.

THE LAW OF POLARITY

The *Kybalion* says, "Everything is dual; everything has poles; everything has its pair of opposites; like and unlike are the same; opposites are identical in nature, but different in degree; extremes meet; all truths are but half-truths; all paradoxes may be reconciled . . . The difference between things diametrically opposed to each other is merely a matter of degree." When we think of temperature, it is really a measure of heat that lies along the scale of degrees of what we would register as hot or cold. The polarity is in the contrast. In other words, we wouldn't know what cold was if we didn't know its opposite of heat. There is no absolute—it is all a matter of degree. Everything has its own pole, such as love and hate, power and force, fear and courage, black and white, good and bad, happy and sad, large and small, and they are all on a sliding scale.

Each plane has extremes along the same continuum. For instance, there is nothing so small that there isn't something smaller, and nothing so large that there isn't something larger. It is just a matter of perspective as to where you are standing. To a human, a cat is small, but to a mouse, the cat is very large! If you don't know what poverty is, you wouldn't comprehend what it's like to be abundant. Where does heat stop and cold begin? We learn to take responsibility for where we choose to live along the spectrum of the poles. Your focus is where you are placing your frequencies, and like attracts like.

Awareness is always key to improving our life. Once you become aware, then you may accept that this is your current reality. What is the polar opposite of acceptance? It is resistance! What we resist is what persists. Understanding the Law of Polarity allows us to raise our vibrations and experiences in life. We choose our reactions and have the free will to change our behavior to a higher or lower level along the continuum of that pole or plane. Staying out of the extremes and remaining balanced in your mind, emotions and actions will, by cause and effect, allow better experiences. What you are currently experiencing shows you exactly where your consciousness lies. What is life is returning back to you? The choice is yours whether to raise the bar or not. This is the power of the Law of Polarity.

Law of Rhythm

It is written in The *Kybalion*, "Everything flows out and in; everything has its tides; all things rise and fall; the measure of the swing to the right, is the measure of the swing to the left; rhythm compensates." This rhythm is found in all things, like the ocean tide with its ebbs and flows. Similar to the Law of Polarity, this law establishes that the swing to the right will be equal to the swing to the left. Like night follows day and spring follows winter, this rhythm is found in all things material, emotional, mental, and spiritual. Just as our moods experience highs and lows, the Universal Pendulum is always in motion. There is no such thing as absolute rest, as we learned in the Law of Vibration (that energy is always moving).

On the mental plane there is high and low consciousness. The pendulum usually swings on an unconscious level; if we are unaware of it, we can feel like we are out of control. There is always an action and a reaction. On a spiritual level there is the "Inbreath and Outbreath of Brahma," as all goes through the cycle of birth, growth, maturity, decay, death and rebirth. We have even witnessed the birth and death of stars.

The key to using this law to raise your vibration is knowing that if you experience the extreme highs then you must, in response, experience the extreme lows. To avoid this, raise your frequency to stay at a higher end of the pole and not allow yourself to participate in the backswing. With the use of our willpower, we can maintain a centered position without experiencing the extreme states. This doesn't mean that you shouldn't feel joy because you will eventually feel the opposite of joy. It means that if you stay consciously aware of your feelings and maintain them at a higher level, you can avoid the extreme unconscious swings to low consciousness. We cannot escape the Law of Rhythm, but we can escape being unconsciously carried along with the pendulum. As stated in the *Kybalion,* "Rhythm may be neutralized by an application of the Art of Polarization." This does not mean that you no longer are affected by the Law of Rhythm, but that you can master your emotions, environments and genetic tendencies rather than be carried along to lower vibrations. You can use the principle of polarity and live within the rhythm of a higher plane.

THE LAW OF GENDER

The *Kybalion* states, "Gender is in everything; everything has its Masculine and Feminine Principles; Gender manifests on all planes." This is not only referring to the biological sex of people; every thing, thought, word, deed and situation also has a gender. Masculine and feminine energies govern all creation, as in heat, electricity, magnetism, light and the bonding of electrons and protons. Every element has a positive (masculine) charge or negative (female) charge, as we know that all is Universal Mind, and therefore there is consciousness in every atom. "Positive" and "negative" here don't mean good and bad. It refers to the principles of "yin" and "yang." Yin is feminine, receptive, potential energy and represents the right brain and unconscious mind. Yang is masculine, active, kinetic energy and represents the left brain and conscious mind. All things comprise of these two energies. We know that nothing is ever truly created and that energy is transmuted and transformed into another form. We use the Law of Gender to catalyze these manifestations.

The feminine principle is the womb that dreams the thoughts, ideas and feelings. The masculine principle is the conscious will, the director that takes the thoughts and dreams and directs the feminine energy into action. The Law of Gender encourages us to balance these two energies. This means to be able to receive ideas and then have the willpower to take the action to bring them into reality. With an unbalance of too much yin energy, we may be content simply with dreaming, as in someone who waits for their ship to come in. You stay in your head without any outward action. In the extreme, you may be so passive that you are susceptible to all thoughts from other, stronger people and don't produce any thoughts of your own. With an unbalance of too much yang energy, there is little attention paid to our feeling and compassionate side. We don't take time to create new ideas and dreams and are only working from our logical, analytical mind. This manifests from the lower ego of pride, force and aggression.

We all have both energies. The goal is to pay attention to our thoughts, feelings and actions and bring these into balance so one gender energy does not dominate. Having too much yin energy is having great inspiration without action behind it, and having too much yang energy is having all action with no creative inspiration behind it. We co-create with Divine Source when we have a harmonious balance of these two forces.

During the most recent era of time, the Earth has been under the dominance of masculine energy. The feminine energy of creativity and compassion have been suppressed while the masculine aggressive energy has dominated. The Earth is in need of balancing, and this will happen as each person balances their gender energies.

CHANNELED MESSAGE FROM GUIDE ON SPIRITUAL LAWS (11/03/2020):

In my meditation, I was shown a place with beautiful marble and gold temples and buildings. I knew that Tristan was communicating with me but he was not giving me the message. Instead I saw a beautiful woman wearing clothes that looked like the ones you see in Hindu texts. When I asked who was giving me the information, Tristan said he was standing by, as he was learning as well as interpreting the information being communicated by one of my guides. (Apparently, I have been given a new guide.) Here is her message:

The Spiritual Laws, as understood by people on Earth who study them and strive to abide by them, are a construct formed to make the Law of Creator into categorized packets of information to be understood by the consciousness of people at this time.

Many great beings in these halls of Wisdom and Planning prepared the way for souls to navigate the unique environment on Earth. As a planet of duality, there must be a road map given to follow to one's final destination—that of reaching a certain level of enlightenment. In truth, there is no final destination except for all being One with the Creator of All. All great mystics and prophets interpreted these ancient laws by what was needed or resonated with the frequency of consciousness at that time.

As you notice, many of the Laws overlap, with each one building upon the last—all emanating from the great Central Thought—the One Great I AM. It is like concentric circles of truth emanating from Source. Each concentric circle is a band of truth of the same aspect of Love. Love your neighbor as yourself is the simple truth underlying these truths, as we are all One. How simply our beloved Master said it so many years ago. Times were simple then, and thus his teachings were simple. This Master you call Yeshua [Jesus]— spoke the Universal Laws through parables and also examples of healing. His love is so great one must feel it as there are no words—much like the Laws.

The Laws must be understood and applied by all the senses. On Earth you learn these intellectually, then one must assimilate and live these Laws in the heart. Souls usually plan on emphasizing the learning of one or two of these Laws in each lifetime, as they are profound and moves one's soul closer to the I AM. The time will come where people will no longer need to read and study these Laws, as they will become these Laws unto themselves. This is the Decree from God: All is One.

I give you my peace this day,

-Adonai

CHAPTER 10

Extra Channelings from Heaven

But you know—what an earthly expression "losing someone"—you can't lose a soul--we hang around. We lose our physical connection but not our essence or love. We don't lose you either. If anything, we find ourselves. We find our love, our peace—our understanding of who we are—and rewire and integrate it all. We truly "find ourselves" again over "on this side."

- TRISTAN

On Tristan's first Christmas in Heaven in 2018, six months after his transition, I missed him so much and the pain was so unbearable that I asked him to come forward and write to me about what Christmas was like in Heaven. (Souls resonate with what they are used to and enjoyed while incarnated on Earth, so, if Christmas held a special meaning for them here, they celebrate it over there as well.)

Merry Christmas Mom and everyone. I am here as always, sending and enveloping you with my love. The love of the Creator really. That is all there is, you know. Yes, I am here to tell you that I have been a part of this family many times. Please let everyone know that there is a Christmas on this side. In a different way though, of course, not commercialized. We gift each other with gifts of our spirit. Gifts of love, our personal creations, we can do that here—gifts from our hearts. It is because we love the season here—truly what it represents. Not just Jesus's arrival day to planet Earth, but truly what that meant to all of us. We are in spirit now but we have all had many incarnations, and truly many of us love that time of year representing family and love. Giving of the heart—not the material presents but what they represent. Of course, as children we love to open the games and toys and tear open the packages. And yet we know there is more than that. The cookies, trees, lights—we know it is special when we are young. Those memories stay with us forever and we can enjoy them when over here at home—our true home. Home is where the heart is, and my heart is here at home, and always with you and my family still on Earth. It is not a difficult thing. You come here to visit but you are not consciously aware—dreams and different frequencies. So much difficulty to grasp when you are in a dense body on Earth.

So Christmas—the Master of Love speaks to us to love. That we must transcend the lower thought forms of what it is today. In spirit we remember and get reminded of our true love—our heart connection with the Divine. The Divine in all of us. Our Creator's love to share and recognize in all. The birth of that love that Jesus, as you call him on Earth, speaks of—the true vibration of Source. He brought that to the Earth plane and that is the Christmas light. The families get together, and even if they don't remember (and they don't) something deep inside, if they are aware, remembers the love they have in common—not only in the current life but in the many other lives they have shared. It is all in the now. All of the love that ever was IS—is now. The Christmas spark—the ignitor spark—like throwing a match on a pile of wood (you know I like that!) it flames in the heart. It is up to you to fan the flames and let it grow—inside and to all. As the Master showed. Bring your presents (presence) to the now—that is all there is—is now. The now moment of the love you express to your family. Your family and the entire family of Earth. Know that I am enjoying Christmas here—you do pop in (you don't know it)—and Christmas at home (Earth home) with my homies—I'm there too.

Take heart—all is as it should be. It's OK to enjoy your Christmas—I want you to because it is a wonderful time. I am not sad—I am having a great Christmas on this side with my family here, too. Merry Christmas, Your son, T.

TRISTAN ON HIS BIRTHDAY, (6/13/19)

*T*ake my hand—do you hear me, feel me? Happy Birthday! *Thank you, Mom and all. My birthday has special meaning to you all. I see and feel your love. It's like a birthday every day here really. We can and do celebrate when we choose to. Birthdays are remembrances of our lives of Earth. We join with you on our birthdays because we are still a part of the family. We are indeed right here! It makes us happy to see you celebrate us—loving us— knowing that you still think of us with love and joy.*

I remember the ice cream cakes—have ice cream today—it is a great way to celebrate—good memories. Celebrate my life—what I did—how I lived—not that I am gone now. That is how to celebrate my day—who I am now—not that I am gone. My life then and now—there is no real time anyway. Celebrate ME! I would love and honor that. Sadness doesn't bring me back, but love brings me closer.

We are all still one big family, just some of us are on this side now. Like a revolving door! If only you could see it from this side. There are no boundaries. We celebrate you guys when you make a step in the right direction. You may feel it sometimes but we are your best and loudest cheerleaders! So celebrate—have a party! Tell Frank not to eat all the ice cream.

Tell Dad thank you for all the love and know I am good here. He did a great job raising me. I wasn't easy this time around. So enjoy! I love you—join the party—you deserve it.

Chris—wow—I am still rooting for you—still have your back. Keep going—listen for me. I am around you, nudging you. Press on—great things are waiting for you. I am lighting a fire under your ass—hahaha. [They went camping and built a huge fire a few days before Tristan crossed over.]

Trish—lightening up—it is good. Keep your ears open—I am around you, yes! I help to take care of the horses.

Mom—hold it all together—both worlds—bring it together. We love that you're listening. Feel my love around you always.

Enjoy my day. I am always with you guys. No pain, no sadness— all glory.

Go celebrate . . .

Tristan (4/27/2020 the two-year anniversary of his crossing)

Hello Momma,

I am here communicating with you now—I communicate a lot—like with the feathers, as you know. On Earth feathers and other signs are a lot easier for you to discern and realize that although we are pretty good—you do miss many of my thoughts I send to you. Stay connected—you get so wrapped up in the goings-on—yes, it is happening—all of those crazy injustices that have existed on this planet for eons of times—or so it seems from an embodiment standpoint or view. From this side it seems like a game—a chess game where you must use great skill and discernment to advance your soul—except we do not win over each other—we win or compete only with our lower selves, egos or lower minds—whatever you wish to call it that makes sense to you. We do get to check mate! Yes—great analogy—we can win but we always have the option to jump in and play again. We can opt out but that is not the higher choice.

Now, getting back to today—this calendar day—it is really just that—a date on your calendar. Mom, I understand it represents the day I left the Earth realm and came home. You focus on me leaving, and I focus on the returning home. Maybe I can impress on you today that part of my life cycle. The coming home to my beautiful family of light here. Oh, I am not saying that it was instantaneous bliss—no, I first was sad at leaving so suddenly, but really, looking at how my life was deteriorating, it really was the better option. Once I realized that—it was a relief to be experiencing my life in a new place—a fair place, a place of justice where people loved me and supported me and truly loved and had my highest and best welfare for me. I hadn't experienced that for a long time on Earth.

Earth was really hard for me this time around—I had a very loving and sensitive heart and a strong will—so my heart had a tough time processing how I was perceived by others when I just wanted to fully experience things—I never meant to do harm. I was so misunderstood on Earth. But when I came home—actually my first stop—you call it rehab—it was a relief, but also it was like a debriefing as you get to reexperience everything about the life you just returned from. Wow—you get to experience all the love you gave and received and process everything not like love. You have the opportunity to expand your consciousness as you integrate all of it into your soul. It is a bit difficult to explain with mere words but you can telepathically understand as you have gone through this process many times but of course, as you know, it is blocked from your mind's memory.

My love for you is so great. I accomplished much this time around—I know it seems short to you, and indeed it was, but from over here it is not ticked off in Earth time elements, it is realized by the heart—the experiences, the joy and heartbreaks and how you learned and processed them. We have jobs to do—there is structure—if you choose. Some at this point have a difficult time and remain rebellious because they cannot shake off the life's occurrences. You are allowed to "wallow" in your anger, sadness, etc., for quite a while, but there is always encouragement to move on. There is always like a carrot dangling. I didn't want to stay at this level long. I healed my energy body—do you understand that? I no longer have deformities—that's how I felt—that I was deformed—no matter how much surgery—I would always be deformed. And—not really rebelliousness—in my self-empowerment—I realized I didn't have to stay that way—that in God's loving kindness I could be restored to fullness. Once I understood this I wanted to heal—I wanted to grow because of how harsh my life had been, I wanted to move on—plus I could see the light. I could feel the encouragement and beckoning from my soul guides and group. Reminders of who I was, where I came from, my truth of who I am and my past/present/future. I dug deep because I never wanted to come back to complete any karma or balancing of this on Earth. It was explained to me that I could advance here and not have to go through this again. Mom, I wish this for you. This is one of life's most difficult aspects or lessons— sometimes we call it a gift—even though I am sure at this moment you are disagreeing with the thought of losing a child is a gift. But you know—what an earthly expression "losing someone"—you can't lose a soul--we hang around. We lose our physical connection but not our essence or love. We don't lose you either. If anything, we find ourselves. We find our love, our peace—our understanding of who we are—and rewire and integrate it all. We truly "find ourselves" again over "on this side."

So no talk of loss—OK? That is a thought you don't want to solidify in your mind as it keeps our connection from fully forming. We have had many missions together on Earth and we aren't done yet—is that good news or does that make you shudder— hahahaha. No—the three of us (Dad) have had many go-rounds. We did a very thorough job this this time. My heart is with you as you are still accomplishing and experiencing in a physical body. We planned it this way—always free will--but always a plan, too.

So, today's date--just a date! Don't take it so hard. I love that you are thinking of me and our life together. I was so cute, I admit, but remember it was a birthday of sorts--a birth from illusion to light. Think of that as you plant my flowers. I went to beauty--to love--to a better, more beautiful life. You can spread my ashes or plant them, and I am moved by that but know that it is an honor to the Mother Earth--my body was just a vehicle for my soul--a vehicle goes to the junk yard to get repurposed or recycled. Like the cells of a body--give them back to Earth as she lovingly let my soul borrow them--and she will lovingly do again when I choose to return. Let her give you the flowers--the beauty, the life. Enjoy it now. I will be with you--not going anywhere. Keep writing--my mission continues--with love--no regrets.

I am still loving the Bruni family and my family here too. We are always connected by thoughts—thoughts of love. Keep going, Mom--you're not done. You will know when the fat lady sings-- you're not fat and you can't sing so you've got a long way to go [inside joke]. Love trumps sadness. My heart I hand to you—hold it—put it in your heart—go there whenever you need to. [I hear the song "I'll Be There" playing]—Michael Jackson--I know you like him.

Love to all on this day. I returned to love—your son, Tristan

TRISTAN (5/25/20, WHILE THE WORLD WAS ON LOCKDOWN)

As I was sitting outside that morning, I was listening to a Seth Speaks video and Seth was speaking of epidemics. This was a channeled message from around forty years ago. I was thinking about the topic and how Seth used the term "a death of protest." I immediately thought of Tristan's life and death and how that would be a fitting term for him. I looked up, and at that exact moment a small feather floated ever so lightly down about three feet in front of me. There were no birds above me in the tree I was sitting under. I knew he wanted to tell me something . . .

Hear me now—My death did serve a purpose. It was a purpose that was well intended prior to my coming to Earth in this lifetime.

You hear a "death of protest" from Seth—yes indeed! It is a protest as that is the Indigo's mission—a huge protest in the energies of the world—a time of mass awakening in each soul. They choose how their death makes an impact as well, the same way a birth makes an impact. Impacts such as how or why people die—we shall use those words—die and death. This world is at a time where the energies are so fractionated that [I couldn't get the wording so he showed me an ice cube cracking, and how ice cracks on the surface of a lake or body of water] *... so many paths of influence of each soul depending on their soul's missions and journeys. Sometimes it is for a greater awakening or topic where many people die of the same thing or their life showed something very valuable and important to the future of the planet. It could be good or bad, but a necessary awareness. Me—injustice.* **Look***—many people dying of the same cause: drug abuse, cancer, guns, wars, it is like their spirit is* ***standing there pointing****... pointing at the cause—the consciousness that needs shifting.* **Look** *.. opioids, corruption, war, the deep state taking us into wars for the opioids. Cancer ...* **look** *... see the poisons, then see the cures that have been suppressed ... see why we have that issue that holds the consciousness down. We die so that others may live more fully. It doesn't seem like that for those who miss their loved ones—like you, Mom, but for the mass consciousness of the planet it is an honor of great importance that we choose before we come into a physical body.*

*Yes, even an epidemic shows something—**see the souls pointing**— what is the learning, awareness, consciousness shift that they are encouraging all to take an awareness of? All must go deep and look inside oneself as well as what is happening on a larger scale.*

I chose much for people to take a greater notice of. As you know, the school system is very destructive, as you experienced and are getting ever more aware of as you research and write the book. The epidemic is showing parents what the effects could be when their children are not subjected to the influence—shall I even say interference—by the many factions who want to program the children's minds and therefore influence society and truly bring the power to an even greater level to the government and those above the government. Hopefully, those who are raising children now will see a positive change in their children enough that they will find alternative ways to educate them. (During the pandemic, schools were closed so children had to stay home and attend classes online.) *Oh, it won't be easy because at this time the culture and families are not set up for this—a huge turn around—like trying to make a U-turn with a big semi-trailer! But sometimes things must turn around—stop going down the wrong road!*

Also, my death showed the injustice system with its greed and avarice. Those in power want to stay in power and will do whatever they are told to do or what makes them look high and mighty to their peers. This has been going on for ages. Every drop on the stone wears it down or smooths it, polishes it. As in my case—the corruption, you call it the Good Old Boy network, was very well established. **We stand and point***—who is aware? Move forward in your consciousness—as it raises, you will vote in men and women of greater integrity. People will demand equal justice of those wearing the robes and the prosecutors and all in the criminal justice system who are acting from their ego and hurting people rather than supporting and helping society.*

Busy, busy, busy . . . people are that—they don't have the time to see these things. It is everyone's responsibility to see this. **We** *are pointing. Now is the time on this planet—the epidemic, the imbalance—love/hate, rich/poor, gluttony/starvation, powerful/ oppressed.* **We are pointing** *. . . our missions continue on this side—we are working to continue our missions and you are all on one too. You still are in embodiment—boots one ground as you call it—I like it—we work together . . . creating evolution. The time is rich for this. It's not always so strong—it is now, however. It is not the time for fear. It is the time for courage. Don't be afraid to die—shine your light—bring forth your greatness in your life now. No time like the present as they say. When your soul is ready to come home, it will—so no fear!*

This is a "war" of the mind—on a higher level than physical war— the battle is real. This is not a time to fight with your neighbor on who is right or wrong on the mundane things. This is a battle for the light—the light to increase in your own mind and heart— **for you to point** *while you are still in a body and can be seen.* **We pointed in death—you point now in life**—*in embodiment. Charge yourself daily. You didn't come into this lifetime to take it easy. Enjoy the moments of beauty and love as that is the way of the new warrior—light over dark. Not hate or divisiveness but ever moving on for the truth, knowing you are aligning yourself with the Divine Plan for planet Earth.* **We stand pointing**—*we are also very busy over here but always loving and encouraging. We will be back to pick up our mantle. It is just a different frequency and a time out too—to upgrade our garments. Oh, love that. We are all one—remember this—remember. Our love for humanity and each other . . . in the end that is what it is all about, then we can say game over—game, set, match. And we all live in peace and harmony.*

Forever loving you and all, Tristan

Tristan on Christmas Day (12/25/20)

*D*earest momma,

Oh boy—what a celebration we had at the Bruni house last night. Of course, I was there and all was how it was meant to be— with my place set. We enjoy this time of year here at home too, as you know. Peace on Earth, that is the theme that we are all working diligently on now. All who have that task and intention, those of us who undertook this mission of seeing the Christ light rule the Earth. We are here now but do plan on re-embodying again. So we are still working on it, as the interest and mission doesn't change when you are here at home. It intensifies, really, as you have the whole picture since you are not under the veil, so to speak.

We do like to get festive here as well with joyful parties. We visit with our loved ones who are still on Earth as well. We have the best of both worlds. It is fun to have those of our loved ones who feel our presence and know we are around with a wink and nod. There is no sadness that we are not in a body though—not like you on Earth who miss us. We are not sad; the expansiveness of joy and love that surrounds us is all joy and bliss. We are "out of the game" here. God is close at hand.

New speaker (it sounds like Tristan's guide, a past family relative):

*M*y Dear,

You know that your son is perfectly fine and quite capable here at home. He is a remarkable builder—his creations are divine! He moves about with such joy, enthusiasm and power. He is in high demand. His stint on Earth was a brief one again and he appreciates you for coming to the task of mothering him. It was one for the strongest as he had so much of his independence and power coming through this time that it could hardly be contained, thus, the short span according to Earth years as you know. There is a different sense of time here.

He had some clean-up work, shall we say, and it was a hot mess. We watched over it closely—even though you didn't believe it and still don't really. But we assure you this great soul had us close by. He said he had it coming to him and knew his time on Earth would be short. He told you himself. [Tristan told me when he was four years old that he wasn't going to be an old man. He told me that again a few years later, saying, "I am not going to live to be an old man, I just need to tell you that." He mentioned that to me again shortly before he passed, "Mom, I told you before that I am not going to live to be an old man."] *We all work together over here in a loving communion of brotherhood and peace. We support each other's growth and missions. There is no judgment—we work with the Christ light as that is the true home and new home of the Earth. We are planning this on this side so we can manifest it when we come back to the Earth plane ourselves. We bring it in with us as that is part of the mission here—to recreate a new Earth, to lift it into a new frequency, closer to the Christ light—the light of God—each time. That is the job of the souls who chose this. It is not one and done. We are planners and builders of the future. We work with you too. We come into dreams, we inspire with thoughts and direction. It is all on the up and up—believe this. The old is breaking down and this is most difficult to exist in while in embodiment and we are cheering you on here. We are here on this side now so we can come back in when the time is right for greater works. This is the truth. Christmas day is but a spark of the joy and brotherhood that will be on Earth to stay. Christmas—the*

heart of Christ—the Christ child alive will be the "new normal,"
nothing else. Rest with peace in your heart, fear not, worry not,
your boy is fine. We are always together.—Your friends and family

After I finished writing the book, Tristan wanted to assure me that just because the book was complete didn't mean he would stop writing me letters (of course he knew what I was thinking.)

TRISTAN (9/05/21)

H*ello Mom,*

Here we are again. We don't need to be writing a book for us to write and communicate like this. My love reaches far beyond the pages of any book. Yes, we all want peace on Earth now. Peace is relative depending where you are on Earth and what one has experienced up to now, is it not? Peace can be sitting still in a garden enjoying the solitude and being with nature. But for some, peace can be an absence of harm, violence, fear, etc. Peace I give to you— yes—what kind of peace are you looking for? Peace of mind, peace for your spirit? Peace comes in many different flavors. What do you ask for? What are your requests and visions? Do you know what peace truly is? Many people ask for peace on Earth yet don't know how to bring it forth in their own heart—in their own world. Peace comes from an understanding of yourself—every thought, word, and deed must be accounted for. One must become aware of what they are attracting into their sphere of influence, we shall say. We become what we think—we are what we think. We are a thought in a flesh suit! All wrapped up and tied with a bow. A bow in the hair can't hide darkness inside. The light must shine forth from the heart. Do you fear, gossip, hate—all these are you. This is your level of peace then. Peace comes from when one has had enough of what they perceive to be "not peace." I leave you with this: there is always peace, you live in peace—be one with it.

Love you . . .

TRISTAN (10/31/21 IN RESPONSE TO MY ASK-ING HIM WHAT LIFE IS LIKE FOR HIM NOW)

I am here, as always, your faithful servant, LOL. These are the times that try men's souls. . . how many years must those on Earth have to comply with this sentiment? It has gone on for far too long. Now is the time for peace—peace within. Peace isn't one and done; like "I want peace, OK, done." Peace is a constant way of living and creating. At this time on Earth, it is a constant endeavor to maintain that peace vibe as there are so many energies on Earth bombarding you and everyone. Find the peace vibe and stay in it as long as you can—it will get easier the more you do it. But as you say, "practice, practice, practice."

This Earth school is having its final exam—did you study for it? Oh yes, everyone on Earth and on "this side" has been studying for years—many lifetimes. If you change your way of thinking that this side and the other side are two different things or places, it will be easier to comprehend the largeness of the current times—and all times really. See the souls entering and exiting [the Earth plane]. It's like going into the classroom and walking back out. Or getting on a plane for a vacation and then returning. Think of all the energies of all the lifetimes on Earth; all the people, all the energies of everything on the planet, all the frequencies of thought and all the energy in the grid system. So you think that you just step into an Earth body and enter into the density of these frequencies and not get affected? It is heavy. That is why we come in as little babies and get swaddled and loved and in the right way, we slowly get exposed to the frequencies. Can you imagine just popping into the Earth as an adult, fresh from spirit? Wow—that would be heavy! No wonder it is said to put on your full armor of God. It is needed on Earth at this time.

But getting back to the two sides [here and the other side]; *there are many sides, really. Many spheres of thought planes. You "earn" your way into higher planes. Just because our spirit leaves the flesh body doesn't automatically place it into the heavenly speres. There is always love and no judgment, but everything is a vibration, and you will find your match. On Earth, we have been so spiritually blind. We see in terms of only one lifetime. The soul is a compilation of its many lifetimes and sojourns into many places and timelines, so we really can't make judgments. We are all together working with Gaia. No one is left out. There are those who have chosen to make it harder for the rest of us. But remember, the pressure on a stone turns it into a precious gem.*

[I asked Tristan to show me what he is doing now. He showed me that he is wearing a hard hat in what looks like a construction site in a beautiful forest with large trees. He is working with others. There is a beautiful lake with mountains far off in the distance.] *I am creating . . . I am a builder. I wish to create beautiful surroundings, like homes for people when they come home and need a place of respite to replenish themselves and heal. A place to learn to nurture themselves after a long, weary life. The unadulterated beauty of nature on the higher-plane planet is pristine and beautiful. Some people need the oceanside to heal but many love the lakes and forests. The projects always turn out great because our thought energy directs the spaces that we build. This is how I help here. I know what it's like to be battle-worn and weary. Many soldiers come here—they seek the peace and beauty and yearn for the brotherhood and unity that was absent in their Earth life. They learn to trust and love again. This is where I am at—unless you call me, or anyone calls me. It's like I sense the call and I tune in. Besides, I like to pop in on the babies and say hi* [my brother's sons]. *They are getting another round—a chance at it again. Fun to watch from here.* [Referring to a new incarnation for those souls.]

In my quiet time—funny, you think [when he said he has quiet time, I thought that it was funny to have quiet time in Heaven, and he picked up on that immediately] *but life is life and I work, yet I have time to travel the Universe or anywhere I "fit" or want to go. There are many places I don't want to go. I know a lot of people over here—many lifetimes, so I have many friends and acquaintances here. I am far from lonely. Van pops in from time to time. We still have a close friendship. That was a wrap-up of many lifetimes; and a doozy, you would call it.*

Mr. Lugner will find his "sphere" and will be directed what to do, how to heal, how to make restorations. Yet still there is free will. He can take all the time he wants to come to see the light. He has been resistant, so we shall see. I wouldn't want his life review—so say a prayer for him. Really, it will be good for your soul, too. Forgiveness is key. You know how this schoolhouse works. You must learn your lessons, study hard and prepare for the tests. You say that there is no way to be prepared for some tests. [Again, he reads my mind.] *Well, that may be so, but not on a soul level. Prepare your soul so you are always ready. That's how you do it. Those are like the trick questions on a test—no one likes those. But if you know your material, critically think and tune into your higher mind you will get through it. Yes, the "two sides"—we'll use that term—will meld—Heaven on Earth. At least the veil will thin for many. Earth will be that [Heaven]—not a home for the dark consciousness. They are about to fail.*

You know I love you. I still love to work hard—working for a brighter future! All for peace.

Till next time—your Tristan

CHAPTER 11

Our Final Thoughts

"Take action—even if it is to shine your love and light on it—because darkness can't exist in the light."

-TRISTAN

BARBARA

People have been led to believe that their feelings and intuition are worthless. We are afraid of what other people may think of us and the public backlash. People quit interacting with their family and give up beautiful friendships over politics and current issues. I believe that is not unintentional. We've been taught to "never talk about politics or religion," so people are uncomfortable with it and keep their thoughts to themselves. How sad. Our country was founded by people who were courageous enough to have free debate about serious matters without getting burned at the stake (well, most of them).

Mature, respectful and informed conversation on important issues is what creates positive courses of action. A whole country that changed the world was born from this! Being taught not to speak up—usually by fear of shame and humiliation—is a form of suppression of free speech. As a society, we have bought this hook, line and sinker.

We have allowed ourselves to fear another's opinion and overreact emotionally when confronted with a differing point of view. The media owes its existence to such bad behavior. It thrives on "shoot the messenger" mentality. This is rampant on social media. The childish hit-and-run statements (actually, we shouldn't put that label on it as children usually have better behavior) never win friends or influence people.

Take your power back! You can hear others' points of view without judgment. There are as many opinions as each unique individual. Accept people for who they are rather than judge them by what they think or how you think they should be. Everyone has a different journey through life; they have created their story through their own perception on their walks through this and many lifetimes. Your perceptions create your beliefs, and your beliefs create your reality.

Although we are unique individuals, we all share common objectives and concerns. As Tristan reminds us, we are co-creators with the unified field, not here to simply support a supreme state or government. Our true objective is to share in compassion and love for all people. We can work individually and collectively. We should be caretakers of our Earth, our children and our communities. Let us awaken to our uniqueness. We can choose hope, inspiration and *true* liberty—not a false illusion of liberty as propagandized by the government. As time progresses, we hope that all awaken to this fact. Be a powerful force for good, not a mouthpiece of the government.

I think we would be surprised to find there are positive solutions to issues that we are not being offered by our current systems, politicians, governments, big business, academia and media. Remember that they want to maintain their power and control. Can you imagine all the inventions ripe with potential that are sitting idle in the minds of men and women because they're in survival mode due to (most often) intentionally created crisis after crisis? These crises keep us in fear, drain our energy, and stifle our ambitions.

Let's play nice with each other on this tiny shiny blue planet and create more effective and benevolent systems beyond our wildest dreams. Let no one diminish your light.

And to my beautiful Tristan: I still wish you were here. . . and . . . keep shining on!

From dark to light. He got this last tattoo just a few weeks before he passed. He took his rainbow heart back home. I am so honored to have shared in his love and rainbow light.

TRISTAN (6/30/21)

While this is the final letter of this book, it is far from the final letter from me. What is done is done, and we move on from where we are. This final chapter is one of hope. It has been laid out in this book how horrendous the Earth is now, and truly not much has changed. Reading the Bible and any history, *for that matter, leads to the understanding that poor decisions, corruptness, and let's just call it what it is—pure evil—exists and has existed from as far back as our written history takes us. So, do we choose to keep circling around and around the merry-go-round ever repeating the same patterns--the same mistakes where only selfishness and caring for only oneself rules the day and being our brother's keeper is last on the list? No, the time has come to move into the next era—the next age.*

Life has reached the boiling point and must be taken off the fire. What you do—every thought, every action, indeed conscious and subconscious as well—is critical. Many people have lost hope, but I say to you now is not the time to do that. You sit in the most miraculous of times. I know it may not appear that way, but I promise you it is. Hang in there. You have been deceived— everyone—even if you think you have all the answers—know that you are living in the age of deception—and coming to an understanding of that is extremely difficult. Know the truth, and the truth shall set you free. What is the truth? Do you have the time to dismantle the generations of corruptness, greed, lies, evil deeds, false history, wars, financial control—keeping most of the world at a simple sustenance level? It was hot, but again I say it is boiling—but the frog stayed in because the heat turned up gradually. It is alarming, but know that in order to turn things around you must become aware of the atrocities you have been living under—lifetime after lifetime—never-ending wars, starvation, slavery, imprisonment, sickness and disease—shall we go on? Yet, within man there is a light—the light of our Creator that always glimmers and keeps us moving forward. Sometimes it is bright but, yet, sometimes it seems like the light has gone out, and there is a darkness and no way out.

I speak to those now who are in that place and wish to leave the life they are in now by their own hand. [Tristan had told me a couple of years prior to this message that young people choosing to leave their lives early is of great concern in Heaven. He said that he would have something to say about it in one of his channelings.] *Know that there is no punishment for that and do not be shamed, but I say to you—NO! Stop! For where there was a way in, there is always a way out. Let no man or circumstance diminish your light. Why come home early when things are just getting good on Earth? Yes, it is hard to believe indeed. I say to balance your energies while you are still in this embodiment. The time is at hand and there is no time like the present. You will learn over here—home—Heaven—but will have to go into a similar situation when you embody again. Go into nature—step away from the turmoil. Yes, of course your inner turmoil will come with you into your voyage but in solitude, in nature, you will learn about yourself. If you read the Bible you will remember the story of Jesus in the desert, alone for forty days and nights, conquering the last vestiges of self. Can you think of anyone else's life to follow as a lesson? Resist the urge to take your life and push through the pain, the turmoil, the feelings of unworthiness. You, my dear friend, are worthy of all good things. Ask for forgiveness. Forgive yourself. Ask to be shown ways to right the wrongs. The world needs your light. As you heal, your light increases. And you can move through lifetimes of karma. Eat clean, ask Spirit for help in getting off of all harmful substances—cigarettes, alcohol, drugs, etc., as these are most likely what has brought you to this place. It dampens your pain and it swells inside you until you can no longer take it. You are loved. Even if you feel alone—you are never alone. In the stillness of nature you can feel the help of Spirit, your angels, the trees, water, sky and Earth. Connect to your Divine*

Source. You are who you are on Earth and in Heaven. Don't be a drop-out! Funny, yes—but seriously, you have what it takes to heal. Breathe—leave all false precepts and pretentions in the wilderness and emerge as a conqueror of self. All of Heaven awaits your next move. You are loved. Move beyond the concept of this one life, this one personality, and know that your soul is eternal and chose to be in this time and space now—you might not have known how hard it would be—I sure didn't—but here you are. Take this life for what it is. Make peace with the higher part of you and put your piece back on the game board. Return to nature as many times as you need to. You still have things to accomplish and yes—enjoy.

Now, for the rest of you who don't have the feeling of leaving Earth early and abandoning ship, I say to you to pass no judgment on your fellow man or woman. Even the ones who, let's say, are dark. Be aware of not sending back the hate, fear and resentment. Look inside—what you are judging? Clean your own windows of your consciousness to see clearly. Send love, light and understanding. How does one do that when confronting those malevolent beings and their actions? First, don't turn a blind eye and walk the other way. Acknowledge the truth of what is happening. If not, you are giving it permission to continue—and it will and it has. Take action—even if it is to shine your love and light on it, because darkness can't exist in the light. When you do this, the energy of life increases on the planet. You are moving into a golden age of love, but how long do you want to wait? Don't wait for an outside source to do your inside job. We are all one, and as the Earth increases its frequency, it goes out in concentric circles and affects the all.

We are all busy—you are the boots on the ground and we work tirelessly on this side, assisting and loving all of you. Remember, what you do now is what you will come back to continue in your next lifetime. That should give you some motivation! Look up, yet also I say look within, go within—ask and believe me you will receive. Pay attention, be aware, heal your judgments and shine your light. Every flicker counts. We are all on standby for your next thought. With love coming from all corners of the Universe, I speak to you from so many of us.

In the greatest of love and blessings, Tristan

P.S. Take the high road—always—and in all ways.

Our loved ones on the other side are always around when we call them. During a walk on the beach, Jack and I aksed him to show us a sign. Right after that we happened to look down and saw this shell smiling up at us.

ABOUT THE AUTHOR

Barbara Bruni has worked in the health, fitness and healing field for thirty-five years. She owns and operates a Pilates and Myofascial Release Studio. She created and filmed a local television show for over ten years. The episodes can still be seen online. She also created a Pilates instructor training school and named it Barbara Bruni's Pilates and Beyond with the idea that movement and healing go beyond the physical body—she just wasn't aware at the time how far the "beyond" was going to take her. Even as a child Barbara was empathic and intuitive. As she got older she shut down her senses as it could be too overwhelming to experience the intensity of others' emotions and energies. In her late teens she became very interested in spirituality and psychic phenomenon which explained much of her early childhood, and soon met her first spiritual teacher. This allowed her to understand more of who she was and to appreciate how she experienced the world. Little did she know that Spirit had been setting up the foundation for her that would allow for the ability to communicate with her son after his sudden death in April of 2018, just a few weeks prior to his nineteenth birthday. He soon was communicating to her from the beyond. Barbara always used her spiritual gifts for her personal relationship to Spirit but never thought that she would be doing it for others. "The tremendous sudden grief cracked my heart open, and my mediumship ability grew. If it wasn't for my continued contact with my son Tristan, I don't know how I would have handled the intense shock and grief. I know that I am here to help people through their grief and ability to move on with their lives without the guilt and sadness that can overshadow every aspect of their lives, especially other parents who have lost a child."

RESOURCES

These are many of the books I read while doing research for this book. You may find them interesting as well.

A New Science of Life: The Hypothesis of Formative Causation by Rupert Sheldrake

Beyond Belief: The Secret Gospel of Thomas by Elaine Pagels

Conviction Machine: Standing Up to Federal Prosecutorial Abuse by Sidney Powell and Harvey A. Silverglate

Divine Magic: The Seven Sacred Secrets of Manifestation: A New Interpretation of the Classic Hermetic Manual The Kybalion by Doreen Virtue

Dumbing Us Down: The Hidden Curriculum of Compulsory Schooling by John Taylor Gatto

Free to Learn: Why Unleashing the Instinct to Play Will Make Our Children Happier, More Self-Reliant, and Better Students for Life by Peter Gray

Good Grief: Heal Your Soul, Honor Your Loved Ones and Learn to Live Again by Teresa Caputo

Growing Up in Heaven: The Eternal Connection Between Parent and Child by James Van Praagh

Happy Teachers Change the World: A Guide for Cultivating Mindfulness in Education by Thich Nhat Hanh and Katherine Weare

Holy Bible New Revised Standard Version

Human by Design: From Evolution by Chance to Transformation by Choice by Gregg Braden

Indigo Adults: Understanding Who You Are and What You Can Become by Kabir Jaffe and Ritama Davidson

Indigos: The Quiet Storm by Kathy Altaras, created by Nancy Tappe

Indigo Warrior: A Guide for Indigo Adults and the Parents of Indigo Children by Lisa Andres

Licensed to Lie: Exposing Corruption in the Department of Justice by Sidney Powell

Mediumship Mastery: The Mechanics of Receiving Spirit Communications: The Ultimate Guide by Stephen Hermann

Messages From The Masters: Tapping into the Power of Love by Brian Weiss, MD

Monumental Myths of the Modern Medical Mafia and Mainstream Media and the Multitude of Lying Liars That Manufactured Them by Ty Bollinger

Myofascial Release: Healing Ancient Wounds: The Renegade's Wisdom by John F. Barnes, PT

Only Love Is Real: A Story of Soulmates Reunited by Brian Weiss, MD

Power vs Force: The Hidden Determinants of Human Behavior by David R. Hawkins, MD, PhD

Shaman Healer Sage: How to Heal Yourself and Others with the Energy Medicine of the Americas by Alberto Villoldo, PhD

The Afterlife Unveiled: What "the Dead" Tell Us About Their World by Stafford Bety, PhD

The Aquarian Gospel of Jesus the Christ, by Levi

The Deliberate Dumbing Down of America: A Chronological Paper Trail by Charlotte Thomson Iserbyt

The Eye of the I: From Which Nothing Is Hidden by David Hawkins, MD, PhD

The Gnostics by Tobias Churton

The Heart of the Shaman: Stories and Practices of the Luminous Warrior by Alberto Villoldo, PhD

The Indigo Children Ten Years Later: What's Happening with the Indigo Teenagers! by Lee Carroll and Jan Tober

The Light Shall Set You Free by Dr. Norma Milanovich and Dr. Shirley McCuneos

The Underground History of American Education: An Intimate Investigation into the Prison of Modern Schooling Volume I by John Taylor Gatto

Weapons of Mass Instruction: A Schoolteacher's Journey Through the Dark World of Compulsory Schooling by John Taylor Gatto

What Great Teachers Do Differently: 14 Things That Matter Most by Todd Whitaker

White Cargo: The Forgotten History of Britain's White Slaves in America by Don Jordan and Michael Walsh

With Liberty for Some: 500 Years of Imprisonment in America by Scott Christianson